MW01026076

ALSO BY GIOIA DILIBERTO

Hadley

Debutante

A Useful Woman

THE EARLY LIFE OF *Jane Addams*

GIOIA DILIBERTO

A LISA DREW BOOK

Scribner

A LISA DREW BOOK/SCRIBNER
1230 Avenue of the Americas
New York, NY 10020

Designed by Brooke Zimmer
Text set in Caslon
Manufactured in the United States of America

1 3 5 7 9 10 8 6 4 2

Library of Congress Cataloging-in-Publication Data
Diliberto, Gioia, 1950–
A useful woman: the early life of Jane Addams/Gioia Diliberto.
p. cm.
"A Lisa Drew Book."
Includes bibliographical references and index.
1. Addams, Jane, 1860–1935. 2. Women social workers—United States—Biography. 3. Women social reformers—United States—Biography. 4. Hull-House (Chicago, Ill.)—History. I. Title.
HV40.32.A33D56 1999
361.92—dc21
[B] 98-31853
CIP

ISBN 0-684-85365-5

Again, for Dick
and for Joe

. . . the good we secure for ourselves is precarious and uncertain, is floating in mid-air, until it is secured for all of us and incorporated into our common life.

—JANE ADDAMS

Contents

PART III Angel of the World

A Useful Woman

Prologue

In 1883, after her first nervous collapse, Jane Addams thought she was "a failure in every sense." She was a pretty, high-strung twenty-three-year-old with no one to love and nothing to do, living with her stepmother in rural Illinois. Within three decades, she was the most famous woman in America. In a burst of courage and will, she triumphed over the invalidism that ruined the lives of vast numbers of Victorian women and transformed herself into an international celebrity. She founded Hull-House, the immensely successful Chicago settlement, worked tirelessly to rid the nation of the worst abuses of industrialization, and wrote best-selling books that became bibles of reform during the progressive era. Though her ardent pacifism caused her popularity to plummet during World War I, the pendulum began to swing back in the thirties and in 1931, four years before her death, she was awarded the Nobel Peace Prize.

Today, Jane Addams is widely recognized as an extraordinary figure in our nation's history, one of a roster of great Americans—Abraham Lincoln and Martin Luther King Jr. among them—who made lasting contributions to social justice. But as with the lives of many iconographic figures, the legend often obscures the real story. That has been particularly true of Jane Addams's early years, when she underwent a remarkable metamorphosis from a frail, small-town girl to one of the most famous women of her era. New family documents, most of which were unavailable to previous biographers, reveal for the first time the story of her difficult girlhood in a troubled Victorian family on the near frontier. They also illuminate the major struggle of her young adulthood—the conflict between her internal drive to power and the stultifying demands of her parents (the dreaded "family claims," which she later wrote about movingly). This conflict manifested itself in a series of physical ailments that tormented her for years.

The idea of writing about Jane Addams occurred to me soon after moving to Chicago with my family in 1991. As a way of introducing myself to Chicago history, I read *Twenty Years at Hull-House,* Jane's autobiography, and was deeply attracted to the story of the settlement's founding. But as I got deeper into the archive of Jane's papers (housed at the University of Illinois in Chicago, a few miles from my home), what most intrigued me was the material about her early years, particularly letters to and from those closest to her. Not only were these documents fresh (most of them were discovered after the last biography of Jane, Allen F. Davis's excellent *American Heroine,* was published in 1973), but they fit into my chief interests as a biographer—the shaping of personality and ambition, how fate plays on character, the delineation of women's lives.

They offered a chance to rescue Jane Addams from her pedestal as a saintly reformer and bring her to life as never before. What's more, they provided a window into a lost world of one-room schools and typhoid epidemics, of grand tours, romantic friendships, and "separate spheres" for the sexes. Yet, the key issues illuminated in this historical context—the struggle to overcome depression during a period of great social change, the battle for power within families, the difficulties of women in convincing the medical establishment to recognize their physical problems—are highly relevant today.

Jane Addams grew up at a time when women had little status in public life, when submissive marriage or retiring spinsterhood was their only option. The aching dissatisfaction that Jane and her friends felt was a forerunner of "the problem that has no name," which Betty Friedan addressed in her classic 1963 best-seller, *The Feminine Mystique.* Friedan argued that women's core problem was the "stunting or evasion of growth" that is perpetuated by the cultural ideal of women as solely sexual and domestic beings. The women of Jane's generation suffered from virtually the same malady, the suffocating demands of a womanly ideal, which required them to be pious, pure, and docile, and which dissolved their talents into "genteel nothingness."

Against terrible odds, Jane found a way to be useful to society. At the same time, she became the world's pioneer in assimilating immigrants into middle-class life. As she readily acknowledged, she founded Hull-House as much to save herself as the poor. (She called her twin motives "the subjective necessity and the objective value" of settlement work.) Even as a child she had ambition, a charismatic personality, and a strong sense of moral duty. But living in a slum on Halsted Street transformed her into a reformer. Throughout her adult life, she worked tirelessly to abolish child labor, sweatshops, tenements, unsafe factories, filthy streets, and corrupt politicians. Though not a particularly original thinker, she was acutely sensitive to the currents of thought flowing around her, and she was a gifted speaker and writer. She traveled the country preaching a "social gospel" demanding justice for all, and she wrote several books that helped set the liberal agenda for the twentieth century.

Jane's career would not have been possible without the bolstering support of close female companions. Like many achieving women of the day, she never slept with a man. The two abiding loves of her life were women—first Ellen Gates Starr, the volatile young teacher with whom she founded Hull-House, and, later, Mary Rozet Smith, a beautiful aristocrat to whom she considered herself married. Jane's letters to and from Ellen Starr and Mary Smith offer a rare chance to look inside romantic friendship, an essentially pre-Freudian phenomenon that has been lost to the modern era.

MUCH HAS been written about Jane Addams, Hull-House, the settlement movement, and nineteenth-century womanhood. I am greatly indebted to the leading authorities on Jane Addams, Allen F. Davis and Mary Lynn Bryan, editor of the Jane Addams Papers Project. I'd also like to thank the scholars Blanche Wiesen Cook, Nancy F. Cott, Lillian Faderman, Joan D. Hedrick, Gertrude Himmelfarb, Helen Horowitz, Donald Miller, David Nasaw, Anne Firor Scott, Barbara Sicherman, Kathryn Kish Sklar, and Carroll Smith-Rosenberg, whose work has helped me understand how Jane's life fits into the broad themes and sociopolitical contexts of the period.

This book spans thirty-nine years, from 1860, the year of Jane's birth, during the presidential campaign of her father's friend Abraham Lincoln, to 1899, when she entered the national stage through her widely read articles in journals such as *Outlook* and *The Atlantic Monthly*—at the time the only national communications media.

My contribution, I hope, is to capture something of the tone and texture of Jane Addams's early life, to give a sense of what she was like as a woman. To that end, I have relied as much as possible on primary sources—letters, newspaper articles, diaries, appointment books, and calendars. Over the years, Jane's life has been obscured by myth and sentimentality and her own extreme reticence. She was silent about many things a biographer wants to know, and she destroyed some material that might have been helpful. Yet, a portrait emerges of a fiercely determined, ambitious, complicated woman—one who, for all her flaws, was unfailingly dedicated to improving American life.

Jane's coming of age occurred against a backdrop of a rapidly changing America, a time when Gilded Age splendor clashed with urban misery. Between her birth and the end of the century, when Hull-House was founded, industrial capitalism came of age. Five transcontinental railroads were built; a national economy was created; the Western frontier was settled and America's boundaries defined. Doubts were first being raised about organized religion, yet many people still retained a powerful commitment to moral duty. Jane was a transitional figure embodying both the purity and innocence of the Victorian angel and the bold independence of the Gibson Girl. In her hopes, conflicts, frailties, and achievements, she speaks directly to modern women.

Today, more than a half century after her death, Jane Addams's place in American history is assured. Her belief that the world is improvable is at the heart of what's best in the American character. Though she has been criticized by some historians for helping to lay the foundation of an overblown welfare system, her ideas of justice and social work, formed in an earlier era when government paid scant attention to the poor, are at the center of today's fierce debate over the underclass. Many people who work with the unfortunate still think settlement-type programs are the best way to cope with urban problems. Jane's career is an extraordinary record of accomplishment and courage, of great odds overcome. And it is a symbol of one of the most important themes of America's second century—the emergence of women into the public arena.

At heart, Jane Addams's early life is a story about the yearning for useful work and the yearning for love; about the tensions between femininity and ambition, family and self; about the meaning of duty and the importance of independence. It is the story of nineteenth-century American women. To a remarkable extent, their struggles and dreams were the same as our own.

PART I

Angels in the House

I

Sarah

Sarah Weber Addams, Jane's mother.
(Courtesy of University of Illinois at Chicago, the University Library, Mary Fry Collection)

In Jane Addams's first memory, she was two years old and standing outside the room where her mother lay dying. She remembered sobbing as she pounded on the door and hearing Sarah Addams cry out, "Let her in, she is only a baby herself." Years later, when her nephew challenged the accuracy of her recollection, Jane insisted, "No one ever told me this, and it is impossible that I could have invented it." It was the only image she had of her mother, and she guarded it fiercely all her life.

The story fits nicely with the known facts of Sarah Addams's last days. At forty-four and seven months pregnant with her ninth child, she had collapsed while helping a neighbor give birth, and the doctor had carried her home to the Addamses' large, Greek Revival–style house in Cedarville, Illinois. For several days she lay under a hand-pieced quilt in the old wooden bed where Jane had been born. Her eyesight was failing, and she slipped in and out of consciousness as violent convulsions twisted her body. Finally, in hopes of saving Sarah, the doctor removed her baby. The infant, a perfectly formed little girl, took a few breaths, then died.

It was the winter of 1863, the midpoint of the Civil War and an era full of dying. Across the Illinois prairie and America, freshly cleared village cemeteries were filling up with the bodies of soldiers and the victims of epidemics, their graves marked by elaborate marble monuments, like trophies. At no other time in American life had death been so glorified—in popular novels with titles like *The Gates Ajar* and in songs in which dead children sang, "We are happy now, dear mother." The closeness of death had sparked waves of Calvinistic predetermination, a poignant need to turn death into a positive blessing, "a reward," even an extension of life itself. Yet, death was no less terrible for being so familiar.

Sarah and John Addams had already lost three babies—in 1850, 1855, and 1859, when cholera swept across the prairie with the spring rains. Each baby had been placed in a tiny, handmade coffin and buried in the family plot at the top of a wooded hill on one acre of land that John had donated for a public burying ground.

The family prayed that those would be the only early deaths. The five remaining children seemed strong, and the parents were in ruddy good health. Both John and Sarah Addams were descended from immigrants who arrived in America in the early eighteenth century and who, in many ways, embodied the spirit of the new republic. They were hardworking and ambitious, and they knew how to make money. Sarah's ancestors were Germans who'd settled near Philadelphia before the Revolutionary War. Her father, Colonel George Weber, helped found Lafayette College and owned a thriving flour mill, as well as hundreds of acres in Kriedersville, Pennsylvania.

SARAH WAS one of six children and the second daughter. The only surviving photograph of her shows a face with a high forehead, straight nose, and round eyes. She had abundant light brown hair, which she wore in the fashion of the day, parted in the middle and combed down over her ears into a loose knot at the back of her neck. Since her family was cultured and prosperous, she was sent to boarding school, where she studied languages and literature and became an accomplished singer.

By the time Sarah Weber met John Addams in 1843, she was twenty-six—old at the time for a single woman with hopes to marry. At twenty-one, John was five years younger. He'd arrived in Ambler, Pennsylvania, after a brief stint teaching school in a nearby town, and apprenticed himself to Enos Reiff, Sarah's brother-in-law, who owned a flour mill. John was the seventh child of Catherine Huy and Samuel Addams, whose English ancestors had been lured from Oxfordshire, England, by a gift from William Penn of five hundred acres of Pennsylvania land. The clan arrived in America with only one *d* in their name; a second *d* was added by an ancestor—a captain for the colonists in the Revolutionary War—to avoid confusion with a cousin.

John Addams was tall, muscular, and dark-haired, with pale, gray eyes and a grave demeanor that made him seem older than his years. He had an overwrought sense of duty and a Quaker's concern with morality. "Integrity above all else," he inscribed in his neat hand in one leatherbound volume of the diary he kept all his life. "What would a man Proffit by gaining the whole world if he lost his soul?" he wrote in the diary. "Am firmly impressed that 'Honesty is the best Policy,' and hope that I may by all means and through all hazards stick to the above Proverb. Let come what may, let me stick to the above."

By virtually all accounts, he did, becoming a direct, plainspoken man whose earnestness—at least in hindsight—often seems to overwhelm his deep love for those close to him. John loathed laziness. Once, after a social gathering, he wrote in his diary, "[S]pent the afternoon rather in frivolous conversation which I hope in future to avoid." As the miller's apprentice, he was required to start work at three in the morning when the mill's operation began. At moments when he wasn't busy, he sat on a tree stump inside the mill reading by lantern light. Eventually, he went through every book in an Ambler library, beginning with the lives of the signers of the Declaration of Independence, and continuing through Pope's translation of the *Iliad,* Dryden's *Virgil,* and Plutarch's *Lives.* In the afternoon, he courted Sarah, who swiftly fell in love with him.

They were married on July 18, 1844, and nine days later set out to make their home in northern Illinois, which they referred to in letters as "the Far West." Eastern settlers had been flocking to the state since the 1830s. Canals were built, plans for railroads were set in motion (in 1848, work would begin on the Illinois Central Railroad), and peace with the Indians had been achieved. Around the time of John and Sarah's arrival, the Pottawatomies, the last Native American tribe settled in the area, had moved from Illinois. The tribe sold their lands east of the Mississippi and settled on the western shore of the river, leaving their home "in fulfillment of their destiny as a fading race," as one newspaper columnist put it, echoing the sentiments of the time.

Part of the Weber clan, including Sarah's father and her missionary brother, George, decided to join the newlyweds. John Addams's brother, James, would eventually follow. For the Webers and the Addamses, as for many Americans, the West represented opportunity. In the Eastern cities, fortunes were being made with the rise of industry. But the great Westward migration was defining the tone of American life—optimistic, energetic, democratic. The Eastern establishment—"Yankee Land," as it was known—still mirrored English society, with all its stiffness and pretensions. The West was America.

Sarah and John set out at four in the morning in a two-wheeled horse-driven wagon. They went first to New York for a few days of sight-seeing (one afternoon they watched workers building Trinity Church). Then they traveled by cart, railroad, and steamboat to Chicago, a journey of ten days. Chicago was a muddy, dusty town, where wolves wandered the streets and bayed at the moon at night. The newlyweds bought a horse and covered wagon, and headed into the wilderness, traveling on the Old State Road at a speed of three miles an hour. They were headed for Freeport, a town on the Pecatonica River, one hundred miles west of Chicago. John had a cousin there with a farm, and the newlyweds hoped to settle in Freeport and make their home.

The country immediately outside Chicago was flat and dull, dotted here and there by a few taverns and farmhouses—in sharp contrast to the rocky hills and pretty villages they'd left behind in Pennsylvania. The farms grew scarcer, and soon the travelers reached the vast expanse of empty prairie. Stretching before them were miles and miles of waving grasses, broken only by small clumps of trees. The many "sloughs"—patches of black mud sometimes a quarter mile wide—made the journey treacherous. The only roads were occasional "corduroy" roads, made by placing rough logs over the mud. Where there were no corduroys, they had to wade through mud sometimes up to their waists, pulling the horse and buggy behind them.

They reached Freeport after several days. At the time, it was a raw, new town of twelve hundred inhabitants. The Addamses arrived in a heat spell and found geese roaming freely, feasting on garbage scraps tossed into the street. Despite a water wagon that sprinkled the streets, clouds of dust hung in the air. Dirt and debris blew into the open stores, where flies swarmed over the produce.

But even by 1844, Freeport was becoming a bustling center of commerce. The wooden sidewalks were crowded with people; in the evening, they carried lanterns to light their way. Political parades, torchlight rallies, circus companies, minstrel shows, and funerals all passed up Stephenson Street, the city's main thoroughfare.

Within eight years, the city's population would grow to seven thousand, swelled by Easterners and immigrants. The largest group came from Germany. After 1848, a wave of Irish escaping the potato famine also settled there.

A friend of the Addamses' counted two hundred people going through Freeport in covered wagons in one week. They were "movers," headed west or north to Iowa or Minnesota, where land could be bought for $1.25 an acre. (In Illinois it was already about $10 to $20 an acre.) "You would wonder where the people all come from that pass by here . . . why the people here all talk about going west," a friend of the Addamses noted in an 1856 letter. All knew that the journey could be perilous. "[T]here was a little boy fell from a team and was run over and killed yesterday not far from Warren at a place called Debuke," the letter continued. Tragedies were common. On their journey, the Addamses met many families who'd lost all their money and several of their children, and were now making the reverse trek, heading home, "begging their way back to the East."

Until they could find a place of their own, John and Sarah stayed with John's cousin. John was homesick for Pennsylvania and so nervous about the future that he was having nightmares. Once, he woke up in the middle of the night after having dreamed that Sarah was dying. Much of his spare time was occupied by performing menial chores on his cousin's farm. "Picked potatoes all day," he wrote in his diary. And on other days, "Made a bench settee after dinner . . . Ploughed for about an hour . . . Felt sad and wished very much for a home."

His only recreation was arguing politics with the other men he met at the general store and attending Methodist meetings on Sunday. At one, he was impressed at the children's good behavior and the adults' seriousness. "All seemed as if they had come to hear the word of God proclaimed and not to see or be seen," he wrote.

He spent months riding across the country on his horse Dolly, studying various sites along the Pecatonica River. Finally, backed by a loan from his father, he decided to pay $4,000 for two mills and several hundred acres of surrounding land on the banks of Cedar Creek six miles north of Freeport. One of the mills was a flour mill, where the neighboring farmers (thirteen other families had already settled in the area) brought their grains, and the other was a sawmill.

The setting reminded John of Pennsylvania, and, though there was as yet no school, church, store, or post office, he pronounced it "a fine site for a town." It would be incorporated as the village Cedarville in 1849. John plowed an acre of ground on a hill beyond the creek and planted a bagful of Norway pine seeds that he'd brought from Pennsylvania. Within a decade they'd grown into trees, which for several generations crowned a hill surrounding the village. Only one stands today.

The couple's first home was a simple two-room house with a dirt floor. "You would no doubt laugh would you see us in our 'log cabin 8 by 10' which serves for Parlour, Bedroom, Dining Room & Kitchen," Sarah wrote to her Eastern relatives, noting that "it is customary in this western part of the world for newcomers first to move [into] log cottages." The cabin was similar to one built by their neighbors, a family of six, who'd also come from Pennsylvania. "We moved to Cedarville and lived in a house with one room below and one above," recalled a daughter in that neighboring family, Mrs. John W. Henney, writing of her childhood years. "We slept upstairs, and it was not plastered. The snow blew in on the beds and we would make snowballs and throw them at each other."

John and Sarah fit the ideal Victorian mold. Sarah was the serenely self-sacrificing wife—exactly the role mythologized by society at the time. In 1856, English poet Coventry Patmore published a book-length poem that immediately became a best-seller in England and America. *The Angel in the House* went on for page after sentimental page, singing the virtues of the "angel":

The gentle wife who decks his board
And makes his day to have no night,
Whose wishes wait upon her lord,
Who finds her own in his delight.

Every respectable Victorian house had an "angel"—a selfless, accommodating, tireless woman who lived to satisfy the needs of others. This ideal of femininity had developed with the rise of evangelical religion at the end of the eighteenth century. Clergymen called on women to be Christianity's most zealous advocates, raising them to the status of angels. Women were morally superior to men, and thus unfit for any pursuit outside the home. Of course, the angel myth overlooked the fact that the glorified role of wife and mother doomed many women to a life of drudgery and early death.

For many women the lack of birth control made pregnancy a perpetual state, and childbirth was still dangerous. Women who didn't die giving birth were an uncommonly sturdy breed—almost a different species from their sisters—and they often had ten or twelve children and lived into their nineties. Sarah, who'd survived into her fourth decade after eight pregnancies, seemed to be one of those women.

Prosperity made her life easier than most. John Addams was a self-made man, the essence of Victorian rectitude. He still got up at three every morning to work side by side with his mill hands, supervising them with those cool gray eyes that confirmed his austere demeanor. He had a reputation for flawless integrity, and people were in awe of him. Around Cedarville, the story was told of the farmer who walked around one icy winter morning with the flaps of his cap turned up. When a friend warned him to pull the flaps down or risk freezing his ears, the farmer replied, "No, I won't; I just saw John Addams and he says 'Tain't cold.'"

Sarah and John quickly had five children—Mary, born in 1845, Georgiana in 1849, Martha in 1850, Weber in 1852, and Sarah Alice in 1853. Mary, like her mother, was an "angel," totally given to self-sacrifice. She was "so far forgetting herself in others that by them she became unforgettable," Jane recalled. She thought of her younger siblings as *her* children, showering on them an affection so intense, she once said, "I could not endure to have it much more keen."

Martha, the next in line (Georgiana had died in infancy), was the family beauty—blond, pink-cheeked, and slim. She was a talented pianist who took lessons every week from a neighbor, the only woman in town who had a piano and a person who would come to have a deep influence on the Addams brood. Following her was Weber. The Addamses' only surviving son, Weber was sweet-tempered and docile, but also lazy and not as quick-witted as his sisters, a source of deep distress to his father. Next came Alice, whose intelligence and energy were marred by a difficult temperament.

By 1854 John Addams had made enough money to build a large house—it remained for generations the grandest in the village. Constructed from painted gray brick in the Greek Revival style popular at the time with the haute bourgeois in England, the house sat on a hill overlooking the mills and on the main road leading north from Freeport to Wisconsin. It had elegant, shuttered windows and spacious rooms. The front door was framed by cranberry glass, which, to those looking out, gave the world an eerie, rosy glow. Here, in the ground-floor bedroom off the kitchen, three more children arrived—Horace in 1855, George in 1857, and Laura Jane on September 6, 1860, two months before Lincoln's election to the presidency.

The new baby was named after Mrs. Laura Jane Forbes, who'd boarded at the Addams home while teaching school in the village. Immediately, the baby's siblings began calling her Jennie, as most Janes were nicknamed at the time, after Jenny Lind, the dazzling "Swedish Nightingale" who'd made a concert tour of America in the 1850s.

Jennie had her father's clear gray eyes and straight brown hair. Early descriptions emphasized her "different" appearance, and her "spiritual" or "dreamy" look. Photographs show that Jennie had a pretty face with deep, intelligent eyes and a sad expression that would grow more pronounced as time went on. Part of the sadness could have been due to her physical discomfort. She suffered from Pott's disease, a notorious child killer since ancient times, which by mid-nineteenth century was still believed to be incurable. The illness, named after the British physician Percivall Pott, who first discovered it in the eighteenth century, was a form of tuberculosis, which when concentrated in the spine caused severe curvature.

Jennie's condition gave her a fragile, sickly aura. Obviously, something was wrong with her. She was thin, pale, and pigeon-toed, and because of the curvature in her back, she held her head to one side. She was the family's "special" child, and like Eva in *Uncle Tom's Cabin* or Little Nell in Dickens's *Old Curiosity Shop,* she seemed doomed—one of the cherished "little sufferers" God had anointed never to grow up.

Within the family, she was treated as an adored pet, hovered over, catered to, and doted on, her every cough and sniffle watched closely by her relatives. "They were all, from John Addams down, lenient with her," recalled Jane's niece Marcet Haldeman. "The way was always smoothed for little 'Jennie.' The others gave up to her and were quickly responsive to her moods and childish tempers. Playing much alone, she grew introspective; uncrossed, she came to feel that her own way was without question the right one. She was lovable but, not surprisingly in this atmosphere of indulgence, she was also willful. She was delicate, too, and the fear that they might lose her often fell like a shadow upon the hearts of her [family]."

THE ADDAMS children knew they had much more money than the other families in Cedarville. Their house, though decorated modestly, was the largest around. Unlike the other children in the village, they enjoyed drawing and music lessons and wore fine clothes. But John Addams would not tolerate pretension. Once little Jennie put on a beautiful new coat and ran to her father for approval. He told her it was indeed "a very pretty cloak—in fact so much prettier than any cloak the other little girls in the Sunday School had, that he would advise me to wear my old cloak, which would keep me quite as warm, with the added advantage of not making the other little girls feel badly," Jane recalled. She ran off to change. When she returned, John Addams added that, "it was very stupid to wear the sort of clothes that made it harder to have equality even there [in church]."

The Addamses never belonged to a specific church, though they always attended Sunday services at one of Cedarville's Protestant parishes. Under John's belief, Christianity demanded a social commitment, and he was intensely sensitive to the injustices of the world, though his ideas were limited by the attitudes of the time. He opposed slavery, but he did not think blacks were entitled to the same full range of civil rights as whites. He supported education for women because he believed it would make them better wives and mothers; beyond that, he held the conventional, Victorian view that women belonged in their separate, domestic sphere. He ridiculed feminists who agitated for the vote as "abominable ugly" women, and he once complained that a speech by Elizabeth Cady Stanton, the famous suffragist, was "mere rambling and rather bordering on the egotistical."

To his neighbors, he was "the king gentleman of the district." He helped build a Methodist church in Cedarville, and in 1846 organized the area's first library, which operated out of the Addams home and eventually circulated 350 books. He invested in the Galena and Chicago Railroad and for weeks rode on horseback from log cabin to log cabin, asking farmers to back the venture, which was needed to send crops to markets in the East. After the railroad finally went through, he helped start the Second National Bank of Freeport.

He also made sure Cedarville had a good school. In Illinois, the free public school system started up only in 1854, and in most communities tax-supported schools were not organized until years later. What schools existed were created and paid for by parents, who for the most part had neither the time nor the money to seek out and hire good teachers. Children often grew up illiterate, taught by teachers who could barely read. Schooling typically ended by the eighth grade.

John Addams, though, raised money from the villagers to build a redbrick schoolhouse (from the Addams home it was a short walk down the hill and across the creek) and searched the Midwest for a competent teacher, finally settling on J. H. Parr, a young man whose brother Samuel later became a professor of Latin at the University of Illinois.

Soon, John Addams was the best-known man in the county, and in 1854 he was elected to the state senate as a Whig. The next year, he joined a group of abolitionists at Ripon, Wisconsin, to launch the Republican party. Afterward, he was elected state senator seven times as a Republican. His honesty was legendary. A *Chicago Times* editor wrote that although there were doubtless many members of the state legislature who had never accepted a bribe, John Addams was the only man he had ever known to whom nobody had ever dared offer one.

Springfield, the capital of Illinois, lay 180 miles south of Freeport, in the central part of the state. When John was there, he wrote his wife daily—affectionate, newsy letters, asking her to "kiss the children" for him and write to him often—"a letter every day would be great comfort if it does not crowd too much on your time," he implored. He sent her the *Springfield Journal* so she could "see what we do" in the Senate, and recounted his new friendship with a successful lawyer named Abraham Lincoln. John was an occasional guest at the Lincoln house on the corner of Eighth and Jackson streets, where Mary Lincoln held lively parties. "There was a great crowd," John wrote Sarah after one fete. "All past [*sic*] off well. The ladies were out in hoops and quite a number of them."

Two pictures of Lincoln hung in John's study, and a picture of Lincoln with his son Tad hung in the Addams family's upstairs parlor. In a locked drawer of his desk, John kept a small packet of papers marked "Mr. Lincoln's letters." They all began, "My dear Double-D'ed Addams," and usually concerned legislative business, inquiring how Addams was going to vote on a certain measure, usually adding the assurance that he knew Addams "would vote according to his conscience," but begging to know in which direction that conscience "was pointing."

At the time of Jennie's birth, political tensions were high in Illinois, as they were around the country. The northern part of the state was pro-Union, having been settled principally by Easterners. Yet there was at least one Southern sympathizer in Cedarville. One night a man on horseback galloped up Mill Street shooting holes in an enormous hand-sewn American flag that had been suspended by a rope over the middle of the street. In Freeport, the telegraph office was burned down by Southern sympathizers, and there were other incidents of vandalism.

The South seceded seven months after Jane was born. With the call for troops after the surrender of Fort Sumter, Stephenson County men began joining the Union army and by April 20, 1861, the first company was organized under Captain S. D. Atkins. John Addams raised money to outfit a regiment called "The Addams Guards."

The *Freeport Bulletin* recorded the regiment's departure to join the main army on April 22, 1861: "They left on the ten o'clock train yesterday. They were escorted to the depot by Cap. Mills' company and attended by thousands of their fellow citizens. At the depot the scene was affecting. Mothers, fathers, sisters, parted tearfully with their sons and brothers. The [soldiers] were in the highest spirits."

Once, during the summer of 1861, Captain Atkins stopped at the Addams house during a recruitment drive. He found John "in the harvest field, driving a reaper," recalled one of Atkins's lieutenants. He appealed to him for aid in enlisting sixty soldiers. "Addams unhitched the team, leaving the reaper in the field, and drove off with Atkins to a recruiting meeting, where, mainly by his influence, twenty volunteers were secured."

One extended family supplied seven of the sixty-three men who'd enlisted from Cedarville. Amazingly, only one of them died in the war. All her life, Jane remembered the "engraved roster of names, headed by the words 'Addams' Guard,' and the whole surmounted by the insignia of the American eagle clutching many flags, which always hung in the family living-room. As children we used to read this list of names again and again. We could reach it only by dint of putting the family Bible on a chair and piling the dictionary on top of it; using the Bible to stand on was always accompanied by a little thrill of superstitious awe, although we carefully put the dictionary above that so our profane feet might touch it alone."

The Addams children idolized the dead soldiers. If the family were going for a drive, the children would beg their father to take them past a farm where a soldier had once lived; if there was a surplus of flowers in the garden, they'd ask if they could deliver them to the mother of a dead hero. The girls were particularly close to Maria Clingman, who lived in a white farmhouse north of the village. One of her three sons had been killed in battle, and her husband had died of pneumonia while on a mission to enlist troops. Maria still had two children at home, and since, under the law, a woman couldn't have legal responsibility for her children or property, John Addams became her guardian.

To his own children, John was the most godlike person on earth, the voice of authority, but also a kind and loving figure. The five-mile trips into Freeport with their father were great events for the children, despite the uncomfortable and often treacherous carriage ride. Except in winter, when the ground was frozen, they often got stuck in mud and had to travel at high speed to keep the momentum up. Mary Addams remembered one unpleasant horse-and-buggy ride through a rainstorm with "the horses going very fast, so that I almost thought I should go out over the wagon." Jane sneezed and coughed the whole way, since she suffered from "horse fever"—she was allergic to horses. Still, she looked forward to these outings as great adventures.

After buying a treat at the confectioner's store, Jennie would walk along the wooden sidewalks, holding her sisters' hands, and watch the people and animals milling about. Herds of cattle, sheep, and hogs were marched down the street for shipment at the railroad. There were also large numbers of beautiful horses with shiny, braided manes and tails that had been wrapped in red flannel.

Once she and Mary stood on the Stephenson Street sidewalk in front of their father's bank and watched for two hours as a parade of 850 horses, 470 wagons, and 400 farmers passed. Mary remembered that she heard no swearing and saw no drunkenness. "It was perfectly safe for a lady to be there."

AT HOME, the family's day began at 3:00 A.M., when everyone arose with John. Sarah started breakfast, and the children did their chores. In the afternoon, the family flour mill became their playground. They romped in the dusty bins full of flour, and used the empty bins to play house. But the sawmill next door was even more intriguing. One of their favorite games was to sit on a log and ride it as the buzzing saw grew closer and closer, jumping off just in time to avoid "a sudden and gory death."

In the evenings the children would read or play chess in the parlor while their parents wrote letters. With John Addams away from home much of the time, it was left to Sarah not only to manage the large household but also to run the family business.

Sarah's tough temperament eased her adjustment from Eastern lady to pioneer wife. She made her own soap, churned butter, baked bread, molded candles (the messiest, most detested chore of the pioneer housewife), and prepared three meals a day for her family and twenty mill hands, assisted only by the family's long-time servant, Polly, and two hired girls, usually the unmarried daughters of neighboring settlers.

Sarah also did much of her own sewing. Like other women of the time, she was an expert at ruffling, cording, hand tucking, hem stitching, and embroidering. Not only did she make many of the family's clothes, she sewed rags into rugs and pieced together squares of gingham, cotton, and calico for quilts. Years after her death, Sarah's children slept under quilts made from scraps of their mother's dresses.

Sarah was hardworking, unselfish, pious, and soft-spoken, an ideal Victorian woman. Sometimes, though, she could be sharp with her children. When they were naughty, she locked them in a closet behind the back stairs and left them there for hours, despite their kicks and screams. (A half century later, gashes made by their boots were still on the door.)

The children were forbidden to play near the rapid stream that ran behind the house and under the mill—had they fallen in they would have been ground under the enormous mill wheel. Once, Sarah saw Alice and Weber at the water's edge. As Alice's daughter recalled the story, "She walked across the yard and with quick, unhesitating strength she pushed the little boy—whom she regarded as the leader—into the water. Alice gazed horror-stricken as her brother struggled helplessly, while their mother ran to the curve of the stream by the bridge. As her son was borne to that spot, Sarah reached out a sure arm and drew him to the bank. He was choking with fright as much as with water—but it was a lesson that neither child forgot. There was no more careless playing by the mill-race."

Sarah's only rest came at the end of the day, when she would sit in the library upstairs in front of the fire, rocking the baby's cradle with one foot, while her other children sat on the floor reading. Downstairs the hired girls cleaned the supper dishes.

Sarah's first eight pregnancies had been easy, but her ninth, in 1862, caused her much distress, and she'd felt ill constantly. Still, when a neighbor's husband asked her to help the doctor deliver his wife's baby, Sarah agreed. She collapsed from the exertion and never recovered. John Addams was in Springfield at the time, and Sarah's brother George Weber kept vigil at her bedside. In a rambling letter, with its run-on, unpunctuated style reflecting not only a strong oral tradition but also his anxiety, George described her final days to their brother and sister in Pennsylvania:

> Oh it was very hard to see her have the convulsions her features had entirely changed she had ten or a Dozen attacks towards morning. . . . Sunday about 11 o'clock the first we noticed of any consciousness was the little daughter Jenny cried with a loud shriek Sarah raised up in bed but oh the wild look she had she soon sank back again I called her by name she opened her eyes I gave her something to drink. . . . John had [arrived] in the Morning Sunday from Springfield towards evening she knew us both we all thought she might possibly get well again I returned home in the night our daughter Mary being very sick of Typhoid fever on Monday afternoon I again went to see Sarah and found the change still for the better as we supposed she named me I said to her the Lord did help she repeated the words . . .

But Sarah did not recover. Two days later, on January 14, 1863, she looked at her husband, recited the Lord's Prayer several times, then breathed her last.

It fell to James Addams, John's brother, to notify the relatives living nearby. He stopped first at George Weber's house, pulling up to the log cabin in a cloud of dust. When George saw the long stick hanging out of James's wagon—a measure for an adult coffin—he knew Sarah had died. George, a Reformed Church minister who was bitterly opposed to the war, regarded Sarah's death as God's "chastisement" for John's support of the unchristian conflict.

Sarah and her infant were buried together next to the three graves of her other babies, Georgiana, Horace, and George, who had all died in infancy. The ceremony was attended by settlers from miles around. George Weber wrote that it was "the largest funeral that I have seen in the West." Sarah "had a very fine no doubt expensive Coffin was dressed in a black [fancy] dress she used to have." His minister's sense of austerity pushed him to add, "I should liked to [have] seen a white shroud & things more plain."

SARAH'S DEATH plunged her family into grief and despair. John Addams consoled himself with work, while the children imagined a reunion with their mother in heaven. With death such a close and constant presence, a belief in an afterlife had immense healing power. In many ways, the family never recovered from the loss of Sarah. Though John remarried in 1867, his new wife, Anna Hostetter Haldeman, was a haughty widow with two difficult, troubled sons. The five surviving Addams children suffered all their lives. Weber's intense grief over his mother's death triggered a breakdown that would keep him in and out of mental hospitals for the rest of his life. Martha would die at sixteen, succumbing to one of the many typhoid epidemics that swept through Illinois. Mary and Alice would be trapped in miserable marriages. Only Jennie would break free.

After her mother's death, she clung to her father. Of all the Addams children, she was the one who most closely resembled him, and John favored her over the others. Yet her father's devotion could not replace her mother, and Sarah's death left a deep imprint on Jennie's life. It was her first experience with what she later called "that mysterious injustice" of life, "the burden of which we are all forced to bear and with which I have become only too familiar." Her commitment to the poor, to justice, to peace, was, at one of its deepest levels, a defense against death. As a child growing up amid the ravages of family tragedy and the Civil War, Jennie became "overwhelmingly oppressed by that grief of things as they are." She "sorely needed" a "sense of universality," a belief in the common humanity of all people, to beat back her feelings of despair.

Sarah Addams's short obituary in the *Freeport Journal* (just beneath a story announcing the Stephenson Insurance Company's "splendid" new sign) stressed her usefulness, a vital element of womanly virtue. "Mrs. Addams was a woman who will be missed everywhere—at home, in society, in the church, in all places where good was to be done, and suffering to be relieved. Possessed of means, and with a heart ever alive to the wants of the poor, she was always present when sympathy was needed or aid required," the *Journal* eulogized. "She lived a life of usefulness, and has gone to her reward, leaving a stricken household and a large circle of mourning friends."

Sarah Addams was the embodiment of the Victorian woman, the ideal Angel in the House. All her life, even as she tried to break free from conventional notions of femininity, Jane would see "the shadow of her wings."

2

Ann

John Huy Addams, Jane's father, and
his second wife, Anna Haldeman Addams.
*(Courtesy of the Jane Addams Collection,
Swarthmore College Peace Collection)*

The motherless children were cared for by Polly Beer, Sarah's governess, who'd followed the Addamses to Illinois and lived with them for many years. Polly was a comfortable presence, but she was more than sixty—too old and tired to take an active interest in the children's lives. The real job of mothering fell to the family's eldest daughter, seventeen-year-old Mary.

Serene and selfless, Mary did most of the cooking and sewing for the family, always keeping in mind how her "mother would have liked it." She helped the children with their homework and tucked them in at night; she nursed them through illnesses and wrote the older ones long, advice-filled letters when they were away at school. "Take good care of yourself . . . be sure to wear your waist under the calico dresses," she once warned Alice, who was studying at Rockford Female Seminary in nearby Rockford, Illinois. "If you bathe and take three or four drops of camphor or white sugar . . . it will almost invariably break up [your] cold."

Though Jennie adored Mary, she never thought of her as a substitute parent. Instead, as she later wrote, she focused on her father "all that careful imitation which a little girl ordinarily gives to her mother's ways and habits."

Jennie's identification with her father was so complete that she had "a consuming ambition" to possess the flattened "miller's thumb" and speckled hands John Addams had acquired from years of rubbing flour between his fingers and dressing millstones. She spent countless days at the mill, she recalled, "sitting contentedly for a long time rubbing between my thumb and fingers the ground wheat as it fell from between the millstones." The faint purple and red dots on her father's hands seemed to her "so desirable that they must be procured at all costs." She'd often run down to the mill to spread her hands out "in the hope that the little hard flints flying from the miller's chisel would light upon their backs and make the longed-for marks."

She struggled to live up to her father's rigid standards of integrity. If, during the day, she'd told a lie, she would spend a "horrid" night tossing about in bed, "held in the grip of a miserable dread of death, a double fear, first, that I myself should die in my sins and go straight to that fiery Hell which was never mentioned at home, but which I had heard all about from other children, and, second, that my father—representing the entire adult world which I had basely deceived—should himself die before I had time to tell him." Her only relief was to go to her father's room on the ground floor and confess. Groping her way down the dark stairs, past the front door, which John Addams refused to lock (his Quaker principles demanded that he trust his neighbors), she'd stand at the foot of the stairs, hugging the mahogany newel post, until she summoned the courage to face him. Finally, she entered his darkened room, approached the bed, and blurted out her confession. Waking suddenly, he looked gravely at her and said he was sorry he had a little girl who told lies, but "he was very glad she felt too bad to go to sleep afterwards."

On Sunday mornings, as the family walked up the dirt road outside their house on the way to church, Jennie imagined that everyone they passed was "filled with admiration" for her father. He looked so "imposing" in his black frock coat and tall black silk hat, his "fine head rising high above all the others." In contrast, she thought of herself as an ugly duckling, a scrawny, malformed little girl whose crooked back forced her to walk pigeon-toed with her head to one side. She couldn't bear for strangers to know that John Addams "owned this homely little girl," so she refused to walk by his side, instead taking the hand of her less imposing uncle James.

Jennie thought her father unshakably strong. But one day she came home from school to see him slumped in his horsehair chair, sobbing. Abraham Lincoln, he told her, "the greatest man in the world had died." At John's feet lay a copy of the *Freeport Journal,* the front page bordered in black and the terrible news emblazoned across the top: PRESIDENT ASSASSINATED.

Lincoln's death was close and palpable to everyone in Cedarville. The war had cruelly disrupted people's lives. Fathers, sons, uncles, brothers, and sweethearts would never be coming back. The deep sadness and confusion of the adults was grimly apparent to the Addams children. They always fell silent as they approached an isolated farmhouse at the end of the village where an old couple lived alone. Five of their sons had enlisted in the Civil War, and only the youngest had returned alive, in the spring of 1865. The following autumn, while duck hunting, he was accidentally shot and killed. Jennie wondered how this accident could have happened to this remaining son "out of all the men in the world, to him who had escaped so many chances of death," and her heart "swelled in first rebellion" against the inscrutable sadness of life.

The lesson was bitterly reinforced in March 1867, when a fresh tragedy struck the Addamses. Sixteen-year-old Martha, a student at Rockford Female Seminary, fell ill with typhoid fever and died within a week. Like the Addamses and most country families, the Rockford school depended for its water on wells and gave little thought to keeping them away from stables, outhouses, manure piles, and cemeteries. The water looked clear and tasted good. It never occurred to anyone that it carried deadly infection.

Jennie, who was six, was left alone at the house while the rest of the family and the hired help attended Martha's funeral. Until the end of her life, she recalled the "horror"—a favorite Addams word—she'd felt at being abandoned. For months she had nightmares that Mary, too, would die, and there would be "no one to love me."

The family consoled themselves by planting roses and carnations along the walk to Martha's grave and by imagining a reunion with her in heaven. "Though [Martha] cannot come to us, we may go to her. I hope we may be an unbroken family circle in heaven," Mary wrote a cousin. "Just one month yesterday since Martha left us. I realize it more every day, but I would not call her back if I could for we know that she is safe from all harm, and is happy."

Martha's death marked the fifth time John Addams had suffered what historian Joan D. Hedrick has called "one of the most common and profound events of nineteenth century family life." Though the infant mortality rate was declining slightly in upper-class America, a new emotional investment in children was growing even faster. Perhaps partly as a result, the status of middle-class children had risen. In previous eras, children were thought to be little adults, whose labor power should be used as soon as possible. The idea of children as precious individuals—the sentimentalization of childhood that has grown steadily to the present day—began around the time of Jane's childhood. Children began to be seen as the treasures of the Angel in the House, to be doted on and fussed over. After Martha's death, John looked at his remaining children and wondered who would be next. Frail, soulful Jennie, the family's "special child," seemed a likely candidate.

Her health was a constant concern. Yet records show that the little girl rarely missed school. It seems her attacks—of whooping cough, flu, backache, stomachache, among other ailments—occurred mostly at night, when her father and sisters were available to nurse her. Decades would pass before psychology would identify the phenomenon of psychosomatic illness, and, at the time, no one in the household recognized the neurotic component of Jennie's ailments. Her sister Alice, however, looking back on these years when an old woman, said Jennie was spoiled and manipulative. "She had everything she wanted, but she was not well," Alice recalled. "And after a time, with so much attention, she began to think it was her due to be waited upon and petted."

THE PETTING, however, was about to end. Soon, Jennie would have a new stepmother, a strong-willed woman with hardly the patience for a sickly child. Anna Hostetter Haldeman was an elegant widow from Freeport, Illinois, who'd been Martha Addams's piano teacher. At thirty-six, she was tall, slim, and fine boned, with hair the burnished gold color of old copper. People often remarked about her smooth, white hands with their long, tapering fingers—the hands of a privileged urban lady, not a frontier wife. "I never saw her do anything more useful with her hands than adjust the objects in a room, care for her flowers and strum a guitar when she sang the ballads of Moore and Burns," recalled her granddaughter Marcet Haldeman.

Like John and Sarah Addams, Ann was from Pennsylvania. Her mother had died when she was a child, the same day as her cherished baby sister Barbara. She never recovered from the twin tragedy, and her relatives blamed it for her sour temperament. All her life, Ann talked about the terror she felt at her mother's deathbed: "Barbara was put on the bed and I sat in a chair beside it, while Mother prayed for us and always asking the good Father to take baby before she died. Then my heart would swell and I would come from the room and go out alone and ponder over the great wrong that was done me for I thought am I not a poor little girl too that will have no mother and my little sister—the light of my life to die too—Oh! . . . Barbara was buried at 3 o'clock in the afternoon and Mother died at nine in the evening of the same day."

Afterward, Ann was raised by her father, a doctor, her older sister, and her six older brothers. At fourteen she moved to Illinois with two of the brothers, who were starting medical practices, and two years later, she married William Haldeman, who owned a mill. They had four sons, two of whom died in infancy. Ann's eldest child, Harry, a brilliant though cocky young man, was studying medicine and violin in Leipzig, Germany, at the time Ann met the Addams family. Her youngest boy, a bright and sensitive seven-year-old named George, was just six months younger than Jennie.

Compared with the other women on the prairie, Ann was sophisticated and well read. She boasted that she taught herself to read at age five, and she subscribed to *The Atlantic Monthly,* the national journal of culture, which had been founded in 1857, in Ralph Waldo Emerson's phrase, "to guide the age." Her self-education, though, was sadly incomplete, as her letters, full of misspellings and grammatical errors, reveal. Still, she thought of herself as an aesthete, and was fond of quoting a German proverb, "Whatever is beautiful—that belongs to me."

Ann was not by nature an Angel in the House. She was high-strung—prone, as her first husband remarked, "in getting up imaginary horrors to weep over." (She knew she was difficult; on insurance forms that asked her to describe her temperament, she wrote "nervous.") She also had frequent bursts of anger. Once, on a visit to her brother's family, her niece complained that "Aunt Ann has been talking so ugly to Mother and it makes me feel bad."

Part of her unpleasantness stemmed from frustration. Ann felt cheated by the limited opportunities of her sex. "Music and drawing when I was a young girl would have made a third heaven for me so did I long to indulge my finer feeling—and portray the inner workings of my finer self," she once told her son George, adding bitterly that "never a time offered itself for such indulgence."

With social acquaintances, particularly attractive men, Ann sparkled. She could be witty and charming, and she was known for her lively conversation. John Addams had enjoyed talking to her when he dropped Martha off for piano lessons twice a week, and after Martha's death, he missed these encounters. Then, one afternoon, as his carriage rolled along the county road to Freeport, he was stopped by a friend with sad news: William Haldeman lay dying of tuberculosis and was not expected to survive the day.

John's first thought—"What a wonderful wife Mrs. Haldeman would make for me!"—was uncharacteristically selfish, and he felt pangs of guilt when Haldeman indeed passed away. He waited almost a year before inviting the new widow to dinner, and, as his letters suggest, he was a stiff and awkward suitor. "Dear Madam," he wrote Ann on September 9, 1868. "From circumstances not under your Control I conclude the contemplated ride for last Saturday was prevented. Am I presuming too much to renew the request for next Saturday say two o'clock? If I hear nothing to the contrary will take it for granted that it will be convenient. With pleasing anticipations I am truly your Friend John H. Addams."

John proposed soon afterward. Though still grieving for her husband, with whom she'd been deeply in love, Ann said yes. Her sons, she told a relative, needed a father. After a quiet November 1868 wedding, Ann moved into the homestead, "now doubly dear" as John wrote her. Soon, however, the couple were quarreling—often over money. After the serenity of Sarah, John was baffled by Ann's "brilliant uneveness."

Ann wanted to impose on the Addams brood "all the tastes and manners" of a new urban era, as the historian Christopher Lasch wrote. First she convinced John to buy a new, expensive carriage. It was essential, she'd argued, to ensure the safety of "the precious freight . . . Pa Ma and children and friends who are dear" who traveled regularly from the homestead to the Red Oak train depot a few miles away. The next change she made was to bring their house into the Gilded Age. An elaborate cornice and a two-story tower with bay windows went up on the south side of the house. The clothes hooks on the bedroom walls came down, replaced by large armoires filled with expensive outfits. A second-floor bathroom was built so the family no longer had to use the privy outside. The trappings of Victorian opulence were installed—a piano, Oriental rugs, mahogany furniture, velvet drapes. Every evening the family gathered in the formal dining room (lit by a fire in a new fireplace) to talk about literature and art over dinners served on gold-rimmed china. Ann paid close attention to the children's table manners, instructing them according to the standards of Eastern society. ("I am very much obliged to you for your kind hint in respect to the use of my fork," Weber once wrote her from college.) After the hired girls cleared the plates, Ann would read from Byron, Scott, Shakespeare, and Goethe.

She also widened the family's circle of friends. She held dinner parties for prominent Freeport couples and sometimes took one of the children with her for the day-long train journey into Chicago to hear a concert or see a play. On winter holidays, sleighfuls of Ann's relatives from nearby Mt. Carroll pulled up to the house and stayed for days.

Ann's pretensions didn't mean much on the prairie, where, unlike in the East, there was no aristocracy based on inherited wealth or pedigree. (One meaningful measure of status, however, was how long a person had lived in the West. Only those who'd arrived before 1840 could call themselves "Old Settlers.") Compared with Sarah Addams's even, homey nature, Ann's manner came off as haughty. The neighbors thought she was "putting on airs" and was a climber.

Ann was well aware that she was a target of disapproval. When she entered church, she complained, she felt the entire congregation's "piercing glances directed at me." She was a favorite topic of conversation at Richart's store in Cedarville, where the hired girls gathered to gossip on Saturday mornings. They were not used to handling fine china, linens, crystal, and paintings, and their casual treatment of Ann's things often caused her to erupt in temper tantrums. Nor was she content with the average prairie girl's standards of housekeeping and cooking. Henry Sill, the family yardsman, wrote a poem about Ann's notorious difficulty keeping help:

Down on the lakefront
Where troubles do brew,

The hired girls are leaving
and the men are quitting too.

Much of the time the children were left alone with Ann, as John Addams was frequently in Springfield attending legislative sessions. During her husband's absence, Ann sometimes slept upstairs in bed with one of the girls. Part of the reason was for security. Though Ann locked the door in her husband's absence, she worried about burglars. From the second floor she could lean out the window and ring her alarm bell, "but downstairs to try such a perilous fete [*sic*]," she wrote John, "one might have one's head snapped off." But she also just enjoyed the physical comfort of being close to another person.

She was genuinely fond of the Addams brood. "To be termed 'Mother' or 'Ma' by such warm-hearted, kind children, (does not after all make the position a hard one) As I had supposed for me to fill," she wrote her husband. "But one day since you have been absent, And it seems an age. Well last night Allie slept with me and in a degree could make amends for her Father's absence, by being so warm and lovingly twining her arms about me."

By 1871 only Jennie and George remained at home. Ann's older son, Harry, was practicing medicine in a nearby town; Alice was at Rockford Female Seminary, and Weber was on his own. Mary had been married in November 1871 to John Linn, the minister of Cedarville's Presbyterian church.

After Mary's departure, Ann's control over Jennie tightened. She noticed that the little girl often feigned illness because she liked to be coddled, but Ann refused to indulge her. She insisted that Jane join her on galloping rides through the meadows and fields around Cedarville. Jennie's sciatica and allergy to horses made riding agony, and she bitterly resented the enforced exercise. Yet she never openly rebelled or spoke harshly to her stepmother—an early suppression of anger suggesting the emotional remoteness that would characterize her adult life.

In many ways, though, Ann had a positive influence on Jennie's life. John Addams had the Victorian notion that reading too many novels was a sign of weakness, but Ann encouraged Jennie to read as much fiction and poetry as she wanted. And Jennie enjoyed Ann's evening readings, when the gas lamps would be extinguished, and the children would sit around the dining table holding lighted candles.

Ann introduced Jennie to Louisa May Alcott, and the child reread *Little Women* several times, deciding that "It never seems to grow old." Once she discovered an author, she read all his or her work. Dickens was a particular favorite—he "never wrote anything stupid," Jennie thought. Still, she felt a bit guilty about too much pleasure reading, writing to a cousin that "as I am a little inclined to 'over do' things when I get started, I now have an arrangement with Pa, that I am to read a certain amount of history first."

Her stepbrother George became her closest companion. A quiet boy, he was passionately interested in science and passed this enthusiasm to Jennie. The children slept in adjoining bedrooms on the second floor and went to school together in the village. "Jennie and Georgie . . . never seem to be quite as contented as when they are here alone, without any company," Mary reported to Alice.

After school the children would run home, to be greeted by their pet chickens (rewards from their parents for writing good essays). They'd spend hours exploring the hills and fields around their house. In the summer they had picnics and went boating. In the winter, they skated on the pond in back of their house. They killed snakes, carrying them dangling between two sticks to an altar they'd built beside the stream, explored caves with lighted candles, and made "sacrifices" to imaginary gods by burning a favorite book on a pyre of stones.

Jennie adored school and could "scarcely wait from one day to another so that she can go," Mary noted. Like most Victorian children, Jane thought a lot about God and worried about the state of her soul. "Long before we had begun the study of Latin at . . . school," she wrote in her autobiography,

> my brother and I had learned the Lord's Prayer in Latin . . . and gravely repeated it every night in an execrable pronunciation because it seemed to us more religious than "plain English."
>
> When, however, I really prayed, what I saw before my eyes was a most outrageous picture which adorned a song-book used in Sunday School, portraying the Lord upon His throne surrounded by tiers and tiers of saints and angels all in a blur of yellow. I am ashamed to tell how old I was when that picture ceased to appear before my eyes, especially when moments of terror compelled me to ask protection from the heavenly powers.

Around the same time, Jennie puzzled over the Christian doctrine of predestination, the idea that God in his foreknowledge of all events infallibly guides those who are destined for salvation. One day she confronted her father with her confusion. To her delighted surprise—"for any intimation that our minds were on an equality lifted me high indeed," she recalled—he told her that they shared a willful bent which made them ill-equipped to accept the doctrine. The important thing, he added, was not to pretend to understand what you didn't understand—"You must always be honest with yourself inside whatever happened." She never wavered from this advice.

Religion was little comfort to Jennie, particularly against death, "that formless peril." She went with her family to the winter revival meetings at the village Methodist church, and worried about what happened to people when they died. Keeping watch at the deathbed of Polly Beer, the family governess, Jennie thought about the futility of most human striving. She was with Polly when "the great change came." The moment of her passing, Jane recalled, "pressed hard;

once to be young, to grow old and to die, everything came to that."

In *The Long Road of Woman's Memory,* her 1916 meditation on memory, Jennie cited this childish search for "magic protection from the terrors after death" as a crucial step in the formation of her conscience. Intensely spiritual, she was searching for something to believe in, and formal religion didn't satisfy her. At fifteen she immersed herself in Emerson. His work appealed to her because, like her father, he celebrated the demise of religious dogma and the rise of a religion based on moral duty.

Once, hearing some Cedarville women gossiping and condemning the kind village doctor for his unconventional beliefs, Jennie "rebelled against their theological bigotry," she recalled. She decided that "the test of righteousness is good works, not divine election."

The injustices of the world troubled her deeply. One day, on a trip to Freeport, as an oft-told story goes, Jennie and her father drove through a slum called Kilgrubbin on the banks of the Pecatonica River. Scores of laborers, most of them Irish immigrants, lived there in filthy, run-down shacks built on logs piled high above the ground to protect the homes against annual flooding. This was the first time Jennie had ever seen the kind of "poverty which implies squalor," and she felt "the curious distinction between the ruddy poverty of the country and that which even a small city presents in its shabbiest streets," she wrote in her autobiography. "I remember launching at my father the pertinent inquiry why people lived in such horrid little houses so close together, and that after receiving his explanation I declared with much firmness when I grew up I should, of course, have a large house, but it would not be built among the other large houses, but right in the midst of horrid little houses like these."

This story has been part of the legend of Jane Addams ever since the founding of Hull-House. Versions of it appeared in newspaper profiles of her dating back to the 1890s. E. A. Berry, who taught in the Cedarville schools while Jane was in college and was a frequent guest at the Addams home, once said he heard it from John Addams himself.

Indeed, the tale could well be true, considering what is known of Jane's childhood personality. Her relatives often remarked on her maturity and self-containment. "She is brave," Mary wrote Alice on May 29, 1872, after taking Jane to the dentist in Freeport. "Dr. Kingsley said she sat in the Dentist's chair for two or three hours & never complained at all. She is a dear good child. [I] think she . . . is a comfort not only to Pa, but also to Ma. She is *true* as she can be, if she makes a promise, she will keep it."

IN MANY WAYS, she grew into a normal, questioning teenager, struggling to find herself and the larger meaning of life. Like every adolescent, she worried about her appearance. Once she wrote to a distant cousin whom she had never met complaining about her nose, "which is simply a piece of flesh, expressing no character whatever, and contains eight freckles! horrible to relate (I counted them this morning)." She disliked her straight hair, and tried to curl it on rollers made by the village tinsmith. Yet, at sixteen, she still couldn't dance. She had no natural grace or coordination, and her pigeon-toed stance made her afraid to try.

Though Jennie learned to crochet, knit, embroider, bake bread (her father required that all his daughters present him with a perfect loaf on their twelfth birthday), and use a sewing machine, she was bored by domestic chores. Nor did she have the typical Victorian girl's passion for hats, camisole ribbons, and pretty dresses. Her chief interests were the same as her stepbrother George's—nature, books, and science. At Jennie's urging, her stepbrother Harry once wrote her a long letter describing various chemicals and later made "a collection" of them for her.

What's more, she was ambitious to do *something* important in the world, as one of her recurring dreams reveals. Beginning at age six, she often dreamed that it was her responsibility to reinvent the wheel. Night after night, she envisioned herself standing in the empty village blacksmith shop. Everyone in Cedarville but she was dead, and she had to learn to make a wagon wheel so civilization could go forward.

On mornings after she'd had the dream, she'd run to town and stand in the doorway of the blacksmith shop, studying the burly, red-shirted man as he bent over his anvil. "I would store my mind with such details of the process . . . as I could observe, and sometimes I plucked up courage to ask for more," she recalled. "Do you always have to sizzle the iron in water?" she'd ask him, thinking how unpleasant it would be to do. "Sure!" the blacksmith answered.

In 1872, John Addams's seventh term in the state legislature ended, and he announced that he would not seek reelection. He never held grand political ambitions, but his decision seems to have been based in part on his dismay with Ann's social climbing, which flowered in Springfield, with its lively press and regular stream of out-of-towners. She often joined her husband there for official functions and parties, for which she enjoyed dressing up. Once she refused to be seen unless he bought her a new outfit. At home, she assured him, she would wear "the gravest and most somber clothes, without the slightest relief of bows or ribbons." In Springfield, though, the newspaper columnists would notice her only if she was dressed beautifully.

Ann was furious that John was cutting her off from Springfield's social life, and she often argued with him about it. Soon, though, they were faced with a worse crisis. Alice and Harry announced that they were in love and wanted to marry. After graduating from Rockford Female Seminary in 1872, Alice made frequent trips into Freeport, where Harry by now was practicing medicine. A romance blossomed. They made an odd couple. He was an accomplished man—a successful professional and a talented musician. But he was also a blowhard, and he did not share the Addamses' democratic principles. "I do hate the nigger above all things," he wrote to his mother after the Civil War. "They have given us more trouble than their heads are worth."

John and Ann did not worry that Harry and Alice were stepbrother and -sister (such unions were common at the time). John's chief objection was that Harry was a drunk. (His alcoholism would eventually force him to give up medicine, and it would contribute to his death from a heart attack at age fifty-six.) Ann was distressed over Harry's drinking, and she worried that Alice, with her prickly personality, was too selfish to help him. In Ann's view, Alice did not possess enough womanly virtue. In particular, she lacked the highly prized quality of "self-rule." She could not control her temper (which had caused her to be in frequent trouble at school); she was a spendthrift; and, as her sister Mary noted, she was overly fond of food, a weakness that eventually would lead her to become grossly overweight.

Nevertheless, in the fall of 1875 the lovers were married at the homestead in a simple ceremony, witnessed only by the family and close friends. (John Addams refused to show up until the last minute.) Alice probably wore a white taffeta dress, the most fashionable gown for rural Illinois weddings, and no veil since the new Eastern custom of trailing tulle had not reached the prairie. After a brief reception—lemonade and ginger cake would have been typical refreshments—the bride tossed her nosegay from the top of the stairs and drove off with Harry in a carriage. As their parents waved to them from the front porch, Ann noticed that John had tears streaming down his face. "I don't feel a bit more sorry for your Allie than I do for my Harry," she snapped.

The following year, in March 1876, Weber Addams married Laura Shoemaker, the daughter of a Lena, Illinois, blacksmith. Jennie and George had the mumps and were unable to attend the wedding. "We have tried about everything to while away the weary hours," Jane wrote a cousin. "Fancy work consoled me for a day or two. . . . [*The Pickwick Papers*] made us laugh which operation was very painful. Yesterday we tried a game of chess, Geo, being blindfolded. George's face looks like a moon and my looks are far from being embellished."

Soon Jennie and George would be leaving home too. Ann and John had high hopes for their futures. George, who wanted to be a doctor, made plans to study science at Beloit College, the small liberal arts school from which Weber had graduated. Jane was more uncertain of her plans. She felt that she was destined to do something important, though she wasn't sure what. She thought perhaps she, too, might like to be a doctor—the profession had been somewhat opened to women since the Civil War.

John and Ann were proud of Jennie's intelligence, and they expected her to do well at school and to think independently. But they agreed that the highest calling for a woman was to raise children. Still, it seems John accepted the fact that his youngest child wanted something more from life. He was proud of Jane's high aims, his son-in-law John Linn noted after his death. "It was his great delight" to prepare Jane "for her mission," whatever that might be.

Jennie wanted to go East, to Smith College in Northampton, Massachusetts, which had just opened in 1872, and was one of a handful of women's schools to offer a rigorous education on a par with that of men's colleges. In the end, though, John Addams thought Smith was too far from home. So Jennie made plans to go to Rockford Female Seminary, where her father was a trustee and where her sisters had gone before her. (John apparently had no qualms about sending Mary, Alice, and Jane to the school where their sister Martha had taken ill and died.) The college choice illustrated a conflict that troubled Jennie for years: on the one hand, she wanted to believe she could accomplish anything she set her mind to do; on the other, she felt pressured by "family claims," by demands that she conform to her parents' wishes.

Still, her determination was fierce. It gave her a presence that many people noticed and remarked upon. Though she was only five feet three inches tall, pigeon-toed, stoop-shouldered, and barely ninety-five pounds, she was "quite prepossessing," recalled one Cedarville neighbor. A phrenologist Ann hired to examine the bumps on Jennie's head found her highly intelligent and original, with her capacity for "conscientiousness great." Displaying the occasional flash of intuition that made these pseudo-scientists so popular with Victorian parents trying to discern their children's talents, the phrenologist thought Jennie's "moral faculties very much larger than religious." Her weaknesses, he believed, were that she was too sensitive and easily mortified, and not as good as others at memorization. But, he continued in his final report, Jennie "[is] steady and persevering, sticking to a thing when the majority give it up. She will come out near the head at last."

3

Rockford Female Seminary

Jane, *standing at right,* in 1881, with a group of friends from Rockford Female Seminary.
(Courtesy of University of Illinois at Chicago, the University Library, Jane Addams Memorial Collection)

On the morning of September 3, 1877, Jane Addams stood in the front of Middle Hall, the brick-colonnaded main building of Rockford Female Seminary, carrying two carpetbags stuffed with her belongings. She was wearing a long calico dress with a high collar and puffy sleeves, and, as usual, she looked a bit unkempt. Wispy strands of light brown hair had escaped from the hastily arranged knot at the back of her neck and fell across her face. Another student who met her that day thought she looked "very trembly."

Jane admitted she was distraught to be starting at "humdrum Rockford." With its weak academic program, its emphasis on religion, and its rigid code of conduct, Rockford seemed stuck in the pre–Civil War past. Across the country, educational opportunities for women were opening up, and for the first time in American history, women were going to college. Dozens of female seminaries were transforming themselves into real colleges, and some of the new state universities accepted women. A few academically rigorous four-year women's colleges also had opened—Vassar in 1861, Smith in 1872, and Wellesley in 1875.

Not everyone thought this was a good thing. Indeed, though only a tiny proportion of women were embarking on higher education, the effect of college on women's well-being was a burning issue of the day, as fiercely debated in the nineteenth century as the effect of TV violence on crime is today. Many thoughtful people agreed with Dr. Edward H. Clarke, a former professor at Harvard Medical School, who'd argued in his 1873 book, *Sex in Education,* that girls were constitutionally unfit to follow the same intellectual regime as boys. Professor Clarke maintained that brain activity by women "diverted" to their heads vital blood they needed for menstruation. Other experts claimed that women couldn't cope with strenuous thinking because their brains were smaller than men's.

This was a moral crisis for the nation. America needed strong families to build a powerful, wealthy society. In an era of epidemics and fatal childhood diseases, large families were a hedge against loss. Women were expected to bear many children, then devote their lives to raising them. (In fact, there was some basis for the widespread concern that the new option of college for women threatened the nation's birthrate. Women college graduates tended not to get married, with estimates, as Barbara Sicherman has noted, reaching as high in some studies as 60 percent. Of the 977 women in *Who's Who, 1902,* nearly half were unmarried; 75 percent of those who received Ph.D.'s in American universities from 1877 to 1924 didn't marry.)

The era's leading doctors believed women arrived at college with their brains already overtaxed from high school, the period of their lives that was most dangerous for them to study since it was when their sex organs were developing. "At no time of life is the nervous system so sensitive, so irritable," wrote S. Weir Mitchell, the nation's premier authority on female nervous disease.

Four books refuting Clarke's and Mitchell's theories were published in the 1870s. Still, the belief that studying could make girls sick persisted, and it deeply affected female scholars. Even trivial maladies like flu or chronic headache were enough to cause some girls to drop out of college. And, of course, engagement and marriage were cause for immediate withdrawal. At Rockford, for example, fewer students returned each fall, with the graduating class of 1881 having dwindled to seventeen from the original twenty-five.

JOHN ADDAMS was rather enlightened about schooling, encouraging his daughters to pursue higher education. Jane even hoped to convince him to let her transfer to Smith after a year. Rockford didn't offer degrees, and more than anything Jane wanted a degree.

For the time being, though, Rockford was the best she could do. The school's backwardness reflected the limitations of its founder, Anna Peck Sill, who could never resolve the deep contradiction in her own nature between fundamentalist religious beliefs and intellectual ambition. "Miss Sill," as everyone called her, would have fit nicely in a novel by Henry James. She was extremely thin and erect, a dignified woman, who always wore a black lace scarf over her head. She came from a long line of New England Puritans, who were known for their religious convictions and strength of character. She was born in Otsego County, New York, in 1816, the daughter of a farmer who died when she was seven. From her hardworking mother she learned the domestic arts, including cooking, candle making, sewing, and braiding baskets. She grew up tall and homely, with a passion for God and education. By her early thirties she had completed her studies at Albion Female Seminary in Albion, New York, and was teaching there.

At the time, the Eastern religious establishment saw in America's great Western expansion a new opportunity for missionary work—the vast frontier was full of souls to be saved. In 1848 Miss Sill was invited by a group of Congregational and Presbyterian ministers to establish a religious school for girls in northern Illinois. The following year she arrived in Rockford by stagecoach, carrying her carpetbags and books. Her piano showed up soon after in a covered wagon. Miss Sill raised $5,000 from the local citizens, and, in 1851, opened the school with fifteen girls.

She modeled Rockford on Mount Holyoke Seminary in South Hadley, Massachusetts, which had been founded in the 1830s by Mary Lyon to educate girls of modest means. Holyoke's tuition was kept as low as possible, and, to reinforce the school's rigid moral code, the girls lived together in dormitories instead of boarding out with local families, as they did at most seminaries. The emphasis was on training girls to be Angels in the House—if not wives, then missionaries and teachers, the vocational equivalents of mothers.

Miss Sill gave Rockford basically the same mission, to teach girls to "elevate and purify and adorn the home and to teach the great Christian lesson, that the true end of life is not to acquire the most good, whether of happiness or knowledge, but to give oneself fully and worthily for the good of others."

By the time Jane arrived in 1877, Miss Sill had built Rockford into a fifteen-acre campus with three large brick buildings housing classrooms, a chapel, dormitories, a library, and a basement gymnasium. Tuition was $275 a year (approximately $4,675.00 in 1998 dollars), including room and board, and there were 180 students, fifty of them enrolled in the four-year academic program. Still, though the physical plant was new, the school was woefully inadequate. Teaching was by recitation instead of lecture; the library was filled with unreadable and useless geological surveys, government reports, and copies of missionary magazines that had been donated by alumnae. Miss Sill's fundamentalism had grown stronger over the years and was in sharp contrast to the spirit of critical thinking that was sweeping the academic world. "She does everything for people from love of God, and that I do not like," Jane wrote in her notebook. As another observer put it, the school "was at least two hundred years behind the times."

A hair-shirt ethic dominated most aspects of seminary life. The staff was overworked and badly paid with little free time and no privacy. Up to four teachers lived together in tiny, monastic cells, where they sometimes also held classes. At one time, Miss Sill shared quarters with three women next door to a room where piano practice started at six in the morning. One of Miss Sill's roommates, Lucy Jones, hid in a closet under the stairs every day for several minutes, just so she could have a bit of solitude.

For the students, the day began at five in the morning, when they dumped out their stove ashes and swept their rooms. Girls with a $30 tuition discount also had to perform an hour of chores daily—setting and clearing tables, washing dishes, baking pies and cakes, ringing the chapel bells.

Each student was required to copy a long list of rules into her notebook and report on her failures each week. The girls also had to keep account books and turn them in for inspection once a month. Demerits were issued to those who were deemed extravagant, or who broke any other rules, and, occasionally, a girl was expelled. (The harsh discipline was still in place seventeen years after Jane graduated, when one of her nieces was kicked out for sneaking into town on a Friday night to meet a boyfriend.) No one could leave campus without special permission, and parents were urged not to send jewelry or expensive clothes to their daughters. Because of the cold, damp climate, the seminary catalog recommended that girls have plenty of flannel garments, wool hose, a pair of India rubber overshoes, a waterproof cloak, and an umbrella. With their hair parted severely in the middle and their shapeless, homespun dresses, the girls were aggressively unstylish. "They all looked as if they had been accustomed to work in the kitchen," recalled one visitor.

Miss Sill outlawed waltzing, card playing, hair curling, and visits to the theater. When Oscar Wilde appeared at a theater in Rockford in 1882, Miss Sill forbade the girls to attend. (A group of boys from nearby Beloit College, including Jane's stepbrother George, did attend the lecture, however. George reported to his mother that the performance "was considered good by some, though [Wilde's] costume and manner was somewhat objectionable.")

In the dining room, a teacher presided at the head of each table; no one sat down until Miss Sill gave the signal. The food, served on brown, badly chipped crockery, was tasteless and sparse. Jane once complained to her stepmother that the girls had been served applesauce "every single night" for a week. The effect was slimming. The *Rockford Seminary Magazine* once published an item noting that not one freshman weighed more than 120 pounds. Sunday lunch of baked potatoes, cold meat, and baked beans was the culinary highlight of the week.

The mandatory physical exercise also was dismal. Every day the girls, dressed in loose white blouses and ankle-length skirts that cleared the ground, had to walk for an hour on the wooden walkway around the grounds, making the same narrow circuit twenty or thirty times, even in rain or snow. Jane loathed this exercise and wrote a poem about it in her diary:

Must I then exercise, said I to myself
With nothing to see or to view
Go round & round the old walk
And encounter nothing new
I put on my hat
I went out the door
I did it without a snarl

Jane's stepmother also insisted she keep a horse at the Rockford stable and ride it regularly, though the sport caused Jane excruciating back pain.

Deep friendships formed among the girls who shared Rockford's dreary existence. Nearly all of them were the daughters of white, Protestant, middle-class families—homemaker mothers, fathers who were clergymen, farmers, millers, and teachers. Most of the girls had grown up within fifty or so miles of Rockford, raised in simple prairie homes, where they returned each summer to help look after their younger siblings. The seminary at least provided these young women with relief from the domestic drudgery that ruled their mothers' lives. It also gave them an all-female culture in which they could develop their talents and intellects and play out their feminist fantasies.

Apparently, Miss Sill didn't object to a bit of railing against male dominance, and the *Rockford Seminary Magazine* contained an occasional article considering the role of women. One was titled "Where Is My Place?" by the pseudonymous writer Jeruska Jane Jones, "a poor, benighted woman, seeking to find that glorious realm for females that everybody talks about and nobody agrees about, called Woman's Sphere." Another article in Jane's time recounted the social contributions and self-reliance of women. And one editor asked in a piece written decades before women could vote, "Why should not a woman of strong ruling mind be our president, when a needy time comes, in place of a man of weak sense and administrative ability?"

The intense female intimacy was encouraged by Rockford's atmosphere of religious fervor. In addition to attending daily chapel services, students participated in regular revivals, during which all classes were suspended, and entire days were devoted to fasting and evangelistic sermons and prayers. Fits of hysteria were not uncommon among the exhausted, starving girls. The father of one student wrote to his wife, "I think it is just wicked the way they go on at the seminary. They are having a revival over there and all the girls are very much excited and some of them are sick of nervous diseases and lots of others so nervous they don't know what to do."

The students were encouraged to confess their sins to one another. Girls like Jane, who were not members of any church and who had never been baptized, were singled out by the teachers during evening services and pressured to declare their faith. Jane found such attention "unspeakably" embarrassing. She had no intention to abandon herself to religion or to become a foreign missionary, as the girls were urged to do. She later came to believe that "this passive resistance of mine, this clinging to an individual conviction, was the best moral training I received at Rockford."

In her religious questioning, Jane was greatly influenced by her reading of Ruskin, Carlyle, and Matthew Arnold, whose humanistic ethics strongly appealed to her. Yet, her father remained her guide in religion, as he did in so many things. Though John Addams was not a member of any church, and though he never mentioned "fiery Hell" at home, he was the most honorable and scrupulously moral person Jane knew. His Christianity was grounded in the moral experiences of small-town life, not on theology.

During vacations in Cedarville, Jane spent hours earnestly discussing religion with her father. At school, she desperately needed someone with whom to explore the subject, someone as interested as she in ideas and the life of the mind. As it turned out, Jane found such a friend during her freshman year. Ellen Gates Starr was the passionately religious daughter of an Illinois farmer. Small, wiry, and restless, she had curly brown hair and wore a pince-nez that kept sliding down her long, thin nose, giving her, even at eighteen, a spinsterish air.

But Ellen was spirited and determined, attractive qualities that seemed to run in her family. Her paternal great-grandfather had walked home barefoot in the snow from Valley Forge to Ipswich, Massachusetts, at the end of four years of service in the Revolutionary War. Around the same time, her maternal great-grandfather died while defending his son from Indians, who'd attacked the little boy as he played in his yard.

Ellen's father, Caleb Starr, left his native New England as a teenager to become a sea captain, traveling to South America, Europe, and Asia. After five years, he returned home to help his debt-ridden father on the family farm. He married Susan Gates Childs in 1848, and soon after moved to Illinois. Caleb instilled in his children a deep love of literature (while at sea, he used to write love letters for his illiterate sailors). Every evening he read aloud to Ellen, her brother, and her sister. Like John Addams, he had a fierce sense of community responsibility—he once organized a farmers' association to improve crop and stock yields.

But unlike John Addams, Caleb Starr had no talent for making money. After struggling for years, he was forced to sell his farm in 1877, the year Ellen entered Rockford. He moved his family to nearby Durand, where he bought and operated a pharmacy. It, too, was a financial failure.

Ellen recalled that her father was a democratic man who was "consistently . . . opposed to privilege." He also was an early and ardent champion of women's rights. At political rallies he was known to cry out, "Give the ballot to women!" And once, in the late 1850s, when suffragists Susan B. Anthony and Elizabeth Cady Stanton gave a talk in Illinois, Caleb introduced them to the crowd. Women, he once told a relative, were "the joy of the whole earth." Men, on the other hand, were nothing more than "lazy creatures."

FROM THE moment they met, Ellen and Jane became devoted friends. There was much to draw them together. Both were intelligent, serious, and idealistic. Both worshiped their fathers. Yet, there were vast differences in their temperaments. Jane was calm, reserved, formal, and cerebral. Ellen was prickly, dreamy, artistic, and highly sensitive. Once, after seeing a production of *Othello,* she told Jane she felt exactly "as if I had participated in a murder [myself]."

Their differences—like so much of life in that era—were sometimes played out in religious terms. Jane was a typical late-Victorian intellectual whose suspicions about organized Christianity eventually would lead her outside formal religion (though without giving up Christian principles). Ellen, meanwhile, became more devout as time went on. To her, God was as real as "certain characters in fiction, Dickens especially."

"You long for a beautiful faith, an experience," Jane once wrote Ellen. "I only feel that I need religion in a practical sense, that if I could fix myself with my relations to God & universe, & so be in perfect harmony with nature & deity, I could use my faculties and energy so much better & could do almost anything."

When Ellen wrote Jane that "God is more a reality to me every day of my life," Jane confessed that she could not accept the divinity of Christ. "I can work myself into great admiration for his life, & occasionally I can catch something of his philosophy, but he [doesn't] bring me any nearer the deity—I think of him simply as a Jew living hundreds of years ago, surrounding whom there is a mystery & a beauty incomprehensible to me. I feel a little as I do when I hear very fine music—that I am incapable of understanding."

The great friendship was disrupted after freshman year, when Ellen was forced to leave Rockford. Though she wrote Jane in August 1878 that she had "voluntarily and willingly" declined to return, in fact, her father could no longer afford the tuition. She became a teacher, first in a small town in rural Illinois, and then at the exclusive Kirkland School in Chicago, where she taught art history, geography, and Latin to the daughters of some of the city's leading citizens. She was a frequent summer guest at the Addams home in Cedarville, and the friends kept up a lively correspondence, writing each other twenty-page letters in which they poured out their feelings about religion. "I have been trying an awful experiment," Jane confessed to Ellen. "I didn't pray . . . for almost three months and was shocked to find that I feel no worse for it . . . I feel happy and unconcerned and not in the least morbid."

Occasionally, Ellen prodded Jane out of her insistent earnestness. After Ellen recounted to Jane how she traveled all over Chicago in a streetcar and went to the theater to see several celebrated actors, Jane wrote, "I was somewhat shocked, but wished that I could do it too."

At school and later these two serious young women would sometimes have sharp disagreements, often ignited by Jane's biting criticism. Once, for example, Jane told Ellen that she'd just read Bacon expressing an idea Ellen had voiced, though "he said it a good deal better than you did." Ellen, always sensitive to slights, shot back that whenever she said something clever, Jane would invariably "remark that it 'sounded like a quotation.' "

Sometimes, Jane's strong personality threatened to overwhelm her friend. In class at Rockford, all the girls were addressed as "Miss." But Jane insisted on being addressed as "Miss Addams" outside class as well—and she told the other girls to call Ellen "Miss Starr," apparently without consulting Ellen. "After I had besought you, as much as I considered consistent with my dignity to call me something else & you had cruelly refused for so long, I didn't expect of you the additional cruelty of misrepresenting me," Ellen wrote her.

With Ellen and others at Rockford, Jane's powerful presence quickly became apparent. One source of that power was her extreme reserve. In the parlance of the era, she didn't "give taffy"—that is, she refused to indulge in the hollow flattery and sentimental flirting that was common among girls in Victorian times. Her cool intellect was alluring.

But there was something else about her—an aura emanating from her strong sense of self that caused her to stand out. She knew she had a destiny—her life would *not* be ordinary—and it created a little light around her, elevating her above the crowd. Jane became the idol of the other girls. They asked for her picture, begged to visit her during vacations, and elected her class president. One student, Sarah Anderson, told Jane that she relied on her help and friendship "as I do on the Sun, as I do on divine help, and I feel just as confident of your never failing me." Another student, Helen Harrington, later said that Jane's room was "an available refuge from all perplexities." Yet another recalled, "However mopey it might be elsewhere, there was intellectual ozone in [Jane's] vicinity."

Throughout, though, Jane always held part of herself back, fearing to become too intimate with anyone. When she learned Ellen would not return to Rockford, Jane wrote her in the summer of 1878, "I am disappointed to think . . . that our social intercourse is probably over for all time, it is queer though, but a fact that I am glad when I know some people just so much and then stop . . . two people honestly going ahead are better if they don't *'meet'* too much—don't need to 'descend' . . . —the condition which high friendship demands."

• • •

JANE FOLLOWED the seminary's most advanced course of instruction. She studied Latin, natural science, ancient history and literature, mental and moral philosophy, large doses of Bible history, and Greek—one of her favorite subjects. After returning to school following the Christmas holiday in 1880, she wrote her stepmother, "[This] will be a week always memorable to me because I began Homer in it. I have never enjoyed the beginning and anticipation of anything as much as I have that." The curriculum was virtually the same as at Mount Holyoke and, though far below the standards of a male college, it was better than that found at most female seminaries. After her first year, Jane dropped music, for which she had no talent, and added mathematics. Like many students of her generation, she was enamored of the new critical spirit, which applied scientific rigor to all areas of life. She pressed plants, examined worms under a microscope, and, she reported to Alice, "I have learned to stuff birds by the new method; i.e. without skinning them. I have finished my lessons & glory in four birds which adorn the room, drying in all sorts of angles and positions. Miss Holmes [the science teacher] has planned to stuff with me every Saturday morning right straight on until June."

One day a live hawk, most likely sent by her father, arrived at her dorm room in a basket. Jane and Miss Holmes killed it by covering its mouth with a cloth soaked in chloroform. After dissecting it and studying its insides, then tanning and stuffing it, Jane mounted the hawk, measuring three feet from wingtip to wingtip, on a wall.

Long stretches of time were devoted to reading. She devoured novels by George Eliot and Victor Hugo, and studied social criticism by Ruskin and Carlyle. Ruskin wrote movingly about the corrupting aspects of great wealth and vigorously asserted the state's responsibility to end poverty and ease human suffering. Carlyle maintained that all history depended on the will of great individuals. He emphasized the importance of duty—an idea that appealed to John Addams's daughter. She wrote Ellen in the summer of 1879, "There is something in Carlyle that suits me as no one else does."

Jane was serious about her own writing and took great pains with her college papers, though they show little of the literary spark that marked her adult works. During her freshman year, she wrote an essay, "The Present Policy of Congress," regarding aid to blacks, which reflected her father's staunchly Republican ideas. After arguing that the Civil War, for all its "butchery," was inevitable, she wrote, "But the Negroes are free, that is a settled fact, and something must be done with them, the plight of the nation reminds us of the Vicar of Wakefield, who paid an enormous price for his family portraits and then didn't know what in the world to do with them."

On the other hand, in an essay on "Tramps," written the following spring, Jane showed little sympathy for beggars. "The country is flooded with tramps," she wrote. "But where they come from and whither they go is a conjecture, we only know they are trying to evade the principle set down from the foundations of the earth, that a man must give a full equivalent for everything he receives; by disregarding this principle they render themselves abject and mean and merit their universal contempt."

Jane was at the top of all her classes, and she was obsessive about following the school's rigid conduct code. To prevent tardiness, Miss Sill advised the young women to see to it "that at least one other girl beside yourself is on time." Most of the girls, the *Rockford Seminary Magazine* reported, decided "to be responsible for Jane Addams."

Jane always took the lead in settling disputes with Miss Sill, "the old cow," as some of the students called her. Once, in a class on moral philosophy, Jane insisted on giving "Don Quixote" the Spanish pronunciation. "We backed her up with laughter at Miss Sill's Don Quix-ott," recalled a student named Eleanor Frothingham. Miss Sill suspended the class for two days. At chapel later that day, Jane grabbed the hymnal of the girl she was sitting next to and wrote on the flyleaf, "Life's a burden, bear it. Life's a duty, dare it. Life's a thorn crown, wear it. And spurn to be a coward!"

Jane wasn't above having some fun, Victorian style. Sometimes late at night the girls would gather for parties in her room. After tacking a blanket over the transom to hide the lamplight, they boiled candy, cooked oysters, and popped corn in a woodstove, fried eggs in buttered boxes of paper held over the oil lamps, and ate cashews from a tin, picking them out with their hairpins. Sometimes, the girls read *Romeo and Juliet* out loud. Other nights, they debated Darwin's theories or discussed one of Carlyle's books.

Jane began writing for the *Rockford Seminary Magazine* her freshman year, mostly stilted essays with titles like "The Element of Hopefulness in Human Nature." She became editor of "Home Items" her sophomore year, and editor in chief her senior year. She also kept a journal, filling it mostly with adages and moral exhortations she'd come across. "Solitude is essential to the life of man," she wrote. "All men come into this world alone and all leave it alone." "Deeds make habits, habits make character, character makes destiny."

Jane's avidity for new experience led her, as it has college students in other eras, to experiment with drugs. One morning she and four friends swallowed crushed opium pills, hoping to induce hallucinations that would help them better understand *Confessions,* by the English essayist and opium addict De Quincey, which they planned to read once the drug took effect. Instead, they became sick and disoriented. A young teacher who found them sprawled on the floor gave them ipecac, an emetic, and sent them to their rooms, as Jane recalled, "with a stern command to appear at family worship after supper 'whether we were able to or not.'"

Jane did not need opium when Amos Bronson Alcott, the famous New England eccentric and Louisa May Alcott's father, arrived at Rockford to deliver a lecture on Transcendentalism. Just being on the same campus with this friend of Emerson's was enough to put Jane in a "state of ecstatic energy," and she vied with the other students "to do him a personal service," she recalled. Jane won the privilege of cleaning the mud off his shoes, a task she performed blissfully.

At the end of her sophomore year, Jane took part in Rockford's public examination, an annual event in which a panel of ministers and politicians tested the girls' knowledge of a variety of topics. The examinations were covered by the press and attended by hundreds of people, including large numbers of young men who fought for front-row seats so they could ogle the "sems." Sometimes the audience was so loud and unruly, *The Rockford Herald* reported, that it was "an impediment to the proceedings." But other times, according to one reporter, the public sat in "breathless silence" on wooden folding chairs as Miss Sill's students parsed sentences, answered questions about the history of the United States, solved difficult algebra problems, played the mandolin or piano, translated Latin, read compositions, sang songs, recited poetry, and held colloquies.

Jane got up in front of the crowd and read her essay on Illinois geography. Afterward she wrote her friend Eva Campbell, saying that she had stayed calm until her time to read had come and "then I was excited for indeed, Eva, the idea of a school girl propounding her ideas to a set of men as smart as they were, struck me as being silly. . . . I knew that they were learned and some of them brilliant [and] that I was very far from being either."

The following year, Jane initiated a junior exhibition, to which her class also invited the public and the press. The girls composed a class song and designed their own class stationery, featuring a picture of wheat and their motto, "Breadgivers," which, Jane told her sister Alice, "is the primitive meaning of the word lady." On the evening of April 20, the seventeen juniors entered the chapel and walked to the front, forming a semicircle to sing their class song. Then Jane, as class president, delivered an address. Her speech criticizing the dominance of men in society drew on ideas that were current at the seminary and increasingly being discussed in the culture at large. She said that over the last fifty years, women's education had "passed from accomplishments in the arts of pleasing, to the development of . . . intellectual force and her capabilities for direct labor." Woman, she reassured her audience, "wishes not to be a man, nor like man, but she claims the same right to independent thought and action." On the other hand, she continued, "We still retain the old ideal of womanhood—the Saxon lady whose mission it was to give bread unto her household. So we have planned to be breadgivers throughout our lives, believing that in labor alone is happiness, and that the only true and honorable life is one filled with good works and honest toil. We will strive to idealize our labor and thus happily fulfill women's highest mission."

The ideas in the speech, though strongly expressed, were fairly typical for the first generation of American college women. Jane and her friends knew they had come of age at a fortuitous historical moment—that never before had there been such opportunities for their sex. For the first time in history, women had the chance to have active lives devoted to work, not family. That in itself was an achievement. Of course, most women found the price of such independence too high: it meant giving up marriage and motherhood, and it often led to conflicts with disapproving parents and siblings. What's more, the employment opportunities were limited—teaching, medicine, and missionary work were about the only options, and there was little hope of earning much money.

Educated women had to stay in their separate sphere since there was great prejudice against women competing directly with men, even in such innocuous areas as college debating contests. In the fall of 1880, a group of men from Knox College in Galesburg, Illinois, tried to block Jane and other female debaters from participating in the state oratorical contest. The men opposed women orators, not only because they thought it unseemly for sexes to argue in public (so did the era's etiquette books), but also, apparently, because they were jealous.

The year before, a female student from McKendee College had been voted first by one of the judges, and the men had complained, suspecting the judge had inflated the woman's score out of chivalry. The judge angrily denied it. "Gentlemen, I graded the girl first because she was a perfect orator and had a perfect oration. . . . I know what oratory is, for I have heard Henry Clay many a time; Daniel Webster many a time," he snapped. "The girl . . . had the only *oration* of the evening. Yates [one of the male competitors] had a *speech* . . . the rest had *essays*." But when Jane showed up at Knox College, a male student on the welcoming committee later admitted, the boys were "scared . . . for fear the judges would award you the prize 'just because you were a girl'!"

As it turned out, Jane was the only woman orator competing that year, the first time Rockford had entered the contest. She felt as though she was representing not only her school but "the progress of Woman's Cause." Her classmates, bemoaning, as Jane put it, her "intolerable habit of dropping my voice at the end of a sentence in the most feminine, apologetic and even deprecatory manner," worried that she'd lose.

They were right. Jane came in fifth, "exactly in the dreary middle." Second place was awarded to a tall, earnest-looking Illinois College student, William Jennings Bryan (the subject of their orations is unknown). Bryan, who as a congressman, a presidential candidate, and a secretary of state would go on to become one of the most famous orators in American history, spent his $50 prize money on an engagement ring for his sweetheart.

As PART OF the first generation of women to go to college, Jane and her friends were filled with a sense of possibility and a common spirit. Their awareness of their unprecedented opportunities and belief in their own moral superiority gave them an intense feeling of solidarity with other women.

Jane was not critical of classmates who dropped out of school to get married. Indeed, she was open enough in her attitudes that girls with traditional ideas still confided in her. One student wrote Jane during a summer vacation, "My highest aspirations now are not any more probable than in my younger days—only a little lower—to marry a rich man and live comfortably."

Hand in hand with this sense of female solidarity often came disgust at heterosexual love; many nineteenth-century feminists believed that women were degraded by having sex with men. Ellen Starr, for example, was dismayed at the idea. "Have you heard from Eva Campbell Goodrich?" Ellen wrote Jane in the summer of 1880, referring to Jane's freshman roommate, who'd dropped out of school to marry and was expecting a baby. "It is just as I expected.

We didn't make our visit last fall and now she is not visitable. I am disgusted."

There's no evidence that Jane shared this feeling, though she apparently had no interest in either an emotional or a physical relationship with a man, and, as far as is known, she never had any serious suitors while at Rockford. Several of her biographers claim that a Beloit student named Rollin Salisbury, who later became a professor of geography at the University of Chicago, asked her to marry him. One polite letter from Salisbury survives in Jane's papers, and although he might very well have been smitten with Jane, there's no suggestion that they became close.

Except for her father and stepbrother George, Jane wasn't close to any man at this time. By her own description, she was a "serious not to say priggish" young woman. Her deepest attachments were to other women, and even then, she believed that it was better to remain somewhat aloof. As she once wrote to her cousin Vallie Beck, "I am a great admirer of Platonic love or rather pure, sacred friendship. I think it is so much higher than what is generally implied in the word love."

Indeed, with her reserved and unemotional nature, Jane was a shining example of "passionlessness," the Victorian idea many women found useful in exerting control over their lives. The belief that women "lacked carnal motivation," as Nancy Cott has written, "was the cornerstone of the argument of women's superiority. . . . It elevated women above the [male] weaknesses of animal nature, stressing instead that they were 'formed for exalted purity, felicity and glory.'"

Passionlessness was particularly useful for women with ambition—women like Jane, who wanted to make a name for themselves in a world hostile or indifferent to female achievement. After Jane became famous, her stepmother told a reporter that even as a child she "was anxious for a career." At Rockford, away from all family responsibilities and in an all-female culture that celebrated woman's intellect and accomplishment, her ambition exploded into a strong desire to do something important with her life.

Around this time, Jane decided she wanted to become a doctor.

The choice was an obvious one, since some of the smartest women of the era were doctors. (In contrast, the profession tended to attract mediocre men, the best male minds being directed toward commerce, government, and literature.) The first women's medical school in the world had opened in Philadelphia in 1850, and, during the Civil War, several female doctors had served courageously for the Union army.

For ambitious women, medicine offered a chance to be dutiful and useful and to right the wrongs perpetrated against their sex by brutal male doctors. They were especially eager to relieve their sisters from the embarrassment of having their breasts examined by strange men and the horrific torment—many thought tantamount to rape—of the gynecological exam.

After the Civil War, several additional women-only medical schools had opened up, and three leading university medical schools—Michigan, Johns Hopkins, and Cornell—began accepting women. Most women doctors went on to practice in hospitals devoted to treating women and children. Overall, the last third of the nineteenth century, as Barbara Sicherman has written, was something of a golden age for women doctors. There were 2,400 registered women doctors in 1880 and 7,300 by 1900. By 1910, women constituted a larger proportion of the medical profession than they would reach again until 1980.

Medicine also offered a great escape from marriage, providing a kind of intellectual nunnery for women who were determined to be independent. Elizabeth Blackwell, generally regarded as America's first woman doctor, deliberately chose the profession, she explained in her autobiography, as a "strong barrier" between herself and "the sad wearing away" of her heart.

As HER senior year wound down, Jane became set on studying medicine at the prestigious University of Edinburgh in Scotland, where the medical department had been open to women since 1869. Her father, however, opposed her plans. When she came home from spring vacation looking pale, tired, and excessively thin, he thought her condition was due to overwork. He wanted her to wait at least a year after graduation before she resumed further study.

Jane's exhaustion, however, no doubt was caused, at least in part, by conflict with her father. During her first three and a half years at Rockford, she'd enjoyed her best health ever. It was only as her college years wound down and she was faced with John Addams's opposition to her plans that she started to feel "unwell"—nervous, headachy, tired, and plagued by sciatica.

Seventeen years later she wrote movingly about the "typical" woman graduate, who returns home after college eager to take an active role in the world, but is stifled by her parents' desire that she be an ornament of the family. Her education, she finds out, is not to prepare her to work, but rather to be a "symbol of her father's protection and prosperity."

Whatever ambitions she held had to be suppressed in favor of this "family claim." As a result the graduate "either hides her hurt, and splendid reserves of enthusiasm and capacity go to waste, or her zeal and emotions are turned inward, and the result is an unhappy woman, whose vitality is consumed by vain regrets and desires."

This exactly was Jane's dilemma in 1881. She tried to fulfill the role of dutiful daughter whenever she could. Once, she even offered to interrupt her studies for two weeks to help her stepmother train a new hired girl. But she wasn't about to give up Smith or medical school without a struggle.

She was angry at her father, and even rebelled a bit by taking a trip that spring without asking his permission or telling him of her plans. By Victorian standards, it was a shocking breach of daughterly duty, though by ours, the trip—to Jacksonville, Illinois, for the championship round of the oratorical competition she'd participated in that fall—was innocent enough.

Also that spring, Jane took on a new cause—a campaign to require her classmates to dress alike on commencement day. "As there are such marked differences in the finances of the members it seems positively necessary to have our gowns alike," she wrote her father. "I never realized before how paramount a girl's interest in dress is to all others & never in my class Presidency have I made such mighty efforts to keep some kind of order and peace." Fashion didn't interest *her.* At a time when an hourglass figure was considered ideal, most Rockford girls cinched their waists by winding their corset laces around their bedposts, then pulling them as taut as possible. Jane didn't even wear a corset. Still, her classmates deferred to her on the question of what to wear commencement day, as they did in so many other areas. "We have finally worked it down to this," she reported to her father. Each girl's graduation dress "shall be white and that the entire outfit—gloves, shoes, fans, shall come within twenty-five dollars."

A few months before Jane graduated, the Rockford board of trustees voted to allow the seminary to confer bachelor of arts degrees on those students who had completed the four-year academic program (until then, graduates received "testimonials" certifying completion of course work). Anna Sill had worked hard to gain collegiate status for Rockford, adding courses in classics and higher mathematics over the years and raising the school's endowment. A degree was important to Jane. But she wanted it from Smith, where she still hoped to go the following fall. She was convinced now of the course her life should take. She would go to Smith for a year to earn her B.A., then "tramp" around Europe a bit, then attend medical school. Only her father's opposition stood in her way. Somehow, she'd find a way around that.

To no one's surprise, Jane was named valedictorian. "Do not think I am puffed up," she wrote John Addams. "I too well realize how little it is worth or signifies . . . [my] only [ground] of satisfaction is that I hope the home folks will be pleased."

By 9:00 A.M. on June 22, 1881, the hour commencement was to begin, the chapel overflowed with the parents and friends of graduates. The year "81" appeared on the back wall in red and white flowers. Huge bouquets and baskets of flowers—gifts to the graduates—covered the altar, windowsills, and hall. The event began with the whole school rising and repeating the Nineteenth Psalm and performing a chant. Professor Joseph Emerson of Beloit College gave a prayer, followed by the salutatorian's address, delivered in Latin, and a piano solo.

Then Jane rose to speak. Her topic was Cassandra, the Trojan woman who had the gift of prophecy and who predicted the victory of the Greeks and the destruction of her father's city, but who was mocked by the men around her and driven mad. "The brave warriors had laughed to scorn the beautiful prophetess Cassandra," Jane told her audience. "The frail girl stood conscious of Truth but she had no logic to convince the impatient defeated warriors, and no facts to gain their confidence. She could assert and proclaim until at last in sooth she became mad."

Cassandra was a brilliant woman. But because she had no education, no training, and no status in society, her talents were wasted—with tragic consequences for herself and her countrymen. Jane's theme—that a woman could be destroyed by the crushing of her potential—seemed pitched to her father, who was sitting in the audience. It was an eerie presage of the crisis she would soon face, and that she would not resolve for eight tortuous years.

4

The Rest Cure

Dr. Silas Weir Mitchell, whose rest-cure treatment for neurasthenics drew patients from around the world. *(Courtesy of the Library of the College of Physicians of Philadelphia)*

In June 1881, Jane returned to Cedarville to live with her father and stepmother, but she did not fit easily into the role of adult daughter at home. She was twenty-one and did not know what to do with herself. She wasn't interested in the picnics and parties that absorbed her friends during the summer, and she loathed sewing, baking, and other domestic chores. Her father still refused to allow her to enroll at Smith in the fall, so she reluctantly resigned herself to a quiet interlude of reading and traveling.

On August 4, she accompanied her father, stepmother, and stepbrother George to northern Michigan and the Lake Superior shore on a trip that was part pleasure and, for John Addams, part business—he wanted to inspect some copper mines as possible investments. After one difficult climb to reach a mine near Marquette, he fell ill, and the family decided to return home. On the way, his condition worsened, and they stopped at Green Bay, Wisconsin, where he entered a hospital. He lingered for several days, then died on August 17 of what appears to have been a burst appendix. He was fifty-nine.

A large crowd was on hand to greet the Addamses when they arrived at the Freeport depot the following afternoon with John's casket—an elaborate wood model lined with blue velvet and bearing the inscription "At Rest" in gold letters. Funeral services were held at the family home. The newspapers reported that fifteen hundred people filed by the open casket in the parlor, before taking their places on the lawn outside. A minister spoke of John's "pure and spotless life." Then the pallbearers carried the casket out of the house, and a procession of men, women, and carriages followed it slowly up a twisting path to the family plot at the top of the hill. John was buried next to his first wife, Sarah, and their five dead children.

John Addams left an estate valued at more than $300,000, a third of which went to Ann Haldeman. Jane, her two sisters, and her brother each received property and stocks worth about $50,000—the equivalent of close to one million dollars in 1998. Jane's share included a 247-acre farm and sixty acres of timberland in Stephenson County, eighty acres in Dakota, Illinois, plus stocks and bonds.

Jane was devastated by her father's death. She'd loved him more than anyone in her life. He was her most powerful influence, as her friends and relatives acknowledged in the condolence letters that flooded Cedarville. "I remember how affectionately you used to speak of him—and the time when we came home together how happy you looked when you saw him waiting outside," wrote one friend. "The poignancy of your grief arises from many causes, principally from the fact that your heart and life were wrapped up in your Pa," wrote Jane's brother-in-law John Linn. Another friend, Caroline A. Potter, noted, "By a word you spoke at one time I know your father's life transfused itself through yours."

Honoring her father's strict standards of rectitude had been Jane's chief motivation. Now, without him, she felt cut from her moorings, "absolutely at sea so far as any moral purpose was concerned," she later wrote in her autobiography. But in characteristic fashion, she kept her pain to herself. In a letter to Ellen several days after the funeral, she spent most of her time comforting her friend, who was suffering a minor ailment:

> Your first letter reached me on Lake Superior when I was as seasick as Mark Twain was crossing the Atlantic, or I should have written to you at once and on the spot. I am so sorry you are tired and wish with all my heart I could do something for you. Two duties I solemnly charge you with—drink a bottle of *malt* every day and use for your chief food *desiccated blood*. . . . I know they will help build you up for I have wilted, tried them & revived.
>
> I wish you could come to Cedarville before you return to Chicago if only for a day or two. . . . I will not write of myself or how purposeless and without ambition I am, only prepare yourself so you won't be disappointed in me when you come. The greatest sorrow that can ever come to me has past [*sic*] and I hope it is only a question of time until I get my moral purposes straightened.

What made her father's death particularly difficult was that he had died in the middle of their conflict over Jane's future, before she could reconcile her ambitions with his expectations. Now she was tormented by fears that she would betray his memory.

In the "black days" following his funeral, Jane quietly made arrangements to enroll at the Women's Medical College of Philadelphia. No doubt, the plans hinged on her stepmother's eagerness to escape Cedarville. Philadelphia offered Ann both a distracting change of scene and the kind of sophisticated social life she'd always wanted. What's more, Ann's son Harry Haldeman already had decided to do graduate work at the University of Pennsylvania. Jane and Ann could live with him and Alice, who would also enroll at the medical school. Alice did not expect to become a doctor—she wanted only to learn enough to help her husband in his practice.

In the fall of 1881, Jane moved with Ann, Alice, and Harry to 1417 North Sixteenth Street, on the outskirts of downtown Philadelphia. The contrast to the alternately dusty and muddy landscape of rural Illinois was abrupt: Philadelphia's wide, leafy streets, grand houses, and historic landmarks suggested an aura of colonial charm.

Six days a week, Monday through Saturday, Jane walked several blocks to the Women's Medical College, a three-story brick building at Twentieth Street and North College Avenue. The school had been founded in 1850 by a young philanthropist named William Mullen. He believed passionately that America needed female doctors because so many women—either from an overstrict sense of delicacy or a dread of undressing before male doctors—ignored the signs of pregnancy and the symptoms of disease, often with fatal results.

Jane's schedule was arduous. Five days a week, she attended lectures and clinics from eight in the morning until six in the evening; Saturdays, the school day ended at one, after a weekly anatomy quiz. The curriculum emphasized female anatomy and diseases; each day began with an hour of bedside instruction at Philadelphia Women's Hospital. Jane worked hard at her studies and wrote to at least one friend that she was enjoying her courses (though she told George she did not like dissecting corpses).

But her heart was not in it. Science, as she later explained to George, "is a trifle esoteric and exoteric in relation to the world." What's more, she knew she would not be happy in a profession that relegated women to an inferior role. Male doctors often were virulently hostile to their female colleagues. Once, when a group of women showed up at a lecture at the men's medical school, they were met by yells, hisses, mock applause, paper missiles fired at their backs, and obscene remarks about their appearance. A few of the men even followed the women into the street at the end of the lecture, swearing and spitting tobacco juice on them.

Soon Jane became exhausted by the effort to excel at something that didn't excite her. She wrote in her notebooks about her "utter failure" and her inability "to work at the best of myself . . . I am growing more sullen and less sympathetic every day."

Her situation was complicated by conflicts with Ann. Her stepmother would have preferred that Jane stay at home playing the devoted unmarried daughter. Like others in the family, Ann thought Jane's ambition unseemly. Jane's brother-in-law John Linn, for one, had criticized her for being too fond of praise and advised her to care a little less for "approbation and more for excellence."

The atmosphere at the house on Sixteenth Street made it hard to study. Ann was suffering from a mysterious bowel ailment and at one point was hospitalized. When she felt well, Ann expected Jane to be a companion at card parties and fashionable dinners—activities that bored Jane and took her away from her studies.

Meanwhile, the prospect of a medical degree grew less appealing. Dr. Rachel Bodley, the medical school's fifty-year-old dean, pushed her students toward missionary work, particularly in India and China, seeing it as a way to find instant employment after graduation and to publicize the school. The reality of life for women missionaries, however, was grim, as Jane well knew. They worked under horrible conditions with little equipment or medicine. And invariably they had to answer to male directors, often arrogant doctors. As Dean Bodley once told Jane's class, the woman missionary doctor needed Herculean strength to combat "powers of darkness [of] gigantic proportions."

This was not the career Jane wanted. Still grieving over her father's death and torn by her own ambitions, by Ann's expectations, and by Dr. Bodley's campaign to make her a missionary, Jane fell into a state of nervous exhaustion. She complained to a friend about losing physical vigor and being taxed "very severely both in study and in doing for others." Typically, her back pain returned ferociously, as it would throughout her life when she was depressed or under stress. (Her childhood Pott's disease was in remission, though it would recur in 1916 in a tubercular kidney.) In December, she saw a doctor who very likely prescribed the era's typical remedies for sciatica—Dr. Chapman's India rubber bags filled with hot water and applied to the spine; the application of leeches to suck out blood at the point of the severest pain; and tartar-emetic ointment spread along the length of the spine.

Remarkably, Jane rallied briefly. She wrote to another Rockford classmate, Emma Briggs, in December 1881 that her "physical strength" was returning. She passed the first term's examinations in March. Then she collapsed completely.

She dropped out of medical school and sank further into despair. There's no evidence of what exactly pushed her over the edge. Her surviving letters of the era don't mention it, and she was silent about it in her memoirs. It was the start of an eight-year chapter of her life that would be dominated by illness and depression, "traces of it remaining long after Hull-House was opened in 1889," she confessed in her autobiography.

There probably was no organic reason for Jane's back to trouble her as it did. Doctors today widely recognize that back pain can be triggered by stress, and even in the nineteenth century, there were glimmers that the key lay somewhere in the mind of the patient. In one study of sciatica victims—all women between the ages of fifteen and twenty-five—Dr. William A. Hammond concluded that they were "hysterical." Any sudden excitement could bring on an attack. Dr. Hammond wrote about one healthy thirty-year-old woman whose back gave out suddenly when informed that she'd lost a large sum of money, and another who felt a sharp pain in her spine when a chunk of plaster fell from the ceiling, landing at her feet. Other patients' sciatica also began with some kind of emotional trauma—their horses running away with them, fights with their husbands, the death of a loved one. In all these cases, the back pain never existed by itself. It always was accompanied by some other nervous symptom—anxiety, loss of weight, vertigo, headache, noises in the ears, blurred vision, scalp sensitivity.

What's more, the mind typically was affected, and, often, Dr. Hammond noted, "the aberration was of such a character as to almost amount to insanity."

Though it probably brought little comfort, Jane needed only to look around to see others suffering in much the same way she was. The distress she felt was epidemic at the time among educated young women, including many of her friends. Mattie Thomas wrote to Jane that she felt sick and lonesome. Helen Harrington confided that she was "utterly adrift." Ellen Starr suffered periods of severe nervous prostration. Sarah Anderson's anxiety attacks became so severe that she was hospitalized for several weeks in the early 1880s.

These young women, like countless others across the country, complained of anxiety, melancholy, exhaustion, headaches, backaches, insomnia, nausea, inability to concentrate, and heart palpitations. The ailments were rarely traced to organic causes. Today, doctors would call these women depressed, and they would be treated by psychotherapy and drugs. But there was no Prozac and no science of psychology in 1882, though doctors were beginning to sense the intricate connections between the body and the mind. Neurology was rising rapidly as a medical specialty, and in 1869 a young neurologist named George Beard gave a name—neurasthenia (literally, an impoverishment of nerve force)—to the strange complaints plaguing many Americans. Beard associated neurasthenia with the stresses of urban, civilized life in the nineteenth century, but he went further, narrowing the trouble down to a quaint list of five particularly harmful factors: steam power, the telegraph, science, the press, and an increase in mental activity among women.

Though most commonly associated with women, neurasthenia struck men, too, a great many of them trained in science. Beard, for example, estimated that 10 percent of his patients were doctors. Here again, changing social roles may have been a factor, as intellectuals who struggled to free themselves from the stern religious teachings of their childhoods found themselves empty and confused from a loss of faith.

Neurasthenia, though, was not considered an appropriate ailment for men, and those who succumbed to it were more likely than women to be diagnosed as insane. But the medical world was perfectly willing to accept neurasthenia in women. In a sense, the illness was an extension of the role society demanded of them. The neurasthenic was a caricature of the docile, self-denying Angel in the House—weak, emaciated, and passive to the point of incapacitation.

Beard believed that neurasthenia was limited almost exclusively to the wealthy and refined. They earned their places in the social order, he reasoned, by virtue of their "nervous organization"—a hypersensitivity that made them susceptible to neurasthenia. This romanticizing of the disease apparently had little basis in fact. Certainly, there was nothing romantic about it among working-class women, who, despite Beard's analysis, also suffered from it.

Over time, a charismatic Philadelphia doctor, Silas Weir Mitchell, became the leading authority on neurasthenia, and his "rest cure" treatment drew patients from around the world. Some of the most accomplished women of the age were his patients, including the writers Edith Wharton and Charlotte Perkins Gilman, whose famous short story, "The Yellow Wallpaper," was inspired by her experiences as Mitchell's patient in 1887. Doctors everywhere adopted his techniques; a young Viennese neurologist named Sigmund Freud used Mitchell's ideas in his new psychoanalytic therapy.

Ann made an appointment for Jane, and the two women showed up at Mitchell's home office at 1524 Walnut Street in March, soon after Jane left medical school. They found the doctor in his book-lined office standing behind a massive mahogany desk. At fifty-two, Mitchell was handsome and lean, with abundant gray hair "like spun glass," as John Singer Sargent, who painted his portrait, described it. He wore a red necktie and in the breast pocket of his velvet coat was a handkerchief dabbed with cologne. A man of extraordinary versatility and vitality, Mitchell was the author of hundreds of articles and books on medical topics (including *Wear and Tear,* which advised people how to reduce stress in their lives), twelve novels (in which female "couch loving invalids" are typically villains), children's stories, several volumes of verse, and a controversial biography of George Washington, in which he portrayed Washington's mother as a shrew. Mitchell's own mother had been the essential Angel in the House, a sweet woman for whom her son felt a passionate love. His father, a well-to-do Virginia doctor, had been disappointed in this "slight, pale lad of no physical strength," as Mitchell described himself. As a boy, Mitchell suffered from a disfiguring case of eczema, which continued to flare up all his life during times of emotional distress. Despairing of his puny son's future, his father predicted he would fail at medicine.

Mitchell proved him wrong. During the Civil War, he worked tirelessly on the front tending to wounded men. After observing how amputees could feel their "phantom limbs," he became interested in the connections between physical and mental health and invented a unique treatment, the rest cure. Under the method, the patient was sent to bed for six weeks of total rest, during which time no visitors or books were allowed. The patient was fed excessive amounts of dairy products, and, to counter the effects of inactivity, forced to undergo several hours a day of massage and electroshock therapy. Mitchell tested the treatment on soldiers suffering from exhaustion and pronounced it immensely effective.

Mitchell's first wife and the mother of his two sons died in 1862, and he later married Mary Cadwalader, a member of one of Philadelphia's richest families. They moved to a fashionable address—1524 Walnut Street—and into the upper reaches of Philadelphia society. He occasionally taught a class at the Women's Medical College of Philadelphia, and he began turning out novels and books on medical advice, all best-sellers. The Mitchells entertained the literary and cultural stars of their day, from the writer William Dean Howells to sculptor Augustus Saint-Gaudens. Mitchell treated Walt Whitman for nervous exhaustion, and later helped support him with a $15 monthly allowance. But the friendship ended when Mitchell learned that Whitman had criticized Mitchell's poetry to a friend.

After the Civil War, Mitchell had turned his rest cure to the treatment of troubled women, many of them unmarried college graduates. (For his male patients he devised what his friends dubbed "the West Cure," a strenuous program of outdoor exercise in places like Texas and California.) Mitchell believed the problems of neurasthenic women resulted from their refusal to accept their subordinate role in society, and he claimed his methods would restore them to radiant physical and mental health. Only women of uncommon strength and determination were capable of holding careers, he thought. The average woman, no matter how well-educated she was, could never be the equal of man, Mitchell insisted. He "obstinately clung" to this view until the end of his life, recalled one of his biographers, and in fact, he became rather a bore about it. "So those who loved him felt it wise to turn the conversation whenever it drifted dangerously in the direction of the New Woman."

If education and ambition were good for women, Mitchell reasoned, why were the college graduates he saw in such terrible shape? His typical patients were "nervous, exhausted . . . weak, pallid, flabby, disfigured by acne or at least with rough and coarse skins; poor eaters, digesting ill; incapable of exercise and suffering from cold extremities. They [are] . . . hopeless and helpless," doomed for life to "the shawl and the sofa."

Mitchell was not interested in what his patients had to say about their health, telling the writer Charlotte Perkins Gilman, for example, that the long letter she wrote him detailing her symptoms was evidence of "self-conceit." He'd already treated two of her relatives, "two women of your blood," as he put it, and that was all he needed to know of her medical history. "Wise women choose their doctors and trust them. The wisest ask the fewest questions," he wrote in *Doctor and Patient.*

The rest cure was designed to "destroy the soil in which hysteric phenomena flourish," Mitchell explained. It was "an effort to lift the health of patients to a higher plane by the use of seclusion, which cuts off excitement and foolish sympathy, by rest so complete to exclude all causes of tire [sic] . . . by massage . . . and by electrical muscular excitation." Rest, as Mitchell explained, "means with me a good deal more than merely saying 'Go to bed and stay there.' It means care that letters bring no worrying news, that they are brief and of such kind as a nurse may read aloud. It means absence of all possible use of brain and body. It means neither reading nor writing at least for a time."

Though Mitchell recognized that neurasthenia could lead to organic disease, he thought it originally arose from psychological causes. The neurasthenic was a "broken down pest," the "despair" of her physicians and family, a "despot" and a "vampire" who destroyed the comfort of everyone around her.

Seclusion was crucial in curing these troubled creatures. It also was the only way to spark the invalid's desire to get well. As Mitchell explained in his 1877 book, *Fat and Blood,* "to lie abed half the day, and sew a little and read a little, and be interesting and excite sympathy, is all very well, but when [the patients] are bidden to stay in bed a month, and neither to read, write, nor sew, and to have one nurse—who is not a relative—then rest becomes for some women a rather bitter medicine, and they are glad enough to accept the order to rise and go about when the doctor issues a mandate." Once, when a recalcitrant patient refused to rise from bed when Mitchell pronounced her rest cure over, the doctor threatened to get into bed with her. When she still failed to move, he started to unzip his pants. At that point, he reported, the patient jumped to her feet.

Since neurasthenia, in Mitchell's view, always resulted in "womb troubles," he thought it essential to "manually adjust" a patient's sex organs at the end of her treatment. "If the patient is a virgin . . . and of the temperament which makes vaginal examinations disastrous shocks to the nervous system, I wait patiently the result of the rest and its aids. Then at the close of two months I like to make an effort at local relief . . . ," he wrote.

No woman left his care without undergoing this "local" treatment, as the internal gynecological exam was called. In an era before the speculum the "local" was for many women a humiliating horror, a kind of pseudo-rape, performed "with bolted doors and curtained windows and with no one present but patient and operator," as the feminist Catherine Beecher remarked.

THOUGH Mitchell's theories sound quaint, and even horrifying, he was considered a genius in his time. And in some ways his research was groundbreaking—he was among the first to recognize the connections between physical and mental health, for example. He also was one of the few physicians of his era to take women's health complaints seriously. He saw that his patients were not malingerers; they were in real pain. The rest cure was used in sanitariums throughout the country well into the twentieth century, and Mitchell claimed a high success rate. No doubt it was effective in some cases, particularly for people who *were* seriously overworked, like Edith Wharton. She had a nervous breakdown in 1898, and was able to resume writing only after undergoing the rest cure. According to *The Boston Medical Journal* in 1898, however, many people relapsed after Mitchell's treatment, and others were made worse by it, becoming even more confirmed in their invalidism.

But at the time Jane met Mitchell, he was glorying in one of the most astounding triumphs of his career, having just saved the life of a nineteen-year-old neurasthenic who'd been carried to his door paralyzed, blind, and near death. The year before, the girl, Miss B., as Mitchell referred to her in his journal, had gone off to college in glowing health, a voluptuous blonde who stood five feet six inches and weighed 156 pounds. Studying had greatly upset her nervous system, however. She became irritable, feeble, and sensitive to noises and light; eventually, she took to her bed, refusing to eat. Within a few months her weight had dropped to eighty pounds, and she was slipping in and out of consciousness. Soon after, she lost her sight and her legs drew up to her chest, locking her into a fetal position.

She was carried to Mitchell's office on a stretcher. He could not straighten her legs, even while she was under anesthesia, and concluded that some organic change had taken place in her joints. He decided an operation was the only remedy, and in two procedures, performed by another surgeon, her tendons were cut at the groin, knee, and ankle, stretched, and sewn back together. Then her legs were extended on splints. A few days later Mitchell strapped her to a board in her bed so that a nurse could raise her inch by inch three times a day. Within a short time, she was standing, and then walking with crutches. Meanwhile, her sight gradually returned, and soon she could write a few words and read a page of large print. Finally, when she was able to stand on her own, Mitchell sent her home restored "to absolutely perfect use of mind and body," he proudly noted in his journal.

Jane walked through his door a few days later. Her symptoms were similar to Miss B.'s. She was thin, pale, exhausted, and severely depressed. Mitchell immediately put her to bed—probably in a hotel near Mitchell's home. Only indigent patients were hospitalized at Mitchell's clinic, The Orthopaedic Hospital and Infirmary For Nervous Diseases. Most of his neurasthenic patients were farmed out to hotels, small, private hospitals, and relatives' homes. She was not permitted to read, write, sew, talk, or feed herself. Every day she underwent a three-hour massage with coconut oil and thirty-five minutes of electroshock therapy. With electrodes attached to his hands and connected by wires to a large battery, Mitchell would knead her body vigorously.

Jane spent six weeks under Mitchell's care. Her surviving letters don't comment on the doctor or the treatment she received. But there's little question she left the clinic worse off than when she'd gone in. She was still exhausted and depressed, and during the following year her spine gave out completely. Back with Ann at the house on Sixteenth Street, she prepared for the long train trip home to spend the summer in Cedarville. After six months of living with her relatives and six weeks of isolation under Mitchell's care, she was eager for "girls' society," she wrote Ellen Starr, and she tried unsuccessfully to arrange a meeting with her in the ladies' lounge at the train depot in Chicago. "I will be dreadfully disappointed if I don't see you at least for a few minutes," she wrote.

As her urgent tone reflected, Jane was in need of a bolstering conversation. Despite her condition, she still harbored hopes of launching a career, yet she was certainly under pressure from Mitchell and her stepmother to abandon such plans. There's no record of Mitchell's parting advice to Jane, though it's likely it was similar to his prescription for another "over ambitious" patient, Charlotte Perkins Gilman: "Live as domestic a life as possible," Mitchell told her. "Have but two hours intellectual life a day. And never touch pen, brush or pencil as long as you live."

AT HOME again in Cedarville, Jane's mood and health didn't improve. She chafed at her stepmother's domination, yet felt guilty that she was not fulfilling her role as dutiful daughter. "I am a failure in every sense," she berated herself in her diary. "People expect things of me. I have every chance to obtain them and yet fall far short."

Above all, Ann expected her to get married, and specifically, she wanted Jane to marry her son George, Jane's stepbrother. Six years earlier, Ann had opposed the marriage of her other son, Harry, to Jane's sister Alice. But as early as the spring of 1882, she began to pressure George to ignite a romance with Jane. Ann's motives aren't exactly clear. It must have troubled her that neither Jane nor George seemed interested in the opposite sex. She was especially concerned about George, a shy, withdrawn young man who had few friends. She encouraged him to be more social. "You will grow as you go with social life more," she once wrote him. "It is not good to keep aloof and remain like a snail in one's shell."

Though George was continuing his studies at Beloit, his mental state was rapidly deteriorating—he was withdrawn and depressed, and he had trouble making friends. Presumably, Ann imagined that a marriage between Jane and George would save both young people—Jane from arid spinsterhood, and George from himself. It was also a way to keep "the children" under her wing.

There is little to document this episode in Jane's life. Though in later years she occasionally spoke of it to friends and relatives glancingly, Jane never mentions it in her surviving letters from the time and refers to it in her notebook in only one mysterious passage: "We can set a watch over our affections . . . as we can over our other treasures—Geo and me both."

In any case, the idea of marrying George almost certainly horrified Jane. Though they had been extremely close as children, they saw little of each other as young adults and grew apart. The tone of their letters to one another, and their mention of each other in letters to relatives, is polite and distant.

Jane was too strong-willed to be cowed by Ann, yet her refusal to do her stepmother's bidding brought on waves of guilt. Her health deteriorated further; her back gave out and once again she retreated to bed. Alice wanted her husband, Harry, who'd recently established a practice in Mitchellville, Iowa, to treat Jane's back. "[Harry] has thought of that back night and day and has tried successfully a similar case," Alice wrote Jane on September 10, 1882. "So come Jane and give us the comfort of helping."

Jane didn't immediately take up her sister's offer, and the distractions of summer eased her pain a bit. In June she returned to Rockford to receive her B.A.—she decided to accept it even though she was still hoping to attend Smith. She helped raise money for a new library at the school and gave $1,000 of her inheritance from her father to buy science books. (The following year she was appointed a member of the school's board of trustees.) In July, she traveled to Northampton, Massachusetts, to visit Smith for a day and take the college's entrance exam, which she passed. Then she went on to Nantucket to be with her childhood friend Flora Guiteau, whose father had been the head cashier at John Addams's bank. It wasn't a happy visit. Flora's insane half-brother, Charles, was about to be hanged for assassinating President James Garfield. Guiteau had shot Garfield the previous July at the Washington train station, and the president had lingered for several months before succumbing to his wounds.

After the shooting, Flora had been shunned by most of her friends. Jane, though, remained loyal. As the hour of Charles's execution approached, Jane sat with Flora, reading aloud to distract her.

When Jane returned to Cedarville, her health was worse than

ever. Once again, she postponed enrolling at Smith and early that winter took up her sister's offer to come to Mitchellville for treatment by Harry. He subjected her to a new procedure developed in Germany. Using needles, he injected an irritant into the tissue around her spine. Jane then lay on her back in bed for eight weeks while the scar tissue contracted to pull the spine straight.

The bleak winter scene outside her bedroom window in Mitchellville mirrored her mood: cattle shivering in the empty fields, chickens frozen dead against the bare trees, a dark gray sky. Jane was so dismayed by her plight that she resolved not to write letters, because, as she later explained to Ellen, she was "ashamed to show even to my good friends against what lassitude, melancholy and general crookedness I was struggling."

Alice hardly left her side. The two sisters passed the time by reading to each other—selections from Carlyle, Mary Shelley's *Frankenstein,* and a biography of Sir Joshua Reynolds, the eighteenth-century English portrait painter. They "grew so interested in [Reynolds's] bright friends and period," Jane reported to Ellen Starr, "that we steadily read all the books we could find on them."

Slowly, Jane started to improve. She assumed—probably correctly—that her back problems were connected to her emotional troubles. Under her sister's loving attention, her discomfort began to subside. "I have had the kindest care and am emerging with a straight back and a fresh hold on life and endeavor I hope," she told Ellen shortly before returning to Cedarville.

At home, however, Jane was faced with a new crisis. Her older brother Weber, who had inherited his father's mills and a nearby farm, where he was living with his wife and daughter, had suffered a nervous breakdown. Not much is known about Weber, but he had been ten when Sarah Addams died, and of all the Addams children, he apparently took her death the hardest. His fragile emotional health was aggravated by trying to live up to his father's high standards. A lack of self-esteem and a timid spirit shine from Weber's letters. He lacked Jane's intellect and her strong will, and possibly he felt diminished by John Addams's closeness to his youngest daughter. Weber's mental health began to deteriorate before John Addams's death. He heard voices, hallucinated, and suffered bouts of deep depression. References in family letters suggest that his "agitation" and "irrationality" were caused, perhaps, by a condition that today would be diagnosed as schizophrenia.

At the time Ann was in Florida and George was at Beloit, so it fell to Jane to help Weber and his family through their ordeal. At first she moved in with them. But after a month, when Weber's condition did not improve, Jane petitioned the Stephenson County court to have him declared insane. After a hearing at which Jane and other family members testified, Weber was committed to a hospital in Jacksonville, Illinois. A few weeks later, he was transferred to the Elgin Hospital for the Insane, north of Chicago, where he remained for two months, most of that time in solitary confinement. He would be in and out of mental institutions for the rest of his life.

As Weber declined, Jane's health improved. For the first time since leaving medical school, she had work to do: It was her job to oversee her farm and other investments, plus Weber's property and mills. Jane was a bit disconcerted to discover she had a talent for business, writing Ellen later that month that she was "becoming quite absorbed in business affairs," and feared she'd "lose all hold of the softer graces." But the purposeful activity was clearly good for her health. She was spending a lot of time outdoors in her "native air," and she wrote Alice that she was "feeling splendidly from the exercise." So marked was the improvement, she added in a subsequent letter, that an acquaintance she met in town didn't recognize her: "She afterwards apologized by saying that the impression she had had of me was that of a delicate looking girl."

Still, Jane continued to be troubled by depression. Ellen's decision to join the Episcopal Church in July 1883 revived Jane's longing for religious faith as a solution to her problems: "My experiences of late have shown me the absolute necessity of the protection and dependence on Christ, his 'method and secret,' as Matthew Arnold put it . . . the good men and books I used to depend upon will no longer answer." But try as she might, she could not believe wholeheartedly in Jesus' divinity.

Sunk in religious doubt and worried that people would think her unchristian, or even an atheist, Jane decided to embark on a European tour, a favored nineteenth-century antidote to illness, depression, boredom, or an unhappy love affair.

Since as far back as the seventeenth century, the grand tour had been the traditional climax to an English gentleman's education. Traveling at a glacial pace by sailing ship and carriage, these well-to-do Englishmen typically spent several years on the Continent absorbing Gallic and Germanic culture, with, perhaps, a pilgrimage to Egypt and the Holy Land on the side. In the 1820s, the birth of railways made grand tours simpler for Europeans. At the same time, the arrival of steamships made the trips possible for Americans.

Many illustrious citizens, especially literary Easterners, traveled to Europe in the nineteenth century, particularly during the economic boom of the 1880s, when newly rich, culture-hungry Americans clamored for steamship tickets. Thousands of people sailed to Europe every week from the nation's ports, and an increasing number of them were women like Jane, who had money and education but nothing to do.

"It seems quite essential for the establishment of my health and temper that I have a radical change," Jane explained to Ellen. "And so I have accepted the advice given to every exhausted American—'go abroad.'"

The summer passed in a blur of preparations. She planned to be gone for almost two years and to visit ten countries. Jane's cousin Sarah Hostetter would join her, as would Jane's Rockford classmate Mary Ellwood and Mary's sister Harriet. Their chaperones were to be the Ellwoods' aunt, a Mrs. Young, and Jane's stepmother—though Ann, who was reluctant to leave home for such a long time, did not agree to go until the last minute. The party, as Jane wrote Alice, would be "large enough to be companionable and happy." Traveling in an entourage was not unusual—Henry James remarked on the women he saw abroad "all traveling in packs"—and it fit Jane's prescription for herself. All her life, she needed to be surrounded by large groups of people—usually women—to beat back feelings of loneliness and despair. Privacy was never important to her; she had a Victorian's comfort in the social bond, first sparked in her large, doting family and later nurtured in the close, all-female culture at Rockford. "I am more convinced every day that friendship . . . is after all the main thing in life," she once wrote Ellen. "And friendship and affections must be guarded and taken care of just as other valuable things."

Jane made elaborate arrangements for the trip. "Ma and I spend a good deal of time renewing wardrobes," Jane wrote Alice on June 5, 1883. She devoured travel and guide books and plotted the group's itinerary. They would start in London, travel to Italy, and end up in Paris.

As the time for departure drew near, Jane closed up most of the family's Cedarville home. She hired an elderly couple from the village to live in the back of the house and keep an eye on things while she and Ann were gone. "They will keep & feed two cows & a horse and pay as rent one third of the produce off of the thirty acres," she reported to Alice. "We sold a good many of the vehicles, etc., and all together it is much simpler and better than ever before."

She left Cedarville in mid-July on her way east with Ann. In Chicago, she met Mary Ellwood at the station, and Mary took her overnight to De Kalb, where Mary's father, a rich barbed wire manufacturer, presided over an opulent estate. Jane's reaction reflected an ambivalence toward wealth that would stay with her throughout her life. As she wrote Alice, "The house is the most elegant I ever was in or saw, the manifest evidence of unbounded wealth is undoubtedly somewhat shoddy but withal there is some thing sort of historic and impressive in tower staircases, a gardener's house on the grounds, stables filled with horses and dogs."

Back in Chicago the following day, Jane was fitted with a complicated back brace made of leather, steel, and whalebone. She wore it for the first time that night on a train ride from Chicago to Albany. It "pounded and rubbed me all the way," she wrote Alice. "But I did not have a backache and although I feel sore to night I have not the regulation pain so I guess we can call it a success. . . ."

She stopped in Philadelphia to pick up her cousin Sarah. A social visit to Dean Bodley of the Women's College of Medicine raised doubts in her mind of the usefulness of the trip. Perhaps Dr. Bodley chastised Jane for dropping out of medical school, for Jane soon wrote Ellen, "I quite feel as if I were not 'following the call' of my genius when I propose to devote two years time to travel in search of a good time and this general idea of culture which in some way never commanded my full respect. People complain of losing spiritual life when abroad. I imagine it will be quite as hard to hold to full earnestness of purpose."

One day on a Philadelphia streetcar, Jane's pocketbook containing her letter of credit was stolen. It seemed like a bad omen. Still, she looked forward to the trip. She enjoyed herself at the round of parties and dinners given in her honor in Philadelphia by the large, noisy families of her relatives.

After a few weeks, she and Sarah joined Ann and their other traveling companions in New York. On August 22, Jane walked up the gangway of the *Servia,* the largest and most opulent passenger ship on the ocean. She was carrying a satchel given her by her sister Mary, and a twice-patched umbrella, a present from Alice. Her back brace strained against her heavy serge dress. She was twenty-three, a tiny woman, standing only five feet three inches tall and weighing ninety-eight pounds, with an attractive face and light brown hair. From the deck of the ship, she waved good-bye to her uncle Harry Weber, to George, and to a group of young cousins who'd come to the pier to see them off. As the *Servia* pulled out and glided past "the big, beautiful, majestic Brooklyn Bridge," as Jane described it to Alice, she was "choked up of course & wept the regulation weep." She would not be home again for almost two years.

5

Grand Tour I

A "companionable and happy" party in London, 1883.
Standing from the left, Harriet Ellwood, Jane, Mary Ellwood, Sarah Hostetter; and the chaperones—Mrs. E. Young and Anna Haldeman Addams.
(Courtesy of University of Illinois at Chicago, the University Library, Jane Addams Memorial Collection)

Jane stepped ashore at Queenstown, Ireland, on August 29, 1883, a warm, beautiful Wednesday. She spent the next week traveling by train through the countryside with Ann and Sarah (the Ellwood girls and their chaperone had gone on to Liverpool), arriving in Dublin on September 7.

The little party checked into the Grisham Hotel, a modest pension, where their accommodations were typical of those they would have throughout the trip. The three women shared a sitting room, where Jane displayed a collection of family photos on the mantel, and a bedroom with two beds, a large one for Jane and Sarah and a single bed for Ann. Jane described the place to Alice: "We have a great big room with a fireplace in which a little copper tea kettle is singing, a big mahogany bed with curtains and a little brass bed in which Ma is propped up nibbling arrow root. There is a round polished table before the fire where Sarah and I are writing."

They remained in Dublin for three weeks while Ann recovered from a digestive ailment. Despite the hardships that typically plagued travelers at the time—wet clothes, damp rooms, freezing train compartments—Jane's health improved steadily throughout the trip. Her weight soared from 98 to 105 pounds, and her back didn't trouble her. Ann, on the other hand, suffered from a panoply of ailments, including fevers, boils, flu, and a bruised and swollen shoulder suffered in a fall from a horse in Switzerland. (She was treated with "blood thirsty little leeches," which, when applied to the affected area, Jane reported to Alice, "at once reduced the swelling.") Jane took over her stepmother's care without complaint. In Ireland she left Ann's bedside for only a few hours at a time—to do some sight-seeing or shopping. She ate all her meals with her stepmother and spent long evenings reading to her in front of the fire.

Ten years later, in her essay "The College Woman and the Family Claim," Jane was highly critical of mothers who relied on their educated, unmarried daughters for companionship and denied them independent lives. But at the time of their tour there's no evidence that Jane openly complained about Ann's demands. Such disrespect for the mother of the house would have violated a strong Victorian taboo. (Nor did Ann whine about being stuck traveling with a stepdaughter instead of her own flesh and blood—though she confessed to Harry, "How I have wished that I could have taken this tour with my boys.")

Jane's relationship with her stepmother was too complicated to be summed up solely in terms of repression and denial. In spite of their differences, the two women cared deeply for each other. In a letter to Harry on January 27, five months into the trip, Ann wrote, "Jane is growing fleshy and looks very much improved tho she is inclined to over tax herself in sight-seeing. [To] stretch [her] neck up to ceilings and high walls in looking at frescoes and paintings is the hardest work for her back and shoulders in the world." In another letter she told Harry, "Jane . . . makes every effort to get the most out of things and we when left alone (which is not our fortune) compare notes and get good out of it."

Jane was equally concerned about Ann. Indeed, when an opportunity arose to break free of her stepmother, Jane did not take advantage of it. A few weeks after they arrived in Ireland, a doctor who examined Ann pronounced her too weak for traveling and recommended that she return at once to America. Jane urged her stepmother to remain abroad. Perhaps she worried that she would be forced to return home too if Ann left. But her letters at the time make clear that she was sincerely worried about Ann's welfare. Jane thought the trip was the best cure for Ann's troubles, particularly Ann's continued grief over the death of John Addams, her concern for George's future, and her general boredom in Cedarville. "I feel convinced that if all disagreeable associations and sickness can be kept away from her for a year, she will be better than she has been for a long time," Jane wrote Harry.

Every day Europe offered something "historic and beautiful" to distract Ann from her troubles. To her delight, she met sophisticated people and bragged to Harry that they complimented her on her deportment. Even living in Cedarville for twenty years, she told him, couldn't obliterate her "refined and high-born manners." Often accompanied by the Ellwoods, Jane and Ann went to the opera and the theater, and toured museums, cathedrals, and literary landmarks, including the homes of Thomas Carlyle, Robert Burns, and William Shakespeare, and the grave of William Wordsworth. They visited the major European universities. At Oxford, Jane signed her name in the guest registry below that of Susan B. Anthony, who had, apparently, just been there, and inspected the entire campus, "from the kitchen in Christ Church College where forty chickens were roasting on a spit, to the fine old theater where the highest scholars in the world have received their degrees," she wrote Weber.

Still, while Ann may have been delighted by the experiences unfolding before her, Jane was feeling increasingly bitter. The grand tour only emphasized the fact that she led a sheltered, pampered life in America. She was repulsed by the "fatuous security" of the other educated young women she met and dreaded becoming like them, "smothered and sickened with advantages." In her autobiography she likened their lives to "eating a sweet dessert the first thing in the morning."

Her long letters home reflect her anxiety over finding something "useful" to do. She wrote Ellen Starr that she was discovering a world that "contains more privileges and possibilities than I had imagined. It enlarges one's vision. But," she added glumly, "there is little chance for solid work."

A "feverish search after culture," to use Jane's phrase, had become by default the most important thing in the lives of many educated, unmarried women. Their days were dominated by a little French, a little art, a little music, a little literature, and much dining, lunching, letter writing, and paying calls.

Jane thought all that was irrelevant, and she later looked back on her tour with contempt, as a time when she "lumber[ed]" her mind with books that only served to "cloud" reality. Her bitterness is a bit startling, as she completely failed to acknowledge the transforming aspects of the experience. Europe's "lighted and decorated stage," in Henry James's phrase, sparked her imagination and sharpened her sense that she must do something important with her life. What's more, her initial glimpses of Europe's urban poverty and suffering fueled her passion for democracy and set in motion the thinking that would eventually lead to Hull-House. Yet, on the evidence of her writing, she thought she was wasting her time.

At the end of September, when Ann had sufficiently recovered, the little party went on to Scotland, then London, where they moved into a boardinghouse for American travelers at 32 Dorset

Square. At first, Jane was intimidated by London. She wrote Weber that it was a "Monster City . . . simply appalling," covered in yellow fog "so dense you couldn't see across the street." Jane also disliked the trappings of British royalty, which offended her republican spirit. After touring Windsor Castle, then home to Queen Victoria, she told Weber, "It seemed a very ponderous affair for one woman's safety & comfort."

One day, the boardinghouse proprietress took Jane and eight other guests into the poorest section of London to see the Saturday food auction, where, for a pittance, the destitute could buy rotting produce left over from the markets and restaurants in wealthier neighborhoods. They took a train to Whitechapel in the East End, then rode on the top of a streetcar for five miles through "booths and stalls swarming with thousands of people," as Jane described it to her brother.

She was horrified not only by the sights of "hideous human need and suffering" before her, but also by her own feeble, literary response to it. As she confessed in her autobiography:

> At the very moment of looking down the East London street, from the top of the omnibus, I had been sharply and painfully reminded of "The Vision of Sudden Death" which had confronted De Quincey one summer's night [when he tried to shout a warning but found] himself unable to make a sound because his mind [was] hopelessly entangled in an endeavor to recall the exact lines from the "Iliad" which describe the great cry [of] Achilles. . . . Suddenly called upon for a quick decision in the world of life and death, he had been able to act only through a literary suggestion. . . . It seemed to me too preposterous that in my first view of the horror of East London, I should have recalled De Quincey's literary description of the literary suggestion which had once paralyzed him.

In November, Jane's party went to Amsterdam, then on to Berlin and Dresden, where they stayed for ten weeks. The six women shared three adjoining rooms. "The white porcelain stoves are heated and actually look warm and the many candles . . . are cheerful, if not very luminous," Jane wrote her sister Mary Linn.

Despite her distrust of advantages, she enjoyed having them, as she admitted in her autobiography. The winter passed in a blur of operas, language lessons, and trips to museums and churches. "We are all making desperate exertions toward knowledge," Jane wrote Mary Linn. Sarah Hostetter took singing lessons every day, while Mary Ellwood painted at a studio in downtown Dresden. Ann reported to Harry, "Jane looks the picture of a little student as she is (and always will be)."

Jane liked the opera, and she and Ann rented a box for the season. They hired a cab to drive them there, wait, and then drive them home, all for a mark and a half. This was the exact daily wage, Jane noted in her journal, that was paid to the women who worked in the breweries transporting large wooden tanks of scalding beer on their backs.

Jane had observed some of these workers from her bedroom window, which had a view of a bustling brewery across the town square. The women's "faces and hands, reddened in the cold morning air, showed clearly the white scars where they had previously been scalded by the hot stuff which splashed if they stumbled ever so little on their way," Jane wrote in her autobiography. One day she and the proprietor of her hotel questioned the owner of the brewery about his treatment of the women. He "received us with exasperating indifference, or rather received me, for the innkeeper mysteriously slunk away as soon as the great magnate of the town began to speak," she recalled.

After such brushes with poverty, she later wrote, "I would invariably suffer a moral revulsion against this feverish search after culture."

In the course of the trip, Jane received "a great many compliments" on how well her traveling party got along. But she did not feel in deep sympathy with the Ellwood girls, who would have fit comfortably in Henry James's novel *Daisy Miller.* "They are perfectly unlimited as to time and money, and see every thing in a good natured happy go lucky sort of a way," Jane wrote Alice on December 14. The sisters had no plans for the future beyond marrying well, and, indeed, they seemed a bit boy crazy. At the theater, Jane told Alice, Mary's "opera glass constantly points at the fine, young officers."

Jane, meanwhile, missed home. Holidays made her terribly homesick and letters from America sparked floods of tears. She was particularly worried and feeling guilty about Mary Linn, whose health was deteriorating. Mary had had four children in quick succession. Her troublesome husband was constantly changing jobs and money was short. "Some days I am so uneasy that it seems to me I *must* take the first ship and go to her. She has spent all her life doing for other people and now when she needs help the most there is no one to go to her," Jane wrote Alice. "She has every claim on me and has a right to demand every thing. If I were more sure of my own strength, I ought to be with her now." Jane urged Alice to warn her if Mary seemed likely to die "so that I can come home before it may be too late."

At the end of February, Jane's party, joined by friends from home, moved on to Florence. As they entered the city by railroad, "spring burst [on] us all at once," Jane wrote home. The stone walls surrounding the city were covered with huge pink roses and the fields were full of purple anemones. Within the city, a carnival was under way. "The streets were packed with people," Jane wrote Mary, "the noise and flags and music reminded one exactly of a Fourth of July."

In Italy, she passed countless hours in museums, studying art. Pondering Michelangelo's "David," she was in awe of the artist's genius, but wondered about "the use and good accomplished" by it. Religious art affected her more deeply. "It may be partly owing to my barbaric instinct for size," she wrote Ellen Starr, "or delight in seeing the story told before my eyes, but the grand series of frescoes" depicting the life of the saints in the Uffizi thrilled her. The paintings, growing larger and more heroic as the story progressed, "never fail to affect me with a tremor and a corresponding desire for the power arising from mere goodness."

Viewing the Italian ruins, she had a different kind of epiphany—a sense of community with the human race. "May be it is because you see that the ground even can not belong long to any one association," she told a friend. Italy also fueled her literary sensibilities, and many of her letters home contain vivid images. After visiting Mount Etna, for example, she wrote Alice, "It smokes sort of calmly and benignly like an after dinner pipe."

After Florence, the group moved to Rome, where they ran into a half dozen or so acquaintances from Cedarville and Rockford. Then it was on to Lucerne, Switzerland, where Jane climbed mountains with no discomfort to her back. She'd stopped wearing her steel brace at the beginning of the trip and never put it on again. Two weeks later, though, in Geneva, she was plagued by toothaches and spent every day for a week at the dentist. "My teeth have never been so miserable," she wrote Ellen. "Do not [be] dreadfully surprised if you see me come home with a new set!"

Finally, in June, the party arrived in Paris. The city "is fascinating, there is no doubting that," Jane wrote Alice. She went on a shopping spree, buying gloves at Bon Marché and new clothes, including a green traveling dress with a fashionable bustle, which was comfortable only, she told Alice, if she sat in it "perfectly quiet." (Bustles the size of small sofa pillows were attached around the waist by ribbons and worn over a woman's undergarments.) Soon the women were joined by George, who came for the summer after completing a year of science study at Johns Hopkins University in Baltimore. George's psychological health seemed to have deteriorated, and Ann was worried about him. She believed that too much studying had sapped him of his "nerve force" and threatened to render him "a melancholy, downcast being no use to the world and a burden to himself."

Instead of bolstering his confidence, the years at college seemed to have made him more timorous than ever. Ann hoped the trip would help him develop his manly side. "T'will be so pleasant for me to lean upon him and have him take charge of us per luggage and tickets," she'd written her other son, Harry. George wanted no part of it and warned her that he dreaded "the role of male in charge."

In any case, George is mentioned only parenthetically in Jane's and Ann's letters home from Europe. His summer with them seems to have passed uneventfully.

A cholera epidemic on the Continent sent the travelers to London for much of August and September. At the end of the summer, George, the Ellwoods, and Sarah Hostetter returned to America. Jane and Ann remained in Europe, committed to another year of self-improvement. Jane hoped a more rigorous study schedule would give her some sense of accomplishment. "As last year was one of unmitigated pleasure and travel," Jane explained to Alice, "this year should have a little more study and profit in it."

In October, the two women moved for four months to Berlin, a city that Jane thought "as modern and busy as Chicago itself." They settled into a charming pension run by an Englishwoman named Mrs. Phillips. As usual, their fellow boarders were other women with money and time on their hands, including a coworker of Emma Willard's, founder in 1821 of the Troy Female Seminary—the first American college-level institution for women—and, as Jane told her sister Mary, "two English old maids about sixty who [are] roaming about the world and having the best kind of time."

Jane attended three lectures a week at the Victoria Lyceum, Germany's first women's college, founded in 1869. She was enjoying "almost a boarding school routine," she wrote George, adding in a letter to Alice on November 16, "I seem to be about as busy as I was at school, with this difference, that there is no necessity about it and the gay operas . . . come in between very often."

Despite her strong democratic impulses, she was dazzled by glimpses of wealth, nobility, and achievement. She heard speeches by Bismarck and Henry Stanley, the African explorer. At a concert one night, she reported to Ellen, she "seriously injured" her eyes directing her opera glass at the Crown Prince, who was seated beside a harsh electric light. Another evening, at a party at the pension, she actually met a relative of Prince Albert's and felt "quite near the throne."

Still, she continued to be troubled by her lack of purpose, and she envied George, who had resumed his studies at Johns Hopkins. "Your kind and regular letters are a constant reproach to my unproductiveness," she wrote him on November 15. And to Ellen she confessed, "I have been idle for two years just because I had not enough vitality to be anything else. I have constantly lost confidence in myself and have gained nothing and improved in nothing. A sad record isn't it?"

On a frigid January day, Jane and Ann boarded a train for their second visit to Paris—the final leg of their grand tour. To keep warm they rested their feet on cans filled with hot water and wrapped their steamer rugs around their shoulders. They moved into two rooms at a pension run by a widowed French woman and her two daughters. Their quarters were so cold that Jane's hands turned numb as she tried to write letters. The tiny fireplace "no more heats [the room] than so much painted scenery," she wrote Ellen. But she was warmed by the pension's lively spirit. Every evening the guests, including two American girls studying for stage careers, gathered in the drawing room to discuss the day's adventures.

Learning the French language "is just now the chief object of my existence," Jane reported to Ellen. But she also studied the paintings at the Louvre and the fashions displayed on the Champs-Élysées. At a performance at the Paris Opera House she was stunned by the "dress and jewelry of the audience [which] exceeded everything I ever dreamed of."

She saw Sarah Bernhardt onstage and toured the palaces at Versailles and Fontainebleau, where she examined "the little round table on which Napoleon signed his abdication." It was, she wrote Alice on May 1, "decidedly the most thrilling piece of furniture to be seen on this side of the water." She and Ann attended a "swell" dinner at the Café de Paris. "All the delicacies out of season were on hand such as melons & late vegetables," she wrote Alice. "The cherries were served growing on a little tree set in the middle of the table. While we were taking coffee, a juggler came in & . . . right at table performed some of the most amazing tricks before our very eyes."

Jane and Ann had planned to visit Spain as their final stop before returning to America in July. But the news from home wasn't good. Mary Linn was expecting another baby—her fifth—and her health was rapidly sinking. After traveling in Europe for twenty-one months, Jane and Ann decided to return to America immediately. They booked passage on the *Servia* and sailed from Liverpool on May 30.

6

Baltimore

Jane with her stepbrother George Haldeman and "Ma," Anna Haldeman Addams.
(Courtesy of University of Illinois at Chicago, the University Library, Jane Addams Memorial Collection)

Arriving in Cedarville in early June, Jane no sooner set down her steamer trunk than she was off again to visit Mary in Harvard, a small Illinois town about seventy miles northwest of Chicago. After a difficult pregnancy, Mary had given birth to a baby boy. She had three other young children to care for and her husband and eldest son were about to go to Dakota, Illinois, for several months to work in a new church. Jane returned to Cedarville within a week, but in September she was back in Harvard for an extended stay.

At the Linns' house, Jane transformed the family study into a cozy bedroom for herself with her favorite books and pictures displayed. Her two-year-old nephew, Stanley, slept with her in a big four-poster and she grew deeply attached to him. Though she adored playing with Mary's children, she disliked most domestic tasks, particularly cooking and sewing. She felt rather helpless when a friend of Mary's stopped by to make over some old quilts, and confessed to Ann, "I am afraid that I will never be the typical old maid."

She tried to study, but felt guilty shutting herself away while so much housework needed to be done. "What reading I do downstairs I like to share with Mary," she wrote Alice. "You know my experience in Philadelphia of trying to fulfill too many objects at once. I am afraid trying to study here would leave me with the same uneasy consciousness that I had not done what I came purposely to do, because I had tried to do something else and failed at that."

A visit from Ellen Starr in November enlivened the routine. For the past six years Ellen had been teaching art history and English at the fashionable Kirkland School on Chicago's North Side. She maintained a grueling schedule of classes, conducted private tutoring in algebra, and at the same time kept up a program of studying literature and languages in her room at night. The strenuous load had taken its toll—Ellen suffered from bouts of nervous exhaustion that kept her bedridden for days at a time. Her students loved her, however. She was a slender woman in her mid-twenties who was passionately religious, emotional, and prone to wild enthusiasms over art, books, and people. In 1880 she'd formed a romantic attachment to a fellow teacher named Mary Runyon and was devastated when Runyon left Chicago in mid-1882. "The first real experience I ever had in my life of any real pain in parting, came with separating from her," she'd written Jane at the time. "I don't speak of it because people don't understand it. . . . 'People' would understand if it were a man."

Now Ellen turned her passionate attention to Jane. The two

friends took care of the Linn children (whom Ellen pronounced very ill-mannered but clever) and read Browning out loud. Jane also read Ellen her essay on her European trip, which was later published in the *Rockford Seminary Magazine.* When Ellen returned to Chicago a few days later, she wrote Jane that she was "positively forlorn" without her friend. "We put so much into the few days that I feel as if we had been together for weeks. . . . I should get to depend on you bodily in a little while. . . . I can't help wishing however that we could be in the same place long enough to do some work together."

Rereading Jane's old letters, Ellen said, the stilted sentences and bad spelling irritated her. But she was moved by the memory of all they had in common. "I had almost forgotten us," Ellen confessed.

Jane, though, was not yet ripe for an intimate relationship outside her family. With her sisters, she openly expressed her deep love. But even among her closest friends, Jane held part of herself back, fearing to give up too much independence and self-control.

Still, Jane relied on Ellen's friendship, particularly in sorting through the religious questions that continued to trouble her. "For many years it was my ambition to reach my father's moral requirements & now when I am needing something more, I find myself approaching a crisis & look rather wistfully to my friends for help," she wrote Ellen on December 6, 1885.

She told Ellen she'd join a church "immediately," if she thought that would "in the least degree" help her find God. The problem was that Jane's questing intelligence made her a bad candidate for deep religious commitment. The humanistic ethics of writers such as Ruskin, Carlyle, and George Eliot stirred her in a way theology never could. After reading *Daniel Deronda,* she wrote Alice, using a favorite expression of the time, "[Eliot's] books give me more *motive power* than any [others]."

Ellen reassured Jane that she didn't need religion to lead a worthwhile life. "[You are] so much above me in goodness," Ellen wrote, adding, "You outside the church, I within it, are simply trying to find the same thing; and you are as much nearer to it than I as the life of self-denial and of pleasing others and not ones' self brings one."

That December, Jane dutifully followed her stepmother to Baltimore, where Ann had rented two rooms at 144 Washington Place to be near George and to partake of the city's lively cultural and social life. Jane, Ann, and George enjoyed "a merry old fashioned Christmas, doing everything possible that we used to do at home," Jane reported to Alice with more bravado than truth. In fact, the life of "pleasing others and not oneself" was taking a serious toll. In Baltimore, Jane later wrote, "I had seemed to have reached the nadir of my nervous depression and sense of maladjustment."

She simply had nothing useful to do. Instead, she filled her time by escorting Ann to card parties, concerts, dinners, and lectures. Ann wanted to launch her stepdaughter into Baltimore society, but Jane had no gift for small talk and no confidence in her appearance, even when dressed in the beautiful clothes she'd bought in Paris. One picture from this time shows her looking miserable in a fashionable hat with absurd feathers plopped on top.

Baltimore society was dominated by an antebellum-South sensibility; the women aspired to be decorative. "There is a sentiment here decidedly against college courses for women," Jane wrote Alice on February 17, 1886. "[There is only one] Vassar graduate in the city and I think Wellesley and Smith are unknown." Jane had trouble relating even to the intellectual women she met, including two "superior" sisters who were staying at her boardinghouse. As she explained to Alice, they were "perfectly rabid on the Southern question. They do not call themselves Americans & claim to have no country save Virginia."

Yet, characteristically, Jane was generous about the Southern belles who called on her and Ann during afternoon visiting hours. "The pleasant ladies one meets, [are] intelligent and thorough as far as they go, [and] almost convince one against his own convictions," she wrote Alice.

But Jane's frustration was beginning to manifest itself in troubling ways. On February 7 she wrote to Ellen, "I have had the strangest experience since I have been in Baltimore, I have found my faculties, memory . . . and all, perfectly inaccessible, locked up away from me."

She had looked forward to returning to Cedarville with Ann for the summer, but when she arrived, she faced a fresh set of problems. Weber had had a relapse and was back in the hospital. Harry Haldeman's drinking had led to his giving up his medical practice and he'd moved to Girard, Kansas, with Alice, where he became president of the Girard National Bank. Mary Linn had recently given birth for the fifth time, and her husband was planning to move the family again. It fell to Jane to smooth over everyone's troubles, and she spent much of the summer shuttling among the homes of her siblings and performing endless errands—ordering monogrammed stationery and silk bookcase curtains for Alice; shopping for a cradle for Mary's baby and interviewing nurses to care for the child. She later referred to this summer when she "did all the housework at Cedarville" as a great mistake, a terrible waste of her talents and intellect.

With each passing year, it grew less and less likely that she would embark on a career. She had given up all plans to go to Smith or return to medical school, and she seemed resigned to living out her life as the family's maiden aunt. Looking back on these years a decade later, she argued that family claims sabotaged feminine ambition. The grown-up son was considered a citizen with well defined duties. The grown-up daughter, however, "who is under no necessity of earning a living," was restless and unhappy after leaving college, she wrote in her 1898 essay "The College Woman and the Family Claim." "It has always been difficult for the family to regard the daughter otherwise than as a family possession. She is told to be devoted to her family, inspiring and responsive to her social circle, and to give the rest of her time to further self-improvement and enjoyment. She expects to do this, and responds to these claims to the best of her ability—even heroically sometimes. But where is the larger life of which she has dreamed so long?"

For Jane, of course, the family claim was not just an obligation imposed from the outside, but sprung from her own devotion. She loved her sisters in particular, with the passion other women heaped on their husbands and children. Jane knew she would never marry and that Cedarville, the village of her birth, would always be her emotional home. She had "all sorts of plans . . . in the dim future," she told Alice, for building a farmhouse near the homestead as a personal retreat. "I . . . have discovered . . . that it is well to hold fast to the place in which you were born and *placed,*" she wrote.

IN THE FALL, Jane and Ann returned to Baltimore, where they rented three rooms on North Charles Street—a bedroom, sitting room, and small dining room. They had dinners sent in from a restaurant nearby. At eight each morning, Jane prepared coffee on a little oil stove and served it to Ann with hot milk, rolls, and preserves. George kept a room on the same floor and joined them for most meals. He and Jane remained fond of each other, but they were no longer close, and their dealings were remote and formal.

Jane resumed a flurry of social activities—organizing an art discussion group that met weekly in her sitting room, taking drawing lessons, making regular trips to the crowded Enoch Pratt library to borrow books. In the afternoon, she and Ann drove around town paying calls and leaving cards at the homes of other idle women.

The manufactured busyness led Jane again to the feelings of desperate emptiness that had been plaguing her since college. But that winter, for the first time, she found a way to open her life a bit through some genteel do-gooding. She started visiting a nursing home for elderly black women several days a week. Soon, she wrote Alice, "I had such a pleasant afternoon yesterday with the old women in the Colored Shelter, they are so responsive and confidential and begin to know me well enough now to be perfectly free." She also began to drop in on an orphanage that trained young black girls to be servants. "I heartily approve of the scheme," Jane wrote Alice on December 28.

The charity work was a revelation. Years later, in explaining to a reporter the motives behind founding Hull-House, Ellen Starr said that Jane discovered in Baltimore that "after a lecture or a social evening she would feel quite exhausted . . . but after a morning with the colored people in the Johns Hopkins home, she was actually physically better than if she had stayed in bed."

Nonetheless, the family claim pulled at Jane. In October 1886 she traveled to Philadelphia to visit relatives from both sides of her family. The colorful trees in the countryside looked like an Impressionist painting, and one afternoon Jane took a long drive to visit the Quaker graveyard where many of her ancestors were buried. She went home "about twilight," she reported to Ann, "filled with country sights and sounds, the men husking corn, chickens roosting on the trees and shouting children out chest-nutting." The following February, when Mary gave birth a month early, Jane rushed to her side. Later, she helped the Linns move to Geneseo, Illinois, where Reverend Linn had taken a new job as minister of a church. Jane spent a lot of time helping care for Mary's children, a job, she confessed to Ellen Starr, she enjoyed immensely. By now Jane was twenty-seven. Though she was not interested in having a relationship with a man, she loved mothering her nieces and nephews, who made her feel connected to the world as nothing else did. "If you don't take charge of a child at night you can't feel a scared trembling little hand grow confiding and quiet as soon as it lies within your own," she wrote Ellen. "If you don't take little children out in the yard to spend the morning you simply can't see their unbounded delight and extravagant joy when they see a bird taking his bath." Later that spring, Alice gave birth to a daughter, her first child after twelve years of marriage, and Jane moved to Girard, Kansas, to be with the Haldemans.

For more than a year, Jane had been hoping to return to Europe, this time with a definite purpose—to collect art reproductions for Rockford College and the Kirkland School, where Ellen taught. But she may have had something larger in mind, too. Her experience in Baltimore had fueled her interest in helping the poor, and she made tentative plans to investigate various urban charities, including London's Toynbee Hall, the world's first settlement. Jane planned the trip with Sarah Anderson, a teacher at Rockford, and Ellen Starr, who had begun to grow as restless as Jane. Jane offered to pay half Ellen's expenses, and Ellen accepted. "I don't often remember that I am using her money, & when I do it is no trouble to me," Ellen once remarked. "I *like* to use it. . . . I love her so much that money makes no difference." In September, Ellen left for Europe ahead of her friends.

When George returned to Cedarville in December 1887 after dropping his studies at Johns Hopkins, he took up responsibility for Ann, and Jane felt free to leave. On December 14, she set sail with Sarah Anderson (who also accepted Jane's offer to pay half of the expenses), and Sarah's brother-in-law, John Bickel. Glad as Jane was to be leaving, she already missed her sisters desperately. As the ship pulled out of the harbor, she was overcome with longing for Alice. "How dear you are to me when I find myself going so far from what I love most," she'd written her sister a day before, adding in a postscript as if to convince herself, "Don't worry about me. I expect to [be] well and happy."

7

Grand Tour II

Ellen Gates Starr as a young woman.
(Courtesy of University of Illinois at Chicago,
the University Library, Jane Addams Memorial Collection)

Jane's optimism was prescient, for, indeed, her 1888 tour of Europe would mark the turning point in her life. Away from her family for the first time since college, she would discover she could live happily on her own with other young women. What's more, the pilgrimage would be the catalyst for her decision to found Hull-House.

Her little party arrived in Southampton a few days before

Christmas. On December 24, the three friends—Sarah, Ellen, and Jane—crossed the English Channel and traveled by train to Paris. The next morning they exchanged presents at their hotel before going out to explore the city. They ate dinner at a fashionable restaurant on the Right Bank and then rode atop an omnibus to the Bastille, finally stopping at the Palais Royale for a Christmas treat of hot chocolate before heading home.

A week later, Jane went by herself to Munich—the first time she'd ever been anywhere alone. "I went to this hotel . . . & ordered a room for the night," she reported proudly to Alice. "Every where it was 'Madame' with the utmost respect and I felt perfectly at my ease and dignified all the time."

She visited the cathedral at Ulm and was moved by the stone carvings and stained-glass windows evoking the history of man's religious quest. By a much later account, the experience had a profound impact on her. She told her nephew James Linn that she returned to her hotel room and stayed up half the night writing in her notebook about her dream for "a cathedral of humanity." Her imagined structure would be "capacious enough to house a fellowship of common purpose" and "beautiful enough to persuade men to hold fast to the vision of human solidarity." She mentioned none of this, however, in her letters home to her family, and her journal of this trip no longer survives.

Ellen joined her a few days later, and the two friends moved into a double room at an inexpensive Munich pension. Their reunion was joyous. "I have seldom in my life had a happier week than we have had together," Jane reported to Alice. They spent most mornings in the galleries studying collections of drawings by Dürer and Holbein, whose works, they believed, held moral as well as artistic value. (In contrast, Jane and Ellen shared Ann's loathing of Rubens's "vulgar nude women.") In the afternoons, Jane told Alice, "we have simply *talked* & visited until we were exhausted."

On their own in Germany, the two friends had the chance to develop their feelings for each other, yet they remained a curious contrast in personalities. Whereas Jane was reserved in her expressions of affection toward Ellen, Ellen openly idolized Jane. In particular, she was in thrall to what she regarded as Jane's moral superiority—especially her ability to get along with almost anyone. As Ellen explained to Ann Haldeman, during dinners at their hotel in Munich, Jane devoted most of her attention "to an absurd old Missourian, who wore a flannel shirt and a paper collar, speared his bread with his fork . . . and picked his teeth . . . and whom nobody else near him would take the trouble to talk to. I never admired her more. She talked to this man as she would have done to a man of the world." Ellen told Ann she was in awe of "the moral effort and self discipline . . . required to develop a character like [Jane's]. It seems more beautiful to me as I know it better, and would be worth more to me than all Europe if I could become only a little like her."

Jane protested that "Ellen always overestimates my influence." But she enjoyed the adulation, and she liked playing the role of protector to her highly emotional friend. One morning, Jane awoke to find Ellen crying because she was cold, so she invited her to share the fur coat in which Jane always slept. As the two women huddled together, Ellen "stopped crying," Jane told Alice, and "the tears dried on her cheeks like a child."

Sarah Anderson arrived a week later, and the three friends moved on to Rome, where they settled into a student's routine, studying and talking late into the night. Sarah was ten years Jane's senior. Like all of Jane's friends, she was smart and high-minded, the product of a middle-class Illinois home. After graduating from Rockford in 1869, she had stayed at the school as the physical education teacher. She was a strikingly good-looking woman, with a robust, athletic figure, heavy red-gold hair, and a rosy complexion that earned her the nickname "pink and white"—perhaps a reference to Harriet Beecher Stowe's 1871 novel, *Pink and White Tyranny*, about a kindly gentleman in thrall to his selfish wife's beauty. The three friends got along remarkably well. Away from Ann's domination, and with Ellen and Sarah's affection, Jane finally began to shake the doubts and depression that had troubled her since college.

But Jane's happiness was soon shattered by tragic news from home. Her sister Mary's youngest daughter, Mary Junior, had died of whooping cough at age four not even a year after the death of the family baby, three-month-old Charles. The little girl had passed away at the end of January, but Jane didn't receive word until February 16, when she stopped at the bank after dinner to find a packet of mail from the Linns.

These letters are as painful to read today as they must have been a century ago. Just before she died, little Mary had asked for "Aunt Dane," who had rocked her to sleep and read her stories during Jane's long sojourns in the Linn household. The parents searched for consolation in their deep religious faith, rationalizing that God had a purpose in calling Mary to him. But that was no solace to their five remaining children. Expressing the sad confusion of a child struggling to understand death, Esther, now the family's only daughter, said she didn't understand "what God wanted with so many little children."

Jane was devastated. "I'm beginning to think that it does not pay to put so much space between yourself and the people you love best," she wrote Alice. Her back began bothering her, and within a week she was confined to bed with "abominable spasms of pain." No sooner had Jane recovered from the sciatica than she was felled by an attack of rheumatism. The English doctor who examined her said he'd never seen so many neuralgic Americans, thus denying her, as Jane joked to Weber, "the satisfaction of being unique in my affliction." The doctor also lectured Jane on "the impropriety of 'so delicate a person—an invalid one might say'—traveling in Europe without a member of her family. He hasn't the remotest idea of the *toughness* of my constitution and was very much surprised by my rapid recovery," she added.

Sarah and Ellen went on to Naples, while Jane stayed behind in Rome to recover. The friends were reunited at Easter in Florence, where the pleasures of studying art and practicing their Italian were enhanced by their delight in one another. They also were joined by a Mrs. Rowell, a family friend from Freeport, and by Helen Harrington, a classmate from Rockford who had come to Europe to get over a "disappointment"—the era's favorite euphemism for having been jilted by a lover. Soon, they moved to Genoa, where one afternoon they saw the visiting Queen Victoria drive by in her carriage. "She is neither beautiful nor graceful," Jane reported to Alice, "but not as red and homely as she is painted."

After stopping on the Riviera so Jane could spend some recuperative time in the warm sun, the travelers landed in Madrid. There, one afternoon, they went to a bullfight—"the great event of our stay," as Jane told her sister-in-law, Laura Addams, in a letter soon afterward. At the last minute, Helen and Mrs. Rowell decided not to go. So Jane, Ellen, and Sarah were chaperoned by a male guest from their hotel.

They arrived at the amphitheater during the opening ceremonies and settled into wooden seats that were protected from the sun by a large canvas canopy. Suddenly, a shiny black bull rushed into the dusty ring. He was "a beautiful creature, as lithe and active as a cat, and as fleet and graceful as a deer," Jane recalled in the letter. The picadores followed on horses, taunting the bull until he charged, killing the horses in a bloody slaughter. Next, six banderilleros entered the arena to taunt the bull, and by the time the matador arrived, "the bull was so tired out that it was a comparatively easy matter to kill [him] by one clever stroke into his spinal cord," Jane noted. She and her friends witnessed the killing of five bulls, and though they "did not stay until the bitter end," they "were rather ashamed and surprised to find that we were brutal enough to take a great interest in it."

Twenty years later, in her autobiography, Jane presented a dramatically different account of the bullfight. In this version, Sarah and Ellen were disgusted by the violence and fled the arena. Only Jane watched the entire spectacle. Afterward, when she met her friends outside the arena, Jane claimed, they were "stern and pale with disapproval" of her "brutal endurance."

"I had no defense to offer to their reproaches save that I had not thought much about the bloodshed," she continued. "But in the evening the natural and inevitable reaction came, and in deep chagrin I felt myself tried and condemned, not only by this disgusting experience, but by the entire moral situation which it revealed."

How could she watch the killing without being appalled? she

asked herself. Why was she so oddly elated at the sight of blood? Was she so caught up in the dry, pale world of books and ideas that she'd become indifferent to real suffering?

By this account, the questions led inevitably to a profound insight: She'd fooled herself into thinking she'd someday accomplish something important. "It was suddenly made quite clear to me that I was lulling my conscience by a dreamer's scheme," she wrote. "It is easy to become the dupe of a deferred purpose, of the promise the future can never keep, and I had fallen into the meanest type of self-deception in making myself believe that all this was in preparation for great things to come. Nothing less than the moral reaction following the experience at a bullfight had been able to reveal to me that so far from following in the wake of a chariot of philanthropic fire, I had been tied to the tail of the veriest ox-cart of self seeking."

The next day, she said in the autobiography, she made up her mind to found a settlement—to rent a house in a part of Chicago "where many primitive and actual needs are found, in which young women who had been given over too exclusively to study, might restore a balance of activity along traditional lines and learn of life from life itself."

JANE PROBABLY exaggerated the importance of the bullfight in her autobiography, which, as historian Deborah Epstein Nord wrote, follows the classic Victorian form of "spiritual crisis" and "conversion." She gave no hint in her letters home that the spectacle was in any way a life-changing event. What's more, the idea of settlement work had almost certainly occurred to her earlier, for in 1888 it would have been hard not to have been aware of this growing reform movement in both England and America. In New York City, Stanton Coit, an Amherst graduate, had moved to the Lower East Side in 1886 and founded a settlement he called the Neighborhood Guild. While Jane's own project was percolating, a group of Smith graduates were plotting a similar one in Boston.

Though the bullfight might not have been the dramatic

epiphany Jane later claimed, certainly it helped focus her thinking and ambitions. Afterward, she quickly confided her "scheme" (a word used widely in the Victorian era for projects to help the poor) to Ellen, stumbling over her words with uncertainty, fearful that in talking about it, her dream would evaporate. But Ellen was wildly enthusiastic. Her warm response gave validity to Jane's plans, and, more important, gave Jane the courage to begin taking them seriously. For the next month, as the two friends traveled throughout Spain, they discussed ways they might carry out the scheme. They parted at some point, the perennially impoverished Ellen going to Paris to take a job chaperoning two American girls. Jane and Sarah Anderson moved on to England, where they stopped at Canterbury. At the cathedral, Jane made a lucky acquaintance—the wife of the bishop of Dover. The good lady invited Jane to tea, where a well-known Anglican churchman, Canon W. H. Freemantle, was also a guest. Freemantle wrote Jane a letter of introduction to his friend Reverend Samuel Barnett, the head of Toynbee Hall.

From Canterbury, Jane and Sarah traveled to London. The city at the time was reeling. For decades, the promise of factory jobs had been luring people from villages and farms, and the widespread agricultural depression of the 1870s set off a further influx. Now, poverty was everywhere, disease rampant. Much of the misery was concentrated in Whitechapel, one of the most wretched neighborhoods of the city's poverty-stricken East End, which held large immigrant (particularly Russian-Jewish) populations. Prostitutes lurked in dark alleys and drunken men stumbled about. Crippled children begged on streets splattered with garbage and animal blood from the open slaughterhouses. A greenish-yellow fog hung over the carriages rattling along the cobblestoned streets. The half-penny press was full of news of unemployment and crime, including a series of brutal slayings of women (mostly prostitutes) by an unknown assailant the reporters called Jack the Ripper.

Jane was shocked and saddened by the scene, as she had been on her first trip to Europe. Urban poverty seemed much more evil than its rural counterpart. "Nothing among the beggars of Southern Italy nor among the salt miners of Austria carried with it the same conviction of human wretchedness which was conveyed by [a] momentary glimpse of an East London street," she later wrote.

A rare spot of hope was Toynbee Hall, which sat in the middle of Whitechapel. One morning, armed with her introduction from Canon Freemantle, Jane called on Reverend Barnett and his wife, Henrietta. Barnett had already earned his reputation as a major figure in London philanthropy. The son of a prosperous merchant from Bristol, he had studied at Oxford, taught at Winchester, and, as the historian Gertrude Himmelfarb wrote, "seemed destined for a conventional career in the church when a trip to America 'knocked all the Toryism out of me,' as he put it." On his return to England, he sought a parish where he could minister to the social as well as the religious needs of his congregation, and after his marriage in 1873, he became vicar of St. Jude's Church in Whitechapel. Eleven years later, he opened Toynbee Hall next to his parish.

Toynbee Hall represented a radically new model for helping the poor. Until the 1880s, and stretching back to the beginning of Western society, most charities and philanthropic endeavors were based on systems for giving "relief" to the unfortunate in the form of money, food, clothes, and other services. As the centuries passed, countless groups came and went to help the full spectrum of needy cases—the young, the old, the sick, the blind, and the infirm. But by the mid-nineteenth century, thoughtful people began to question the effectiveness of traditional charity, drawing the lines of philosophical and social dispute that are still alive today. Support for traditional charity was grounded in the biblical dictate "the poor ye have always with you." The most that could be hoped for was to relieve their distress.

But critics of traditional charity believed the root causes of poverty could be alleviated with new approaches. In fact, doling out relief, these critics argued, seemed to encourage the poor to be more dependent. What's more, the religious zeal underpinning traditional charity seemed out of touch with the brutality of nineteenth-century urban misery. William Booth, founder of the

Jane's father, John Huy Addams, the "king gentleman" of Stephenson County, Illinois. *(Courtesy of University of Illinois at Chicago, the University Library, Jane Addams Memorial Collection)*

Jane Addams's stepmother, Anna Haldeman Addams, standing on the balcony of the family home in Cedarville, Illinois. *(Courtesy of University of Illinois at Chicago, the University Library, Jane Addams Memorial Collection)*

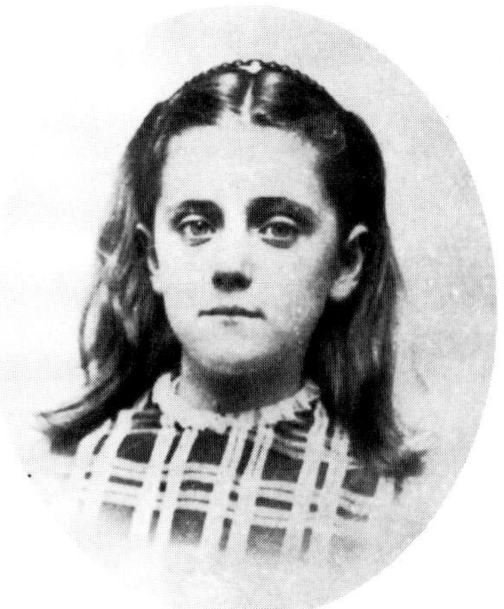

A frail, soulful child. Jane Addams at eight. *(Courtesy of University of Illinois at Chicago, the University Library, Jane Addams Memorial Collection)*

Jane Addams at four. *(Courtesy of University of Illinois at Chicago, the University Library, Jane Addams Memorial Collection)*

From a family album: Jane Addams's birthplace in Cedarville, Illinois, with views of mill and rear of the house. *(Courtesy of University of Illinois at Chicago, the University Library, Haldeman-Julius Family Papers)*

The student body of the Cedarville Village School with their young teacher, J. H. Parr. Jane Addams is standing second from the left in the middle. *(Courtesy of Cedarville Museum, Cedarville, Illinois)*

The four surviving children of Sarah and John Addams:

A. Jane. *(Courtesy of University of Illinois at Chicago, the University Library, Jane Addams Memorial Collection)*

B. Alice. *(Courtesy of University of Illinois at Chicago, the University Library, Haldeman-Julius Family Papers)*

C. Weber. *(Courtesy of Jane Addams Collection, Swarthmore College Peace Collection)*

D. Mary. *(Courtesy of Jane Addams Collection, Swarthmore College Peace Collection)*

Jane Addams's troublesome male relatives:
A. Stepbrother and brother-in-law Harry Haldeman. *(Courtesy of Jane Addams Collection, Swarthmore College Peace Collection)*
B. Stepbrother George Haldeman. *(Courtesy of University of Illinois at Chicago, the University Library, Jane Addams Memorial Collection)*
C. Brother Weber Addams. *(Courtesy of University of Illinois at Chicago, the University Library, Haldeman-Julius Family Papers)*

A

B

A

B

C

E

D

The women of Hull-House:

A. Florence Kelley. *(Courtesy of University of Illinois at Chicago, the University Library, Jane Addams Memorial Collection)*

B. Louise de Koven Bowen. *(Courtesy of University of Illinois at Chicago, the University Library, Jane Addams Memorial Collection)*

C. Julia Lathrop. *(Courtesy of University of Illinois at Chicago, the University Library, Jane Addams Memorial Collection)*

D. Alice Hamilton. *(Courtesy of University of Illinois at Chicago, the University Library, Jane Addams Memorial Collection)*

E. Ellen Gates Starr. *(Courtesy of University of Illinois at Chicago, the University Library, Jane Addams Memorial Collection)*

A typical yard in the Hull-House neighborhood. *(Courtesy of University of Illinois at Chicago, the University Library, Jane Addams Memorial Collection)*

Jane Addams in 1896 in the dress with "monstrous" sleeves that offended Leo Tolstoy. *(Courtesy of University of Illinois at Chicago, the University Library, Jane Addams Memorial Collection)*

Turning swarthy immigrants into polished Anglo-Saxons. How one Chicago cartoonist in the 1890s saw Hull-House's mission. *(Courtesy of University of Illinois at Chicago, the University Library, Hull-House Association Records)*

The Hull-House nursery in the 1890s. *(Courtesy of University of Illinois at Chicago, the University Library, Hull-House Association Records)*

Mary Rozet Smith and Jane Addams in the 1890s. "There's reason in the habit of married folks keeping together." *(Courtesy of Jane Addams Collection, Swarthmore College Peace Collection)*

Hull-House Coffee House at the turn of the century. The Coffee House provided cheap meals for working people. *(Courtesy of University of Illinois at Chicago, the University Library, Hull-House Association Records)*

The reception room at Hull-House. A photo of Tolstoy hangs above the desk. *(Courtesy of University of Illinois at Chicago, the University Library, Jane Addams Memorial Collection)*

A Hull-House parlor. A painting of a nursing mother by Alice Kellogg Tyler has pride of place over the mantel. *(Courtesy of University of Illinois at Chicago, the University Library, Jane Addams Memorial Collection)*

Salvation Army, was often singled out for particular disdain. Booth, as historian John Richard Green described him, was a "ranting preacher of the neighborhood whose one notion of relieving distress consisted in giving enormous breakfasts to the poor and regaling them meanwhile with the Revivalist effusions."

Earlier in the century, reform activities in England and America, particularly the fight to end slavery, had been inspired by deep religious faith. But as the century drew to a close, Charles Darwin's theory of evolution, and the progress of science in general, had steadily unraveled the Christian underpinnings of middle-class life. Jane's generation was the first to question seriously the role of religion in morality. With no deep faith in God to bolster and guide them, many educated young people felt adrift and searched for something else.

The books of Matthew Arnold, Thomas Carlyle, and John Ruskin helped point to a new way by evoking what French philosopher Auguste Comte called "the religion of humanity," a secular creed that called for breaking down the barriers between classes to improve life for all. Adherents of this "religion that was not a religion" were dedicated to the service of others based on a conviction that all people—regardless of class, birth, or wealth—have the capacity and, indeed, the duty to "evolve" into their "best selves." This became the distinctive reform spirit of the Victorian age—an earnest combination of self-improvement and duty to others—and it was epitomized by Toynbee Hall.

The settlement was named after Arnold Toynbee, a charismatic social philosopher who'd been a close friend of the Barnetts. In 1883, Toynbee had suffered a nervous collapse after delivering an impassioned lecture on social justice, and he died two months later at age thirty-two.

Soon afterward, Barnett raised money to buy an old industrial school for boys near his church. He had the school torn down and in its place built a neo-Tudor mansion with gables, diamond-paned windows, a lecture hall, and a dining room decorated with the Oxford and Cambridge crests. Barnett installed fifteen or so male residents, all recent university graduates, who paid a modest room and board, and who had been chosen out of a field of applicants to live there for varying periods of a few months to a few years. They pursued paying jobs on the outside, but devoted their free time to community service.

Basically, the residents provided the people of Whitechapel with the kinds of services that would "uplift them," that is, help them partake of bourgeois life. That included giving lectures and classes to working men and their families on hundreds of subjects. In one month alone, the calendar showed classes for writing, math, chemistry, drawing, music, sewing, nursing, hygiene, composition, geography, bookkeeping, citizenship, French, swimming, singing, reading, needlework, and cooking. In the evenings, more advanced courses were offered on subjects such as geology, physiology, botany, chemistry, Hebrew, Latin and Greek, European and English history, and a host of literary subjects from Dante to Shakespeare to Molière.

The Toynbee residents also sponsored social groups (including a Smokers' Club, since tobacco was believed to suppress anarchist tendencies among workers), a Travelers' Club that arranged trips, concerts, art exhibits, a library, and a program that sent children for a week to the country every summer. To improve conditions in the neighborhood, the residents lobbied officials and worked with local charity organizations for cleaner streets, better schools, and the establishment of libraries and parks.

The settlement quickly drew attention, and many well-known people came to study the facility or lecture there—Charles Booth, who used Toynbee Hall as a source for his study *Life & Labour of the People of London;* Leslie Stephen, the writer and editor and father of Virginia Woolf; Mrs. Humphry Ward, the novelist; the Liberal party leader Herbert Asquith; and, before he was jailed for sodomy, Oscar Wilde.

The chief purpose of Toynbee Hall, as Gertrude Himmelfarb wrote, was to humanize and civilize charity. The settlement "implied no denial or even denigration of the distinctions of wealth, occupation, class or talent. It was meant rather to be a civic community, based upon a common denominator of citizenship in the largest sense of that word, a citizenship that made tolerable all those other social distinctions which were natural and inevitable, but which should not be exacerbated and should not be permitted to obscure the common humanity of individuals. The settlement house was not an experiment in socialism; it was an experiment in democracy—which was no mean feat at that time and place."

THE BARNETTS gave Jane a tour of the premises and allowed her to interview the residents. The visit was a revelation. Jane was most impressed that the settlement seemed designed primarily as an aid and outlet to educated young men. The benefit to the workers was regarded as almost secondary. Indeed, the warden insisted that they sacrifice the very feeling that they were sacrificing.

Jane believed the key to its success was its nonstructured, homey ambiance. "It is true of people who have been allowed to remain undeveloped and whose faculties are inert and sterile that they cannot take their learning heavily," she said. "It has to be diffused in a social atmosphere."

While in London, Jane also attended meetings of the World Centennial Congress of Foreign Missions, including one on the Chinese opium trade and another on the liquor traffic in the Congo. She also toured the People's Palace, a massive new community center that held meeting rooms, a gym, a pool, and a well-stocked library.

By the time Jane left London, she was resolved to duplicate Toynbee Hall in Chicago, with this key difference—her settlement would be for college women, not men. Jane had begun to see in the religion of humanity an answer to her spiritual quest, and, in the founding of a settlement, an end to her uselessness and depression. In "the solace of daily activity," she believed, she would escape her physical infirmities and the family claim. She would become the remarkable person she had always wanted to be.

PART II

Angel of Halsted Street

8

Chicago

Charles J. Hull's once proud home as it looked in 1889, when Jane Addams discovered it.
(Courtesy of University of Illinois at Chicago, the University Library, Jane Addams Memorial Collection)

On a warm Sunday morning in 1888, two months after she returned from Europe, Jane knelt at the altar of the steepled, wood-frame Cedarville Presbyterian Church as a young minister sprinkled her hair with a few drops of water. After years of religious questioning, she'd finally decided to declare her faith by accepting the traditional rites of baptism. Writing in her autobiography twenty years later, she presented the event as a triumph of Christian community. "At this moment something persuasive within made me long for an outward symbol of fellowship, some bond of peace, some blessed spot where unity of spirit might claim right of way over all differences."

But it is hard not to see a hint of opportunism in her sudden decision to join a church. Jane knew a baptismal certificate would give her credibility with Chicago's most powerful clergymen, the city's chief agents of reform and the group whose support she would need for her settlement. Despite her baptism, Jane had not resolved her religious doubts; indeed, she never would. Her faith would gradually diminish over the years, and toward the end of her life, when pressed by her niece Marcet Haldeman, Jane would confess that she could not believe in the divinity of Christ or in a personal God.

"But do you believe in any God?" Marcet demanded.

"Part of the time I do and part of the time I don't," Jane answered.

She passed the next few months earnestly reading everything she could about European social movements and plotting her own "scheme." She was determined it would work. Jane believed she had inherited her strong will and need to achieve from her father, and she justified her ambition, not as a modern feminist would—arguing that it was her right as a human being to fulfill her talents and intellect—but on the grounds that it was her father's legacy. "It seems to me almost impossible to constantly repress inherited powers and tendencies & constantly try to exercise another set," she told Alice.

Yet, Jane had not totally repressed the pull of her family, and excitement over her project was muted by worry over her siblings, particularly George and Mary Linn. Jane had returned from Europe to find George living as a recluse at the homestead following a bizarre incident in which he had disappeared for three weeks. Apparently, one day in June, after an argument with his mother, George had left the house and walked more than a hundred miles to Iowa, stopping along the way for a week to work on a farm. A Freeport sheriff and Harry Haldeman finally found him near Waterloo, shuffling along the road looking "ragged and dirty and . . . out at the head and feet," according to one newspaper account.

Mary was suffering, too, still grieving over the death of her baby son and youngest daughter. What's more, Mary's third son, Stanley, was ill. At the end of December, having spent Thanksgiving and Christmas in Kansas with Alice and her family, Jane moved to the Linn household in Geneseo. Ellen awaited her anxiously in Chicago, but Jane could not bear to leave Mary. In principle, Jane decried the family claim as a hindrance to feminine ambition. But Ellen's impatience seems shallow against Jane's deep devotion to her sister. She mourned Mary's fragile, brokenhearted life with sisterly passion, and her own happiness was tied up in part with the well-being of Mary's family. In this spirit, she wrote Ellen on January 24, 1889:

"I am dreadfully disappointed. I was quite sure I would be in Chicago Sat. but simply cannot leave Stanley, the little fellow has been threatened with diphtheria and looks like a ghost. I owe so much to Mary in so many tender ways that I feel now as if I ought to stay. I know you disapprove dear heart, and I appreciate your disapproval, I disapprove myself in a measure, but 'God has made me so' I suppose . . . Have patience for a few days longer and I will work with all my might and do my best."

The letter concludes with a declaration of her affection, a rare expression in Jane's surviving papers. "Don't scold me dear, I am awfully sorry about the delay. Let's love each other through thick and thin and work out a salvation."

Throughout her life, Jane's extreme reserve made her reluctant to reveal her feelings, but clearly, planning the settlement had drawn her closer to Ellen. She felt responsible for Ellen's emotional and financial welfare, and she asked Alice to make sure Ellen received $1,500 if Jane died unexpectedly. At the same time, Jane depended on Ellen's companionship and support, and relied on her thrifty friend to keep her spending in check. After impulsively giving $25 to Beloit College, Jane wrote Ellen, "I must stop doings of that kind and save for our affair. I don't know why I am so weak and need you to help me from my weakness."

But she was not in love with Ellen in the way many romantic friends of the era were—indeed, in the way Ellen was with her. "I don't know now, just at this point how I could live in my life without [Jane]," Ellen confessed to her cousin, Mary Allen. A woman of strong, poetic emotions, Ellen needed to have passionate attachments. Yet, her high-strung nature also pushed her to be a bit of a nag. She confessed to Allen her "attacks of obstinacy, peevishness, conceit & what not . . . I scold [Jane] & oppose her, but outside of that I always feel that rare, & by me unattainable character." Many years later, recalling their early relationship, Ellen wrote Jane, "I remember an amusing thing you said to me once. I had said . . . of somebody, that I *liked* and respected her thoroughly [but] didn't love her, and you said you respect me and love me, but you don't *like* me."

When people asked about it, Ellen described her relationship with Jane as the "ordinary" one of "friends who live together." In late-nineteenth-century America, it was indeed "ordinary" for two unmarried women to share a home. So many women, particularly those in the new class of female college graduates, lived in long-term unions with other women that, as the historian Susan Ware noted, "the term 'Boston marriage' was coined to describe [them]. Such a relationship with a companion or friend offered elite women a socially accepted alternative to the traditional route of marriage and children." Turn-of-the-century America, as Ware wrote, was "something of a golden age for female friendships . . . women who chose not to marry were respected for their choices rather than pitied for their state of singlehood."

Indeed, the spinster had her place in nineteenth-century America. "The ideal old maid," according to *The Ladies Guide in Health and Diseases,* a popular manual of a century ago, "is one who is scrupulously neat in appearance, by most people considered very nice, possibly somewhat prudish in her notions of modesty and unwilling to place any confidence in the opposite sex, but a very useful sort of person in cases of illness, a ready worker in Sabbath-schools, home missions, and temperance organizations, and, in fact, on the whole, quite an indispensable member of society. There is certainly nothing to be abhorred in this, and a woman would better by far be an old maid and die homeless and childless than to live the life of wretchedness and unhappiness sure to result from an ill-mated marriage."

After Stanley recovered, Jane felt free to join Ellen in Chicago. One icy morning at the end of January she boarded the Rock Island Limited outside Geneseo and settled back against the plush seats. Outside her window the wintry prairie sped by in a blur of whiteness. As the train approached Chicago, the snowy fields gave way to little towns and then factories, grain elevators, and stock-yards, until, finally, the clock tower of the Board of Trade Building came into view—rising against the dull nickel sky, a stolid symbol of the commercial power of a new financial age.

"Chicago!" boomed a brakeman as he parted the steel doors. Jane stepped into the cavernous Rock Island train shed and out into the street. The heart of the city stretched out before her—blackened, smoke-belching factories, ten-story office buildings, streets jammed with people. Carriages pulled by tired horses rattled on with shivering passengers, their feet sunk in mounds of straw to ward off the bitter cold. A few miles away on Prairie Avenue, on the city's South Side, the castlelike mansions built by Chicago's industrial titans, with their massive stone facades behind towering iron gates, stood as monuments not only to Victorian architecture, but also to the faith and strength of the era.

Fifty years before, Chicago had hardly existed. The city had grown from a desolate trading post in the middle of an Indian camp to the bustling center of the West's grain and lumber trade, thanks largely to outstanding railroad connections. Then, on October 8, 1871, a fire broke out in the West Side cow barn of a housewife named Mrs. Patrick O'Leary. Fed by fierce winds off the prairie, the fire quickly spread across the city, burning everything in its wake. It was at that time the worst national disaster in American history, an inferno that killed three hundred and left ninety thousand homeless.

The next day, the city began to rebuild itself, and within a few years it had become the nation's "second city" in population and wealth (after New York). The city limits expanded from 35 to 185 square miles as the population exploded. By 1890 there were ten thousand manufacturing establishments in Chicago and vast stockyards with sprawling mazes of open pens, where herds of animals waited to be butchered. On the dirty green Chicago River, fleets of barges and scows hauled coal and produce. The city was steeped in an orgy of "cunning and greed," wrote Rudyard Kipling after visiting Chicago. "Everyone is fighting to be rich," announced another English tourist.

A few had succeeded grandly. Marshall Field, who'd managed a small retail store in Pittsfield, Massachusetts, pioneered in Chicago the idea of a large department store and grew immensely rich, as did George Pullman with his sleeping cars, Philip Armour and Gustavus Swift with meat-packing operations, Cyrus McCormick with the reaper, and Potter Palmer with real estate. After a stint in a Pennsylvanian prison for his corrupt business practices, Charles Yerkes had arrived in town to monopolize the Chicago railway system. His network of elevated tracks spread throughout the city and included a circle around the business district downtown, giving the area its nickname, the Loop.

The wild growth of the city created a huge demand for labor, and thousands of immigrants poured into Chicago. By 1890, 68 percent of the population had been born abroad and another 10 percent were the children of foreign-born parents. The vast majority of these people existed in crisis, living in, as Justin Kaplan wrote of New York's immigrants, "some of the conditions of life on the harsh frontier . . . epidemics of all kinds, crime, pauperism, alcoholism, sweated labor, hopelessness, and a frightful mortality rate." Half the children born in Chicago in 1889 died before age five.

The gulf between rich and poor fostered rampant political corruption and horrific labor violence. Beginning with the great strikes of 1877, during which the streets of Chicago's riverfront wards were seized by angry mobs of workers, and culminating in the Haymarket affair of 1886, in which a bomb thrown by anarchists killed several policemen, Chicago became the headquarters of America's socialist and anarchist movements.

The city was considered "demonstrably male—all shove and muscle and brawling," in historian Garry Wills's words. Yet it was also a city of feminine force. The growth of higher education for women and the pressing need for reform of the abuses of industrialism had galvanized middle-class women. Emancipation of the immigrant workers, these women believed, was only possible through their own emancipation, and, in growing numbers, they began agitating for the vote. The era's view of women as the world's moral guardians became their justification for entering public life.

In Chicago, as in other American cities, a strong tradition of volunteer work by women had been growing since the Civil War. Widows, young matrons, and schoolgirls had served as nurses, set up a "soldiers' rest" to provide meals to troops passing through town, and organized two sanitary fairs, in 1863 and 1865, to raise money for hospital supplies. President Lincoln donated the original draft of the Emancipation Proclamation to be auctioned off at the second fair.

In 1873, Illinois passed a law allowing women to serve on school boards, giving them a powerful voice in school reform, which led to activism in other areas—housing, child labor, anti-sweatshop efforts, and the reform of prisons and mental hospitals.

Respectable Chicago matrons, many of whom had been raised in evangelical Christian homes, considered it their religious duty to protect their less fortunate sisters, and dozens of relief efforts sprung up to help "deserving" poor women. A Mrs. Denis, who worked for the Young Women's Christian Association, called herself "the Stranger's Friend" and haunted the city's railway stations looking for penniless girls from outlying farms who'd arrived in search of work. She offered the girls hot meals, baths, and a place to stay until they found jobs.

The Erring Woman's Refuge, housed in a massive brick building on the city's South Side, was typical of the era's shelters. It took in unwed mothers between the ages of twelve and thirty, and offered them lodging as well as training as seamstresses and laundresses. The refuge had a nursery where, as a *Chicago Tribune* reporter wrote, "thirteen blessed babies kicked and crowed as joyfully in their cots or upon the clean floor as though they were not the symbols of degradation."

Across the country, the decades after the Civil War saw a proliferation of women's clubs devoted to self-improvement, charity work, and the causes of the day. In Chicago, these groups were particularly strong. Paradoxically, a more provincial, conservative sense of women's separate domestic role seemed to make women's activism in Chicago more effective than it was in other parts of the country. In Boston and New York, for example, ambitious women were starting to work with men (though not as equals) in long-established, male-run civic institutions and charities. In Chicago, however, women created their own institutions for reform.

One of the most powerful was the Chicago Woman's Club—"the mother of woman's public work in Chicago," as journalist Julian Ralph put it. The five hundred or so members met once a week on the top floor of the Art Institute of Chicago, where they read papers on topics such as "Is it punishment for criminals or their reformation for which we are striving?" The club was much more than a study group for dilettantes, however, and took up countless activist causes. "Our manner of getting what we wanted was spectacular and speed[y]," recalled one member. "When one of us was aroused to the existence of a wrong, we took down our bonnets, tied the strings under our chins, harnessed the horse and buggy . . . and drove to the place where we needed to do battle." Once, during an icy winter, a group of club members showed up at the mayor's office demanding better coal for the poor. A female probation officer they'd brought along carried a huge slab of the inefficient slate typically doled out in the tenements. The mayor agreed to help, but only after she dropped the slate on the floor, narrowly missing his toes.

The club also pressured male politicians into hiring women

doctors in the Cook County Insane Asylum and night matrons in the city jails, which put an end to the nightly rapes of women by male guards. In 1891, after an Internal Revenue Service inspector fired three women in the Chicago office, stating that only voters—that is, men—should hold government jobs, a Woman's Club delegation marched on Washington to deliver a petition to President Benjamin Harrison. The Chicago women were led by Lucy Flower, a lawyer's wife who once deposited an abandoned baby on the bench of a Chicago judge to protest the lack of facilities for orphans. After meeting with the Woman's Club members, President Harrison ordered the IRS inspector to stop the firings, though he did nothing about reinstating those who'd already been let go.

The club drew strength from its ability to forge alliances across racial and class barriers. Fannie B. Williams, a black woman who raised money for a nurse-training school for Negroes, was a member, as was Corinne Brown, the working-class daughter of a shipbuilder, who became the wife of a banker and a teacher active in school reform.

Similar alliances formed to take on sweatshops and abusive factories. In response to a woman journalist's exposure of "City Slave Girls" in the garment industry in a Chicago newspaper, a group of women organized the Illinois Woman's Alliance (IWA). Under the motto "Justice to Children, Loyalty to Women," the IWA fought to improve conditions for working women and children. The year Jane Addams arrived in Chicago, the organization pressured the city council to appoint five women health inspectors for factories and sweatshops, and the next year it pressured the city to pass an ordinance prohibiting the employment of children under fourteen, though the ordinance was eventually overturned.

WHEN JANE and Ellen arrived in Chicago in January 1889, they settled into cozy and cluttered boardinghouse quarters. The building, at 4 Washington Place, sat in a modestly fashionable enclave of graystones and leafy streets a few blocks from Lake Michigan. Immediately, they got to work paying calls to raise money and build support for their scheme. Every morning, before the sun was up, a maid came into their bedroom to light a fire. They dressed by its warmth, standing with their backs to one another as they donned fleece-lined vests and drawers and several layers of petticoats before slipping heavy wool dresses over their heads. After breakfast with the other boarders in the common dining room, they stepped outside into freezing temperatures and icy winds, where a hired carriage was waiting to take them on their rounds. Every night they returned exhausted, the hems of their skirts damp and dirty from the snow.

Jane and Ellen visited churches, missions, charity organizations, and schools; they met with ministers, politicians, reporters, philanthropists, and society ladies. Ellen's friends through her former employer, the Kirkland School, provided some initial contacts, and the two young women also got leads from Ellen's aunt Eliza Starr, who taught art lessons to wealthy families. Some of the city's richest women, including Ellen Martin Henrotin, wife of the president of the Chicago Stock Exchange, were early and ardent supporters. A Chicago club woman later recalled the first time she met Jane in the spring of 1889: "I was hurrying from one committee to another when someone came to walk beside me and began to talk. . . . I turned . . . to face a frail, sensitive girl. She looked anything but the reforming type."

Jane wasted no opportunity to get practical experience in social work. She attended Sunday school lectures at the exclusive Fourth Presbyterian Church on the corner of Washington and Paulina streets (she had her Cedarville church membership transferred there). She and Ellen volunteered at the Armour Mission, a settlement founded by Joseph Armour that offered classes and meals to the poor out of a massive brick building at Thirty-third Street. They taught classes at the Moody Church School and the Industrial Arts School.

They visited the Maurice Porter Memorial Hospital, a small, private facility for sick and disabled children, and made arrangements for a nine-year-old blind Italian boy to enter. Jane had no qualms about separating the unfortunate child from his loving parents and wrote confidently to Mary Linn that he was better off at the hospital. "I took him this morning," Jane reported. "His father went with me and was delighted with the house and the assurance that the child would always have enough to eat."

Key support for their scheme came from the city's liberal, Protestant clergymen, who believed that injustice, rather than immorality, was at least partially the cause of poverty. Many of these ministers were outspoken critics of industrialism and preached "a social gospel." As Richard Hofstadter wrote, "They saw the living conditions of the working men, their slums, their pitiful wages, their unemployment, the enforced labor of their wives and daughters. Many ministers were troubled because the churches were out of touch with the working class and sensed the unreality of talk about moral reform and Christian conduct in such an oppressive and brutalizing environment." The two women called on William M. Salter, a onetime Unitarian minister who had become head of the Chicago Ethical Culture Society. Salter had helped start a visiting nurses program for the sick and a legal-aid bureau for the poor, and he was enthusiastic about Jane's plans. Charles Frederick Goss, the minister of Dwight L. Moody's revivalist church and a passionate advocate for the poor, made "all sorts of rash promises," Jane reported to Mary Linn. The charismatic Reverend David Swing, whose congregation at the Central Church included many Chicago millionaires, offered "money or moral support."

Another pastor to a rich congregation, Dr. Frank W. Gunsaulus, of the Plymouth Congregational Church, warned the women to be wary of "saintly drivellers, who go out harpooning for souls" and stuffy committee men who liked to write bylaws and form committees and "get money and spend a great deal of it on the organization."

Though some of the men they consulted, including an elderly board member at the Armour Mission, thought they were "vaporizing," as he put it, most people who listened to their ideas were enthusiastic. "The scheme is progressing at an astonishing pace," Jane wrote Alice on February 19.

In the beginning, the project had few specifics beyond Jane's lofty ideals. Her plan, modeled on Toynbee Hall, aimed to do more than provide the poor with money and other assistance. Rather, she wanted to create a bond between the classes that would alleviate hostility and unite them in their common citizenship. She assumed that the poor would be receptive to cultural and educational uplifting, because they were, as Gertrude Himmelfarb wrote, "rational moral being[s] capable of realizing [their] best sel[ves]." The rich, as represented largely by the new class of educated young women, would participate because they had no other outlet for their talents and energies.

Jane and Ellen had no grand theories of how to run a settlement beyond a general intention to have as much personal contact as they could with the poor. This, they believed, was crucial to making life more worth living both for themselves and the people they hoped to help. Jane was adamant and would continue to be throughout her career that she had opened the settlement as much for herself and other young women like her as for the unfortunate—this she called the "subjective necessity of settlements." She was throwing in her "lot" with the rest of the population, struggling with them toward "salvation."

Jane was offering women like herself a chance to escape their suffocating lives. She differed from modern feminists in her sense that women's fulfillment lay not in personal success, but in accepting the great opportunity for usefulness by going to live with the poor. The idea had a powerful appeal in 1889. Jane and Ellen became, as Jane put it, "a fashionable 'fad.'" They were invited to join the Chicago Woman's Club and were celebrated at parties in graystone mansions where butlers answered the door and singers performed after dinner. News of the young women reached the newspapers, and reporters from some of the city's dozen or so dailies sought to write about them. Though Jane would later develop an extraordinary ability to manipulate the press, at this time she and Ellen shared the typical Victorian's horror of publicity. They begged a *Chicago Tribune* reporter not to publish their names in a story she was preparing. "The reporter came twice and it was only by much browbeating that we finally got her to mention no names & keep to generalities," Jane wrote Mary. Yet, she clipped the story and sent it to her sister. Under the headline A PROJECT TO BRING THE RICH AND POOR CLOSER TOGETHER, the story described Jane as "a young lady of independent means and generous culture," and her scheme as "an interesting departure" from traditional charity work, one that would be "a mutual exchange of the advantages of wealth and poverty."

Organizing the project brought about an extraordinary transformation in Jane. The depressed, emaciated invalid turned into an energetic, busy woman, slender and attractive in the high-collared, big-sleeved dress of the day. Her brown hair, pulled into a knot at her neck, glistened, and though she rarely smiled because of her misshapen teeth, her large, soulful gray eyes radiated kindness and intelligence.

She had not, however, totally cured herself of depression. Traces of it remained "long after Hull-House was opened," she wrote in her autobiography. Her way of coping with it was to distract herself with work, pushing herself to the point of collapse, and then retreating to a friend's house to rest and be coddled. But she never again experienced the kind of paralyzing despair that had troubled her after college, and she no longer had back trouble. In fact, her health was excellent.

Jane and Ellen were launching their project at a time when the public was fascinated by stories of feminine achievement. The papers were full of articles about women writers, lawyers, doctors, and adventurers, like the famous *New York World* reporter Nellie Bly, who in 1890 circled the globe in seventy-five days—five days faster than the fictional hero of Jules Verne's 1873 best-seller, *Around the World in Eighty Days.* Nearly every week, newspapers featured reports of feminine "firsts"—the first woman to argue a case before the Illinois State Supreme Court, the first woman elected president of a company, the first woman to carry mail on horseback across the Oregon wilderness.

The articles typically remarked on the heroine's youth, beauty, goodness, modesty, and spirituality—the buzzwords of Victorian womanhood. In particular, the word "spiritual" was hopelessly overused by reporters in much the same way "charisma" was a favorite cliché in the heyday of President John F. Kennedy seventy years later. But the elevation of "spiritual" offers another sign of the era's ambivalent attitude toward accomplished women. The feminine ideal was still the accommodating and selfless Angel in the House. Independence and worldly ambition were equated with coarse masculinity. What's more, as scholar Nancy Cott has written, religious conviction, though declining, was still potent, and an awareness of "the supposed treachery of Eve in Adam's sin" caused women who strayed from the feminine ideal "to appear shrewish, treacherous or witchlike." It took the quality of spirituality to cleanse, so to speak, feminine accomplishment.

An 1889 article by Leila Bedell in the feminist magazine *The Woman's Journal* was typical of the stories written about Jane. Bedell was a homeopathic physician associated with the Chicago Hospital for Women and Children and a past president of the Chicago Woman's Club. She wrote that "Miss Addams's rarest attraction—although possessing a generous share of physical beauty—is her wonderful spirituality. One cannot spend much time in her presence without wondering by what process she has attained to such a remarkable growth of soul." The article was read before a woman's convention in Freeport and then republished in its entirety in the Freeport newspaper, which was read by all of Jane's family and childhood friends. Jane was somewhat upset by the attention. "I positively feel my callers peering into my face to detect 'spirituality,'" she told Ellen.

Still, as Allen F. Davis noted, "the conception that [Jane] was somehow different, that she had a quality of soul that made her close to God with special saintly powers," became a powerful factor in her life. Even Ellen remarked on it. "Everybody who comes near [Jane] is affected by her," she wrote to Mary Blaisdell in 1889. "It is as if she simply diffused something which came from outside herself of which she is the luminous medium."

Jane's photographs capture a quality which to a modern sensibility seems more melancholy than spiritual—what Leonard Woolf called "the neurotic turmoil of doubt and discontent . . . an ego tortured in the old fashioned religious way almost universal among the good and wise in the nineteenth century." What seemed at the time the mark of ethereal spirituality might in fact have been the look of intense religious doubt.

To explain Jane's drive and powerful personality as "spiritual," as Davis wrote, "was to deny the break she was attempting to make with the past and to interpret her innovation in the context of the old ideas of the genteel female." Yet it was an interpretation that Jane herself encouraged. Time and again she presented her work as an extension of women's traditional moral and nurturing roles, a self-justification for the ambition that made her feel guilty and unwomanly.

GRADUALLY, the details of a plan started to take shape in Jane's mind. She and Ellen would settle in a poor neighborhood in a rented house big enough to hold classes and lectures. The house would also have several bedrooms to house the well-to-do young women they hoped to persuade to live with them—a key element of the plan. As Ellen explained to Mary Blaisdell,

> After we have been there long enough and people see that we don't catch diseases and that vicious people do not destroy us or our property, we have well-founded reason to believe that there are at least a half dozen girls in the city who will be glad to come and stay a while and learn to know the people and understand them and their ways of life.
>
> We don't wish the girls who come to us to feel that they are doing anything queer & extraordinary, turning themselves into sisters giving up the world or society or cutting themselves off from the things of the flesh or any such sentimental nonsense. We don't intend to.

Reverend Melancthon W. Stryker, pastor of the Fourth Presbyterian Church, thought they would never find women to join them. "He said he had a perfect horror of the 'modern fashionable young lady' that they were the most hard hearted creatures in existence," Jane wrote Mary Linn. "Ellen championed them valiantly and finally declared that it was time someone did something for them if their very pastors talked about them like that." On the other hand, Allen Pond, a young architect and member of the board of the Armour Mission, assured Jane "that he could send me three young ladies at once who possessed both money and a knowledge of Herbert Spencer's 'Sociology,' but who were dying from inaction and restlessness."

With their scheme taking shape, Ellen and Jane embarked on a search for a place to put the settlement. With newsmen, truant officers, ministers, and charity workers enlisted as their guides, they toured Chicago's worst slums, where, in the words of one reporter, "English speaking persons are as rare as strawberries at this time of year." At one point, Jane visited an anarchist Sunday school, where she was greeted with great suspicion and told that "'Americans' never came up there, except the reporters of the capitalist newspapers and they always exaggerated." She found about two hundred children speaking German in a hall in back of a saloon "with some young men trying to teach them 'free thought without any religion or politics.'" The Sunday school, she decided, "was very innocent."

Ellen favored settling in a French-German enclave, while Jane wanted to live among Italians. She told Mary Linn about a visit with a truant officer to the Italian section of south Chicago. "It was exactly as if we were in a quarter of Naples or Rome, the parents and the children spoke nothing but Italian and dressed like Italian peasants. They were more crowded than I imagined people ever lived in America, four families . . . of six or eight each living in one room for which they paid eleven dollars a month and were constantly afraid of being ejected. Yet they were affectionate and gentle, the little babies rolled up in stiff bands and the women sitting about like mild eyed Madonnas. They never begged nor even complained and in all respects were immensely more attractive to me than the Irish neighborhood I went into last week."

One Sunday afternoon on the way to a Bohemian mission, Jane's carriage rolled down Halsted Street, a long north-south thoroughfare abutting the stockyards and shipbuilding operations and running through one of Chicago's worst slums. This particular slum was broken up into fetid immigrant ghettos rigidly separated by ethnic groups. Here, as Jane wrote in her autobiography, lived

> about ten thousand Italians—Neapolitans, Sicilians, and Calabrians, with an occasional Lombard or Venetian. To the South on Twelfth Street are many Germans, and the side streets are given over almost entirely to Polish and Russian Jews. Still farther south, these Jewish colonies merge into a huge Bohemian colony, so vast that Chicago ranks as the third Bohemian city in the world. To the northwest are many Canadian-French, clannish in spite of their long residence in America, and to the north are Irish and first generation Americans. On the streets directly west and farther north are well-to-do English speaking families, many of whom own their houses and have lived in the neighborhood for years; one man is still living in his farmhouse.

In her book, Jane fails to mention the small community of blacks on the eastern edge of the neighborhood.

Halsted Street was rife with despair. Three or four families lived together in filthy, dilapidated wooden houses. The sidewalks were wormy, soggy planks, the streets rivers of mud. Once, after a week of rain, a resident posted a sign at an impassable intersection: THE MAYOR AND THE ALDERMAN ARE INVITED TO SWIM HERE. The houses had no indoor toilets, no running water, and poor ventilation. Children played around piles of rotting garbage and, occasionally, the bodies of horses that had collapsed while pulling carts loaded with junk or vegetables. Sometimes, to amuse themselves, the children fished for rats under the sidewalks.

In the middle of this wretchedness, sandwiched between a saloon and a funeral parlor, Jane spotted a large, beautiful old house. Though grimy with soot and falling apart, the house featured high windows, a wide, wraparound porch, and exquisitely carved wooden columns. Once the home of Charles J. Hull, a rich real-estate developer, the place had miraculously survived the Great Fire of 1871, which had burned to the ground everything around it.

By 1889, it was hard to imagine that Hull's mansion once had been shaded by oaks and surrounded by verdant countryside. When he built it in 1856, Hull had hoped to attract other rich families to settle west of the Chicago River, several blocks away. That never happened, and instead developers put up tenements and cheap housing. Waves of immigrants moved in. Property values sank and Hull himself moved out in 1868. Afterward, the house ran through a series of tenants. For a time, the Little Sisters of the Poor used it as a home for the aged; later, it became a secondhand-furniture store and a tenement. By the time Jane came upon Hull's proud home, part of the first floor was empty, and the rest was occupied by an office and by storage rooms for the Sherwood Desk Company, which made school desks. The family who rented the second floor believed the place was haunted and kept a pitcher of water on the attic stairs—an old folk trick for warding off ghosts.

As it turned out, Charles Hull, the lone survivor of his immediate family, had died in Houston on a business trip just a few weeks before. His cousin, Helen Culver, inherited his estate, including the mansion, $4 million, and a thriving real estate business. At fifty-seven she became one of the richest women in Chicago—a feisty entrepreneur who operated quite well in a man's world without a man and who played a key role in founding Jane's project.

Even before the inheritance, Miss Culver, as everyone called her, was a great success—Chicago's first female real estate mogul and an activist for liberal causes. She'd grown up in a small valley in the remote, unsettled wilderness of western New York. From her ardent-abolitionist parents, she'd inherited a fiercely liberal temperament and extraordinary intelligence, though she was largely self-taught. As a child she was an avid reader and kept a book on the head of her spinning wheel. After her parents died, she moved west, eventually ending up in Chicago, where Charles Hull had already started his real estate business. She worked as a teacher, a high school principal, and, during the Civil War, she ran a Union hospital in Murfreesboro, Tennessee.

After Charles Hull's wife died, Helen moved into the large house on Halsted Street to care for his two children. Later, she set up housekeeping with a younger woman named Martha Ellen French, who'd been a classmate of her niece's at Oberlin College. The two shared a Boston marriage that lasted until Martha's death many years later. In 1869, Charles Hull brought Miss Culver into his business, which had suffered during the financial crash of 1857. Over the years, she helped rebuild his fortune through wise investments.

Miss Culver never seemed to age. She walked briskly into meetings with clients and bankers—a slender, copper-haired woman with large gray eyes and pink skin—and impressed everyone with her astounding memory and gift for numbers. Her office at 614 West Lake Street, where she employed women only, was a model of feminine efficiency and independence. Miss Culver's interest in making money was matched by a dedication to social causes. She spent many of her evenings teaching in a night school for newsboys, and in the South, where she and Hull owned hundreds of acres, she opened a night school for blacks who'd bought land from her on the installment plan.

After Charles Hull's death, Miss Culver became the owner of much of the housing around Halsted Street—a fact of which Jane probably was aware, and which might have influenced her choice of neighborhoods. Throughout her life, Jane would show a genius for befriending important and helpful people.

After several meetings with the grand lady, Jane arranged to rent the second floor and a large first-floor reception room of the old house for $720 a year. To oversee renovations she hired a young architect named Allen Pond, who was deeply involved in reform politics and who would go on to design university buildings and another Chicago settlement, the Chicago Commons. Then Jane returned to Cedarville for the summer. Ellen stayed a bit longer in the city before returning to her family in Durand, Illinois. Throughout the summer, the two women bombarded each other with letters full of plans for their project. Two chief concerns were recruiting other young women to live with them and publicizing their venture. They hoped to attract a few women as paying boarders, and a group of volunteers who would come and go as they were needed. As far as publicity was concerned, they wanted, in particular, to thwart articles that described their project as a traditional charity and that ignored the dual motive of the settlement as an aid to both young women and the poor.

As the summer drew to a close, Jane was preoccupied with the final arrangements for moving to Halsted Street. Though many rich Chicagoans had promised financial support, Jane worried about money. Much to her disappointment, her stepmother, who had inherited two-thirds of John Addams's estate, refused to help her. Ann blamed Jane for George's problems—had Jane married him, he would have settled into a career, she believed. What's more, Ann was against careers for women and also opposed the ideas underlying Jane's project—particularly the notion of closing the gap between rich and poor. Class distinctions, Ann thought, were essential to preserving the moral order. "'Tis the struggle from the common needs of life that moves the world," she once wrote her son Harry. "If everyone was fed and clothed alike their sensual and selfish tendencies would 'run riot.'"

Jane and Ellen returned to the city in August and moved in with the family of one of their chief supporters, Roswell B. Mason, the white-bearded former railway engineer who had been Chicago's mayor during the 1871 fire. Every day they drove out in a carriage to shop for furniture and stop by Halsted Street to oversee the final renovations. Jane had spent a great deal of money—more than $3,000 on repairs and $1,800 on furniture. The walls and ceilings had been cleaned, and the marble mantels polished. The halls and gingerbread woodwork on the door frames had been painted with an ivory and gold motif, recalling Louis Sullivan and Dankmar Adler's Auditorium Theater downtown, which had been built to great acclaim that year.

The two women were as thrilled as newlyweds who had just decorated their first home. On September 15, Ellen wrote her cousin Mary Allen, "I stood about all day before yesterday, ate a cold lunch on a plate held in my hand while I directed a man doing the frieze. . . . I feel at home in Halsted St. already. It seems perfectly natural to be there. And it is so pretty!—Our house."

Jane and Ellen had separate bedrooms upstairs, down the hall from the dining room, of which Jane was particularly proud. She had decorated it with new leather chairs, a large oval table, and her writing desk from the Cedarville homestead. The room also contained a large oak sideboard given them by the Masons; Jane placed a few pieces of family silver on it. In all, Jane told Alice in a September 13 letter, the mansion is "by *far* the prettiest house I have ever lived in."

9

Hull-House Opens

Halsted Street in the 1890s. The view from Jane's front porch. *(Courtesy of University of Illinois at Chicago, the University Library, Jane Addams Memorial Collection)*

On September 19, 1889, Jane and Ellen awoke after their first night at 335 Halsted Street to an empty, silent house. They dressed quickly in their separate bedrooms and met in the dining room for breakfast. As they sat at the oak table, sipping tea from blue china cups, a rooster's crowing wafted through an open window, and, in the distance, a sawmill whirred. It was the last peaceful hour they would have for months.

No sooner had they finished breakfast than a group of mischievous boys—no doubt trying to scare the two upper-class women who'd invaded their neighborhood—began bombarding the house with stones, one of which broke a freshly washed parlor window. Then the doorbell rang. News of the young women's project had intrigued many of the neighborhood's adults, and over the next weeks, dozens of immigrants called at the house. Sweatshop workers, washerwomen, maids, factory laborers, street cleaners, taxi drivers, and peddlers—some with their entire families in tow—stopped in. The "transfigured few," as Jane called the most ambitious foreigners, those who were eager to shed their old ways and to assimilate, signed up for the clubs, classes, and lectures Jane and Ellen had advertised in the various ethnic newspapers. The Russian-Jewish taxi driver who dropped by one evening when Ellen was at the door was typical. He spoke English "in a most formal manner," Ellen reported to her parents, and "informed us that he always made it a study to be as much of a gentleman as he could. He succeeds to a certain degree & we signified our willingness in polite terms to give him any assistance in our power." Some adults in the neighborhood, however, were hostile to the newcomers. One day a man Jane passed in the street spat in her face.

Though Jane and Ellen had made sketchy plans over the summer, modeling their settlement on Toynbee Hall, they had no definite program in mind, and, essentially, they made it up as they went along. A housekeeper, Mary Keyser, had moved in with them, and the settlement's first resident, Anna Farnsworth, would join the household before Christmas. Meanwhile, despite their worries and the skepticism of some of their supporters, they had assembled a small army of volunteers to help them. Most were educated young women from Chicago's prominent families who were unmarried and had time on their hands. Many of these young women had gone to the same elite Chicago schools and lived in the same fashionable neighborhoods, and they traveled back and forth to Hull-House in their parents' carriages.

From the start, the settlement was a refuge for the neighborhood children, whose harsh lives were often cut short by industrial accidents and the many epidemics that raged through their squalid homes. As yet, there was no compulsory education law in Illinois, and only about a third of the children under fourteen in the area went to school.

On their first Monday morning on Halsted Street, Jane and Ellen opened a kindergarten, the first in the city, with twenty-four children and a waiting list of seventy. A society girl, Jenny Dow, was the teacher. She arrived every morning at nine, when, as Jane later remarked, "miniature Italians, Hebrews, French, Irish and Germans assemble in our drawing room and nothing seems to excite admiration in the neighborhood so much as the fact that we 'put up with them.'" In the afternoons, the children played outside, making sand pies on the pillared porch or pulling wheeled toys up the inclined walk.

For the older children, Jane and Ellen initiated an ambitious educational program, adding classes and clubs every week to meet the neighborhood's growing demands. Some of the classes were utilitarian and educational; others were broadly cultural. Within weeks, children of all ages and ethnic backgrounds were flocking to the settlement. "Friday afternoon we have little girls in every room in the house and Tuesdays we are overwhelmed with boys almost as much," Jane wrote Alice on November 23. Older boys who worked as bootblacks, street cleaners, and factory laborers came in the evening. "[They're] harder to manage," Jane reported, though they've "given up spitting tobacco, or keeping on their hats—two things that we almost despaired of curing them of."

Monday afternoon was devoted to a sewing class for 120 Italian girls, taught by a volunteer who spoke Italian. (Classes were often segregated by ethnic groups, primarily because of language problems—most of the recent immigrants did not speak English.) Wearing dowdy print dresses that dusted the heels of their heavy cowhide boots, the girls sat on chairs in the parlor surrounded by photographs of Jean-François Millet's etchings of peasant women and children. At 5:00 P.M. they trooped into the dining room, where a huge tin dishpan overflowing with marigolds, geraniums, and mignonette sat on the oak sideboard. Jane stood nearby, and, as each girl walked past, handed her a small bouquet.

In 1894 Jane and Ellen transformed a vacant lot near Hull-House into a playground. It was the first one in Chicago, and the neighborhood children were ecstatic over it. Before the facility was even opened, a group of youngsters had dug out the sand around the playground's chain-link fence and crawled underneath to get inside.

At Christmas, there were parties, candy grab bags, and dressings and undressings of the tree (a handyman carrying a bucket of water and mop stood by to put out any fires caused by lighted candles). Over the years, the Christmas celebrations became more elaborate. One year, the neighbors made a *tableau vivant* of Jesus' birth. A young immigrant wife, draped in a piece of embroidered Turkish cloth, played the Madonna, with a live baby laid in a manger before her. "The little Italians made a rush toward the stage & fell on their knees!" Ellen reported to Mary Blaisdell. "The baby raised its little hands toward her mother & never made a sound. It was a marvel."

Jane and Ellen were as concerned with "uplifting" the adults in the neighborhood as they were with helping the children, and to this end, they'd organized an impressive schedule of programs. During the first year of the settlement, a group of women came one night a week to view colored slides of Florentine art. Another night, a group largely made up of men came for the Working People's Social Science Club. They heard a forty-five-minute address on topics such as child labor and the Chicago police, followed by an hour of discussion. Two women's clubs were organized, one that met in the afternoon for stay-at-home mothers, and one that met in the evening for working women.

Some late-twentieth-century historians have criticized Jane for encouraging her Hull-House neighbors to embrace the culture, language, manners, and dress of the Anglo-Saxon establishment. At the time, however, as historian Alan Ryan has noted, "multiculturalism was not an aspiration." An immigrant's best hope for American success was to fit in as soon as possible.

A Chicago newspaper cartoon from the 1890s depicts this ideal "Hull-House Evolution." A series of six drawings shows the transformation of two immigrants—a man and a woman—from disheveled, slack-jawed new arrivals to prosperous, neatly attired citizens. In the first picture, the couple are extremely ethnic-looking, with large noses and dark eyes. They appear increasingly Anglo-Saxon as the pictures progress, until in the final drawing they look like the WASP paragons in illustrations by Charles Dana Gibson.

In reality, Jane was deeply sensitive to her neighbors' ethnic pride and cultural differences, and her celebration of this diversity pushed her to organize a series of special parties. Dozens of families came to the house for Italian nights, "with the rich and vulgar Italians in the back seats & the peasants to the front," as Ellen reported to Mary Blaisdell. Alesandro Mastro-Valerio, editor of *L'Italia,* a Chicago newspaper for Italian immigrants, became a close friend of Ellen's and Jane's and helped recruit and entertain guests for these parties. (Jane and Ellen had a rule that children weren't welcome at the adult events unless accompanied by their parents. But a *Tribune* reporter was there one night when three small boys appeared at the door meekly asking for admission, and Jane relented, demanding only that they first wash their hands and faces in the laundry tubs outside.) Sitting on folding chairs in the long parlor, the families watched magic-lantern pictures of Italy. Then the gas lamps were relit, and a singer, standing on a raised platform in an alcove at the end of the room, performed traditional Italian songs.

Another night was devoted to Germans, who drank coffee and studied German history. Eventually, the women added similar evenings for the Irish, the Greeks, the Russians, and the French, whose lecture subjects ranged from the nineteenth-century Paris salons to Marie Antoinette.

WITHIN two years, the settlement was offering more than fifty clubs and dozens of classes; one thousand people used the house every week. Monday through Friday, from nine in the morning to nine at night, every room of the house—bedrooms, guest rooms, dining room, kitchen, and parlors—overflowed with people. Children enjoyed a kindergarten, a baby nursery, and classes on sewing, drawing, gymnastics, piano, Latin, art history, cooking, and crocheting, to name a few. There were reading parties, English lessons, and clubs with quaint Victorian names organized around everything from literature to flowers to boys' games—a Fairy Story Club, a Jolly Boys' Club, the Pansy Club, Red Stars, and the Story Telling Club.

In the evenings, working children and adults could find social clubs, debating clubs, art classes, athletic classes, singing groups, and cooking lessons. Among the working girls, one of the more popular programs was the 3P Club, which organized its discussions around fostering the virtues of purity, perseverance, and pleasantness. Through the settlement's college extension program (begun in the spring of 1890), twelve-week courses were offered in chemistry, electricity, history, Shakespeare, arithmetic, and Latin, among other subjects.

Hull-House was a bubbling center of vitality and self-improvement. A *Chicago Tribune* reporter who lived at the settlement for a week in 1891 described a typical evening. It included "the rollicking crew of . . . girls who come to Miss Addams's Monday Night Club [to discuss] Longfellow . . . Someone tells the story of Longfellow's life; another girl adds something new to the account; a third reads one of [his] descriptive poems. Meanwhile, algebra and geometry have been going on in the dining room. Up-stairs in one of the chambers an ex-Wellesley girl has been teaching half a dozen other girls 'how to put words together.' In the reception room Miss Ellen Starr has been conducting a class in art history, assisted by some photographs."

Abraham Bisno, a young Jew who had escaped the pogroms in Russia and settled near Hull-House with his family, taught himself to read with Ellen's help. "Bisno has renewed his study of Grammar & is as clear as before. He is really an intellectual person," Ellen told Mary Blaisdell. Bisno went on to become a labor organizer and even wrote a book—a posthumously published memoir.

The underlying purpose of Hull-House's frenetic activity was to show the poor the possibilities of a better life, a life that they might never be able to duplicate on their own, but one, nevertheless, that would enrich them. At heart, the settlement was profoundly democratic, because it assumed that the poor immigrants "had the yeast within them to rise," as Florence Kelley, one of the settlement's most famous residents, put it. What's more, it operated on a conviction that the educated had an obligation to share their privileges with the unfortunate—not simply by lecturing them or doling out services to them, but by living among them, getting to know them, and by trying to create with them a sense of community. It was to be the opposite of what Emerson, speaking of the abolitionists, had called "love afar."

It also was to be the opposite of traditional charity, which in Jane's view emphasized the differences between rich and poor, thus widening the gap between them. In her view, Christmas newspaper appeals for the "neediest" cases were examples of well-meaning but misguided philanthropy. "Let us not acknowledge that we are divided into two classes, even in order to make a plea that the superior class should overlook the differences at Christmas time. To accent in any way the sense of separation even when done in the name of philanthropy is to postpone the final realization of the common life," Jane wrote in an article for *Unity* magazine.

Yet, even Hull-House couldn't escape its paternalistic underpinnings. During their second Christmas on Halsted Street, Jane and Ellen agreed to help out a rich North Shore matron named Mrs. Hoswell, who wanted to throw a party at her house for twenty- five poor children. Since Mrs. Hoswell "seemed to incline to Italians," as Ellen explained to a relative, they found twenty-five Italian children and gave Mrs. Hoswell their ages and sizes so her staff could buy them appropriate presents. When the parents of the children realized that the party was to be held on Christmas Day, however, they asked Mrs. Hoswell to change the date of her event. The rich woman refused, and the Italian parents withdrew their permission. "It ended . . . in . . . our scratching round to get some non-Italian children of the same age, size & sex—matching them in fact to fit into the list just so that the [presents] bought for the first list will do for the second," Ellen explained to Mary Blaisdell.

Perhaps a bit belatedly, Ellen had come to understand the dynamic of the party. "The truth of the whole matter is that Mrs. Hoswell is doing all this for the development and improvement of her own children, which is very fine," Ellen wrote, "but meanwhile, because it is more ideal that the Hoswell child should spend Christmas day in making 25 poor children happy, the parents of the 25 on the only day they would enjoy that felicity, are to do without it. People will have to learn that the poor sometimes have the same parental feelings they have."

Tensions also broke out occasionally among the various nationalities. Though Jane had organized separate events for the adult ethnic groups, the children were often thrown together during the daytime programs, and sometimes unpleasant scenes resulted. One morning in the kindergarten, as Ellen reported to her sister, "a German parent came . . . & demanded the removal of *all* the 'Italianische Kinder' on account of their being so dirty, having bugs. . . . if she were in our place, she wouldn't let any of them stay. She explained . . . that they were *all* that way."

JANE'S HOPEFUL ideals and the lively activity at the settlement clashed harshly with the sordid facts of life in the nineteenth ward, where disease, filth, and unspeakable suffering were always close by. Jane and Ellen considered it their moral duty to help whenever there was a crisis in the neighborhood. Once, early on, they sheltered a young Italian woman who came staggering up the steps of the house, her face bleeding and swollen from a beating inflicted by her husband. Another time, drawing on her medical-school training, Jane delivered an illegitimate infant born to a young Irish immigrant. Jane was pressed into service because "none of the honest Irish matrons would 'touch the likes of her.'" And at least once Jane stayed up all night with an alcoholic suffering from delirium tremens to keep him calm. They took in homeless children, and once for six weeks nursed a baby who'd been operated on for cleft palate, only to see him die from neglect a week after he returned to his family.

They were often called on to comfort the heartbroken parents of dead children. One immigrant girl remembered arriving at the house of a friend who'd died from consumption, an Italian girl who worked at home with her mother making fabric flowers for a living. Her small coffin, covered in white velvet, was carried out of the house, followed by her weeping mother on the arm of Jane Addams.

Jane had a striking ability not to be dismayed by the pain and suffering around her. Indeed, she had a deeply human fascination with cruelty, a fact she'd acknowledged after the bullfight in Spain. As Herb Leibowitz noted in his analysis of Jane's autobiography, "The appeal of the bloodshed was perhaps the appeal of the extreme, of the barbaric person within, which she normally repressed, but which fascinated her more than she cared to admit. Perhaps her lack of disgust enabled her to draw close to those who lived on the margins of society."

The emotional remoteness that was part of Jane's character helped her to confront daily horror and withstand the endless demands on her time and resources without using herself up or losing her focus. People noticed, however, that she was difficult to get close to. Florence Kelley said she only once saw Jane holding a baby. To most people, even those she worked beside, even members of her own family, she was forever "Miss Addams," or "Miss A." There was "something impersonal" about Jane's warmth, like the sun's rays, which "shone alike on the just and unjust," one friend noticed. As time went on, and Jane became a public figure who wrote and traveled extensively, her prolonged contacts with individual immigrants became rare.

Though she had difficulty becoming intimate with anyone, she could never be alone, and she was happiest surrounded by many people. What's more, Jane became famous for her thoughtfulness and kindness, qualities that seem to have been real and consistent, not just part of her myth. She could talk to people of any station and put them at ease, shrewdly appealing to each individual's personal interests and sense of self. She had "an almost indescribable personal magnetism," as one reporter put it. Another reporter, in disguise as an ordinary citizen, visited Hull-House to see for herself if Jane was as saintly as everyone claimed. The reporter, Agnes Leonard Hill, who wrote for several Chicago dailies, was amazed to see Jane behaving "wonderful[ly]" to the Halsted Street immigrants and other "unimportant people."

"She is the greatest of mortals, and far indeed from domineering over anybody," gushed one Hull-House resident, Madeleine Wallin Sikes. Jane's soulful face peers out from photographs radiating sympathy and intelligence. Wearing a high-collared, big-sleeved dress with a bustle in back, Jane moved through the cluttered Victorian rooms of Hull-House with a serenity and composure that nearly everyone who met her remarked upon. There are few accounts of her ever losing her temper, a manifestation, perhaps, of the self-control she'd practiced since childhood, when her stepmother's bursts of temper shook the harmony of the Addams homestead.

Jane's generosity also became part of her legend. Her friend Louise Bowen recalled that "Miss Addams was very provoking at Christmas. While she loved pretty things, her passion for giving them away to others was so great that it was difficult to get her to keep anything. I remember one year when she had complained that she had no nice underwear. That was at a time when women wore considerably more than they do at present, and I had a dozen of almost everything worn by women made up to fit Miss Addams and marked 'JA' so that she could not give it away. On Christmas day she asked a number of residents to her room and was handing out all these carefully made pieces, when I bounded in."

Unlike Jane, Ellen Starr was tormented by the wretchedness around Hull-House. She regarded her sensitivity as "an infirmity" and relied on religion to see her through. Once, she spent the night in a tenement caring for a dying woman. After lying down for a half hour on a filthy cot, she got a "necklace and bracelet" of bug bites, so she stayed awake the rest of the night reading the Bible.

Ellen was as intense and volatile as Jane was distant and cool. Small, wiry, and restless, her pince-nez sliding down her nose and her brown hair in a loose knot at her neck, she scurried through the house quoting George Herbert, a seventeenth-century minister known as "Holy Herbert" who was a model of pastoral solicitude of the poor. At the end of the day, she would flop into a chair by the window and read Fabian essays.

Her clothes reflected a meager budget and a quirky sense of style that had nothing to do with current fashion. For a time she dressed almost exclusively in shades of lavender, repairing the same dresses over and over, sometimes adding bits of family embroidery as fichus. For years she wore a fraying raincoat that had belonged to an elderly machinist who frequented Hull-House events. The man, a bachelor named Mr. Dodge, left all his possessions and $3,000 to Ellen when he died—a token of his gratitude for Ellen's help in finding him suitable chess partners.

Wearing "Mr. Dodge," as Ellen referred to her raincoat, and a small hat with a purple veil that streamed out behind her, she strode purposefully through the neighborhood, shocking many with her outspokenness. Once on a streetcar, Ellen watched a woman plop down in a seat with no word of thanks to the man who'd given it up for her. "Thank you very much, sir, for giving this lady your seat," Ellen loudly announced. Another time, standing on the corner of Halsted and Polk, a young, heavily made-up woman walked by. Ellen shouted at her, "My dear, you look like a clown in the circus, all red and white."

Ellen felt the ugliness of Halsted Street as a personal assault. At Hull-House, she made it her mission to advance the sacred cause of art. As her niece recalled, "She believed with Victorian certitude in the ennobling power of the great paintings, sculptures and literary creations of the past, and she was appalled by their absence from the Westside. The immigrant had lost his capacity to create folk art, and yet had no access to the treasures of classical art and literature."

Ellen devoted herself to changing that. Her first task after Hull-House opened was to lead a reading party of George Eliot's *Romola* (the story of a privileged Renaissance girl who goes to live with the poor), chosen in part because of Ellen's love of all things Italian. No doubt, Ellen, whose religious fervor was deepening, also identified with the book's heroine. Though Romola had no "innate taste" for helping the sick and poor, she believed it her religious duty to do so.

Soon Ellen branched out from the reading parties to more formal lectures on Homer, Browning, Dante, and Shakespeare. Also, she gave lessons on art history, oversaw art exhibits and classes, and organized a collection of photographs and paintings that were loaned to local families and schools.

Since she wasn't from a rich family, she needed to earn money, and she held a series of jobs arranged by her friends. She gave lectures at Rockford College and taught art to a group of girls on the South Side, assuring her mother that "they are all from the 'best families', & I didn't feel any fleas on myself while there." She also accepted money from the widow of a Chicago real estate magnate, who for years gave her an allowance.

Despite her persnickety nature, Ellen—unlike Jane—was capable of forming deep emotional attachments. Early on she came to adore a toddler named Francesco, the son of a woman who occasionally cooked at the settlement. For reasons that are unclear (perhaps an illness in the tenement), he lived with her for several weeks, sleeping in her bed. Ellen bought him new clothes, bathed him, put an anti-lice solution on his black, curly hair, and yearned to adopt him.

"I love Francesco better than any child in the world," she wrote her cousin Mary Allen on December 7, 1890. "I would like to own him if I could make enough money to buy his clothes & food . . . we omit the small circumstance that his parents probably want him." She was right. Francesco returned to his home. As Ellen sadly told her cousin, "Italians never give up their children."

• • •

THE FIRST months at Hull-House, Jane later recalled, were "blurred by fatigue." When she wasn't overseeing activities at the house or tending to a neighborhood emergency, she was writing letters to raise money or was out speaking to groups to recruit volunteers.

On free evenings, Jane and Ellen paid calls on their neighbors, often taking a male friend as chaperone. They'd walk on the soggy wooden sidewalks, past the tobacco shops, the coal stores, and the dingy saloons, where beer was sold for five cents a pail. The women were horrified at the squalor and foul air inside the immigrants' rickety tenements. "One is so overpowered by the misery and narrow lives of so large a number of city people, that the wonder is that conscientious people can let it alone," Jane wrote to her stepbrother two months after she moved in.

She was determined to make her own house a model of bourgeois comfort and clung to the standards of gentility she'd grown up with in Cedarville. But Halsted Street made it hard. Soot from tenement and factory coal fires drifted into the house through every crack, covering the mantels, pictures, tables, and beds with a thick black dust. What sweeping, dusting, mopping, and washing the housekeeper, Mary Keyser, didn't have time for, Jane and Ellen did themselves.

They shared their exhausting routine with Anna Farnsworth, the only young woman who actually lived as a resident during Hull-House's first year. Anna was a strange character. The daughter of a rich lumber manufacturer, she was escaping an unhappy love affair and a stepmother with whom she didn't get along. She paid for her room and board out of an allowance reluctantly given to her by her father, who didn't approve of the settlement. She had to spend most of her first month's stipend on new clothes, since the ones she brought, including a dress trimmed in sealskin and gilt buttons, "wouldn't do at all to go about" on Halsted Street, as Ellen put it.

Anna was typical of the type of "sexually unemployed" woman, in one later resident's phrase, who was attracted to Hull-House. As Ellen described her to Mary Allen, "she highly disapproves of the wedded state & 'overpopulation' is her hobby." Ellen suggested to

Anna one day that God intended married people to have children. But Anna disagreed. "I don't believe he intends it as much as he did," Anna argued. "He probably sees that there's overpopulation!"

Anna turned out to be a good resident. She kept her room clean, helped with the housework, and got along well with people from the neighborhood. Her duties included teaching English to Italian children and calling on the neighbors in the evening. She "hobnobs delightfully & intimately with young & old, men & women without the least indication of patronage, or I believe, without feeling any," Ellen noted. "It is my conviction that no amount of good manners will conceal the feeling when it exists." But when there was no work to do, Anna seemed lonely and bored. She couldn't amuse herself as Ellen and Jane did with books and conversation. Yet she declined invitations to attend parties on the fashionable North Side. As Ellen remarked, "She seems to have renounced society for the time being."

Since Hull-House was clearly a feminine enterprise, it's not surprising that few men applied to become residents. Those who joined boarded out in nearby houses, until 1896, when special quarters were built for them. The male residents tended to be weak, shadowy types—"self-subordinating," as Fabian socialist Beatrice Webb noted on a visit to the settlement. They "slide from room to room apologetically," she wrote, while the "strong minded, energetic women" bustled about. Sometimes, the men were handed the settlement's most menial tasks. A young college graduate named Edward Burchard, for example, took dictation from Jane, guarded the paintings in the art gallery, and marched around the neighborhood wearing a sandwich board to advertise the exhibit.

Then there was Edwin Waldo, a young minister who couldn't cope with his duties working with outdoor relief cases for the Chicago Bureau of Charities. He joined the settlement, but after he was found one day wandering the neighborhood in a daze, the Hull-House women packed him off to a sanitorium.

The men who lectured at the settlement were a different story. Indeed, they were among Chicago's leading lights, and they proved to be important connections for Jane. Henry Demarest Lloyd, pioneer muckraker and author in 1890 of *A Strike of Millionaires Against Miners,* came often to talk about reform politics and introduced Jane to Governor John Peter Altgeld. Clarence Darrow talked to the social science club about labor strikes, and political economist Richard T. Ely lectured on social problems. Jenkin Lloyd Jones, minister of All Souls' Unitarian Church, Chicago's most liberal pulpit, spoke about Emerson. His sister, Mrs. Russell (Anna) Wright, mother of Frank Lloyd Wright and a progressive educator, became an ardent supporter of the settlement. (Frank Lloyd Wright himself lectured at the settlement in 1897.) John Dewey, the country's leading educational philosopher, came up from the University of Chicago in Hyde Park to talk about his ideas; he later named his daughter after Jane.

Jane and Ellen soon became the darlings of the city's liberal rich. Society women dropped by out of curiosity, pulling up to the house in their shiny carriages, often with two white-gloved footmen on the box (one to open the door of the lady, and the other to deliver her card to the hostess).

"Curious visitors . . . overran the place in those early days," wrote Jane's nephew James Weber Linn. They "simply poked their inquisitive noses in everywhere, as if the settlement were a sort of museum, and the residents and neighbors alike were specimens of one sort or another." One day, James was reading a book in the corner of the dining room when a well-dressed matron put her hand on his shoulder, demanding, "Are you one of the dear boys who have been saved here?"

"No, ma'am, I am just visiting my aunt," James replied.

"You see," said Jane tartly, "he is not saved yet."

JANE WAS eager to improve and expand the settlement, and she got an opportunity in March 1890, when the Sherwood Desk Company moved out. That freed up the south side of the mansion's first floor, which included a double parlor and an octagonal office opening onto a veranda.

The day the desk company left, a storm spilled two feet of

snow on Halsted Street. Because of the move, the front door was open for hours, and Jane, whose resistance was lowered from overwork, came down with a fierce cold. Still, she threw herself into renovation plans, consulting with carpenters and architects and working to raise money to pay their bills.

Jane believed firmly that beauty was a way of beating back sadness—of refining the human spirit. And because her house was a settlement, its decor had a social purpose: to create a pleasing environment that enhanced the immigrants' sense of community.

She was not shy about asking for donations, and she could be officious in making demands. In late winter she asked Helen Culver to pay for two new bathrooms as well as repair the front piazza and cellar. When Miss Culver responded by sending a check for only $100, Jane threatened to have the beautiful but crumbling piazza torn down.

It was the first of many battles Jane would have with Miss Culver, who, as Jane told one friend, "just naturally loves money [and] cannot bear to give even small sums [away]." Miss Culver's cheapness was encouraged by her companion, Martha French, who not only was extremely tightfisted, but also had, for unknown reasons, "a great prejudice against the House."

For her part, Miss Culver was baffled by Jane's handling of financial arrangements, noting that the settlement's accounts showed "a great mingling of economy and lavish expenditure." Miss Culver was appalled that Jane had spent close to $5,000 on repairs and furnishings. Yet she marveled that Jane could run the settlement on less than $1,000 a year and was impressed by Jane's unselfishness and the "large minded, large-hearted" people she'd attracted. In May she gave Jane the use of the house rent-free for four years—a savings of $2,880. In return the two young women christened their settlement Hull-House.

By 1891, two years after Ellen and Jane moved in, Hull-House had been restored to much of its original splendor and stood proudly on Halsted Street, a Gilded Age home in the middle of a slum. On the first floor, to the right of the curving mahogany banister, was the long drawing room, used in the morning for the kindergarten and in the afternoon and evening for classes and receptions. Extending the entire north side of the house, the drawing room had two marble fireplaces and tall, elegant windows on the north and east ends. In a concession to the house's location, Jane had taken down the beautiful brocaded drapes given to her by Alice Haldeman and returned them to her sister, explaining that "the moral effect of them down here is not good."

To the left of the staircase was a double parlor separated by massive pocket doors, two more marble fireplaces, and, opening from the first parlor, a charming octagonal room that Jane used for an office. A two-story addition at the back of the house held a kitchen and, upstairs, a formal dining room. Throughout the first floor, the arched doorways, ornate ceiling moldings, and trim had been painted white and gold. The walls were covered with a William Morris floral print. On the floor were dark Turkish rugs. Oak rockers, Windsor chairs, and claw-footed sofas and pedestal tables were scattered about. The rooms were filled with glass-enclosed bookcases and decorated with pictures, potted ferns, and plaster busts, many of them bought by Jane and Ellen in Europe. The effect was relentlessly Victorian—cluttered and cozy, much like the interiors at the Cedarville homestead; indeed, like every house Jane occupied.

"Miss Addams was really a home lover and delighted in the arrangement of a room," recalled her friend Louise Bowen. "Whenever she was disturbed or depressed she would move the furniture in all the rooms. She got the janitors together, and as many of the maids as she could, and had the pictures rehung, and the position of the chairs, tables, and everything movable in the room changed. If there was no one to help her, she did it herself. Twice she fell off the tall step ladder, once breaking her arm."

The second floor held Jane's and Ellen's rooms, a bathroom, the dining room, quarters for the housekeeper, and several guest bedrooms constantly occupied by a revolving group of residents, friends, and visitors. In the rear of the house were five bathrooms for the use of the neighbors. Against the back wall of the house sat several laundry tubs.

In 1891, Edward Butler, a Chicago businessman, gave Jane $3,000 to buy McGeeny's livery stable on the south side of the house and turn it into an art gallery, studio for classes, and a reading room. The public library furnished books, periodicals, and two men to care for the place. Around the same time, Jane acquired the lease to the saloon in the building just north of the house. Allen Pond transformed the space into a "diet kitchen," where cheap meals were prepared for the sick and poor and cooking classes were held. The settlement also took over a six-room cottage behind the main house, which was painted pink and blue and used as a day-care center for babies.

From her bedroom on the southeast corner of the house, Jane looked out onto rows and rows of falling-down tenements along garbage-strewn streets. She had a Darwinian conviction that the future of America lay with working people. Because they were living life at a deeper emotional level than the comfortable classes, Jane believed, they were at the forefront of progress. "While the strain and perplexity of the situation is felt most keenly by the educated and self conscious members of the community," she wrote, "the tentative and actual attempts at adjustment are largely coming through those who are simpler and less analytical." What's more, their deep sense of responsibility to one another put the reformers to shame. Their charity "was simple and true, not because it sprang from piety but because it was democratic."

Jane was thrilled to be living among them. She was exactly where she believed she was destined to be, drinking "at the great wells of human experience."

10

Women Without Men

Mary Rozet Smith with an unidentified child in 1896.
(Courtesy of University of Illinois at Chicago, the University Library, Jane Addams Memorial Collection)

On a snowy morning in 1891, Jane answered the jingling doorbell to find a Kickapoo Indian and a pale, blue-eyed woman shivering on the front porch. The odd pair—who'd never before met—had arrived at Hull-House at exactly the same moment, tired, hungry, and looking for work.

Jane invited them in, and over breakfast with a group of Hull-House regulars, the visitors told their stories. The Indian was Henry Standing Bear, whose ancestors had lived around Fort

Dearborn (the city's first white settlement) until ceding their land to the United States and spreading out across the prairie. One of the few Kickapoos to remain in the city, Henry had been living under a wooden sidewalk in the neighborhood and had recently lost his job selling hair tonic for a pushcart vendor. Jane arranged for him to work as an assistant to the Hull-House engineer, a job he kept until the spring, when he moved to a reservation in Kansas.

As the woman visitor listened to Henry Standing Bear's story, she grew agitated. She was outraged that Henry had not learned a trade at the government Indian school from which he'd graduated and that he had no marketable skills. It "was a dreadful human commentary upon Uncle Sam's treatment of his wards," she later remarked.

The woman's name was Florence Kelley, and her passionate commitment to social justice would deeply influence Jane, pushing her away from high-minded do-gooding and into active political reform.

Florence was a large woman, with fine, dark blond hair that she wore in a knot on top of her head and round, somewhat heavy features. Like Jane, she'd grown up in the comfort of Victorian America's educated middle class. Her father was William Kelley, a famous Democratic politician from Philadelphia, who was nicknamed "Pig Iron Kelley" for his ardent support of high tariffs to protect the iron and steel industries. Her mother was a devout Quaker. In 1876, Florence graduated with the first class at Cornell University to include women. Refused permission to study law at the University of Pennsylvania because of her sex, she enrolled at the University of Zurich, where she earned a degree in economics. She became a socialist and met Friedrich Engels, who hired her to translate into English his *Condition of the Working Class in England in 1844*.

In Zurich, Florence married a doctor, Lazare Wisniewski, with whom she quickly had three children. The couple moved to New York, where they joined the Socialist party, and Florence began spending most of her time lecturing and writing articles on the evils of child labor. Wisniewski, though, turned out to be abusive, and the marriage soured. Florence decided to flee to Chicago because of Illinois's liberal divorce laws and the city's lively reformist spirit. After she'd arrived in the city, contacts at the Women's Temperance Society steered her to Hull-House. When she showed up on Halsted Street, Florence, who'd resumed using her maiden name, was in the midst of a legal battle with her husband and desperate for work to support her children.

Jane arranged for the youngsters to live at the suburban home of Henry Demarest Lloyd, the muckraker whose books and articles attacked classical economic theory with its emphasis on competition. Lloyd and his wife, Jessie Bross, daughter of William Bross, founder of the *Chicago Tribune,* were ardent Hull-House supporters. Jane also created a job for Florence as head of a Hull-House bureau that trained young immigrant women in domestic work. At night Florence studied law at Northwestern University, eventually earning her degree in 1895.

She approached her responsibilities with great energy and enthusiasm. "She has to pay the board of her three children & their nurse & the nurse's wages & it takes all she can earn, but she is awfully sorry for people who have no chicks," Ellen Starr told Mary Blaisdell in July of 1892. With her outspoken socialist beliefs, her worldly experience, her "bigness, manliness and warmheartedness," in the words of one resident, Florence Kelley stood out in Hull-House's world of genteel spinsters. Of the dozens of women who worked at the settlement, she was the only one who dared challenge Jane Addams, and her sense of humor mitigated the atmosphere of earnestness. Once, contemplating her swollen feet as she soaked them in a washbowl after a long day, she remarked, "I wonder if those are ever coming back to their natural size or if they're going to remain, like everything else in Chicago, the largest of their kind."

During the spring of 1892, Florence was appointed by the State Bureau of Labor Statistics to investigate sweatshops, and her work led the following year to the formation of a legislative commission to study the employment of women and children.

In the fetid slums around Hull-House, hundreds of men,

women, and children worked night and day sewing garments that would soon be sold in Chicago's finest shops. Because the "sweaters" were paid by the piece, the more items they finished, the more they were paid. Consequently, they worked as much as their bodies could stand, and often pressed their entire families into work. "From the age of eighteen months few children able to sit in high chairs at tables were safe from being required to pull basting threads," Florence wrote.

A tour Florence led for a group of Illinois legislators and reporters turned up horror after horror in the disease-infested tenements where the clothing was made. One reporter wrote of children with smallpox crawling among piles of jackets that would be sold at Marshall Field's; old people dying of typhoid lying on beds with coats destined for State Street shops; filthy rooms so dank that the plaster oozed from the walls and everywhere a "stench that shouts to heaven for vengeance."

Florence's report, plus the shrewd lobbying of her friends at Hull-House, led to the passage of the Illinois Factory Act of 1893. The law limited the working day for women and children to eight hours for women and set out safeguards for children in factories. On Henry Demarest Lloyd's recommendation, the newly elected Illinois governor John Peter Altgeld appointed Florence chief factory inspector of Illinois, a new position for a woman.

UNLIKE most of the residents, Florence had joined Hull-House without making a formal application. Typically, those who wanted to live at the settlement had to apply to Jane, with the promise that, if accepted, they would stay for at least six months. Though Anna Farnsworth was the only woman who lived at the settlement the first year, by 1895 so many women wanted to become residents that a third story was added to the mansion so it could accommodate about twenty-five residents.

The application process was rigorous. After being screened by Jane, applicants had to be approved by the other residents and then pass a six-week probation period. The settlement drew several women who went on to become celebrated for outstanding accomplishments. Among them were Mary McDowell, an early Hull-House volunteer, who became head of the University of Chicago settlement, founded in 1894; Harriet Monroe, who founded *Poetry: A Magazine of Verse* in 1912; and the feminist Charlotte Perkins Gilman, who spent three months at Hull-House in 1896 and returned in 1898. (Still, philosopher John Dewey thought too many mediocre women slipped through. Many of the residents, he told his wife, "do not seem particularly intelligent except in quite particular ways.") Some residents paid for their room and board, mostly from salaries they earned as teachers, nurses, doctors, and charity workers. Others were supported by "fellowships" paid for by rich Hull-House donors. All residents devoted their spare time—mornings, evenings, and weekends—to working on Hull-House programs and projects. Everyone had to endure a turn on door duty—an endless stream of callers showed up at the house—and a stint "toting" interested dignitaries around the settlement. One applicant who thought she could live at the settlement as a boarder and "sit around" relaxing in her spare time recalled being "distinctly told" that "one is expected to do part of the work."

At Hull-House—and at dozens of other settlements springing up around the country—the residents created their own independent world, working, traveling, and managing their money unencumbered by husbands and other family claims. Settlement work was, as J. Ramsey MacDonald put it, "a revolt of [America's] daughters" against the straitjacket of conventional womanhood. It was a way for women to take on "new and more worthy duties." These women were not interested in promoting their own "selfish ambition"—a loathsome vice to educated women of the late nineteenth century—but in becoming a force for good in the world. Indeed, at no time in American history have so many women been so actively committed to elevating the poor and helping the unfortunate. And at no time have so many women felt a common sisterhood with others of their sex. In an example of political correctness

1890s style, Jane struggled to avoid using the term "young lady," favoring instead "sister," and apologizing once to a friend for a lapse into "false social distinction, a remnant of former prejudice."

The women of Hull-House *did* feel like sisters, and a few, like Julia Lathrop, made Hull-House their permanent home. Julia arrived in 1890 as Hull-House's second resident, and, except for an interlude working in Washington, D.C., she remained until her death in 1932. Her background was remarkably similar to Jane's. She had grown up in Rockford, Illinois, one of two daughters and a son in a prominent family devoted to women's rights and public service. Her father, William Lathrop, a representative in the state legislature and a passionate abolitionist, had written the law allowing women to join the Illinois bar. Her mother, Adeline Potter, was a member of the founding class of Rockford Female Seminary; her mother's sister, Martha, became one of Miss Sill's missionaries in India.

A gifted student and her father's favorite, Julia had spirit. She spent a year at Rockford College, where she first met Jane, then transferred to Vassar in 1878. Following graduation, she returned home to ten years of boredom and nervous collapse. She helped out from time to time in her father's office, read a little law, and worked as a secretary to two local businesses, where she developed a talent for managing.

In 1890, when she moved into Hull-House, she was thirty, a small, dark-haired woman with slightly protruding eyes, the result of a thyroid abnormality. At first her duties consisted of "friendly visiting"—calling on the neighbors—and teaching. She also organized a club for the neighborhood's elderly men dedicated to studying Plato. Then she got a job investigating families in Cook County who received relief. In 1893, Governor Altgeld appointed her to the state board of charities. Wearing a dark-blue tailored suit, she trudged through poorhouses, orphanages, hospitals, and insane asylums investigating conditions and fighting for more humane care. Her intelligence and energy were greatly admired by the women at Hull-House (who indulged her eccentric habit of going to sleep right after dinner and then getting up in the middle of the night to read and write). She could be sharp with the neighbors, however. Once, when a group of Jewish refugees showed up at Hull-House to complain that the soup given them at a nearby shelter contained non-kosher lard, she snapped sarcastically, "Of course, you would *rather* starve."

Julia Lathrop and Florence Kelley were feisty, aggressive women who were unafraid to appear unwomanly, and they were not shy in confronting male officials about the horrors of sweatshops and poorhouses. Florence, in particular, showed Jane the hard truth of being an independent woman. "She was not playing at life, not trying to escape boredom," Allen F. Davis has noted. "She had not only been married and had children, but she had broken almost every tenet of the genteel code. She had taken part in radical politics, published her political views, and was in the process of getting a divorce. While [Jane] had searched desperately for something meaningful to do in life, she had lived."

FLORENCE and Julia challenged and stimulated Jane and pushed her to be more politically active. But they could not give her the uncritical, loving support she craved. The woman who could—and who would become the love of Jane's life, locked with her in a passionate, caring, and (by today's standards, anyway) somewhat mysterious romance—arrived at the settlement one morning in 1890 with her friend, the kindergarten teacher Jenny Dow. Tall, blond, and willowy, Mary Rozet Smith was twenty-two—eight years younger than Jane—when they met. She was the only daughter of a prominent paper manufacturer, Charles Mather Smith, and she lived with her parents and two brothers in a huge stone mansion on Walton Place on Chicago's North Side, one of the few houses in the neighborhood to survive the 1871 fire. She had graduated from the elite Kirkland School, where Ellen Starr had once taught, and spent her late teens traveling around the country and to Europe with her parents. The purpose of many of these trips was to give Mary, who suffered from asthma, a restorative change of scene. Sometimes, she would be gone from Chicago for months.

Asthma had made Mary unfit for any regular work or activity. She'd been rattling around her parents' mansion with nothing to do for several months, when Jenny Dow, with whom she'd gone to the Kirkland School, suggested she help out at the settlement. On the first day Mary visited Hull-House, she met Jane.

It's not hard to understand why Jane was taken with the young lady. Mary not only was lovely, but bright, sweet-tempered, and, unlike the prickly Ellen, she was eager to play the role of docile helpmeet. Mary had not gone to college, and she had no ambitions for a career. Her primary interest, as James Linn wrote, was "in making life easier for Jane Addams." Over time, she virtually came to act the part of a traditional wife, tending to Jane when she was sick, handling her social correspondence, and making her travel arrangements. One friend noted that Mary often followed Jane around the drafty Hull-House rooms with a shawl in case Jane was chilled. Mary also had a habit of jumping to Jane's side with a handkerchief whenever the great lady sneezed.

Mary liked playing this subservient role, but she was not in awe of Jane, and she wasn't afraid to tease her. Once, when Jane was hurrying to an appointment, she tripped on the top stair at Hull-House and fell, tumbling down the stairs and landing with a thud at the bottom. Amazingly, she was unhurt. When Mary arrived a few minutes later, she smiled at Jane and said, "Why didn't you wait till I could get here? Didn't you know that severe shocks are good for my asthma? If I saw a thing like that my adrenaline glands would open up and I would be free from asthma forever more!" Jane promised that the next time she'd wait to fall when Mary was around.

Mary also could be playful. Urging Jane to take a European trip with her, Mary wrote, "This is a very fine plan and you'd better consider it. I will offer you bribes to the extent of my fortune. I'll even build a third floor on the Butler Gallery if you'll come—otherwise I won't." Jane was charmed.

Throughout her life, Mary was known for her soft-spoken kindness. She "never did anything conspicuous [and] always gave me the lift one feels in contact with a character perfectly and loftily poised," recalled Harriet Monroe, the editor of *Poetry,* who lived at Hull-House for three months after 1900. Mary could also be a strong-minded advocate of women's rights. In the 1890s, she badgered her male relatives until they agreed to put rest rooms for women in the offices of the family firm, the Bradner-Smith Company. For years, she hosted a feminist salon in her family's elegant parlor, decorated with eighteenth-century antiques and green velvet draperies. While Mary smoked mentholated cigarettes specially designed for asthmatics, Jane and other friends sipped orange blossoms from long-stemmed glasses served to them by Irish maids.

MARY WAS not the only woman who made Jane the center of her life. Another was Dr. Alice Hamilton, a tall, determined blonde who grew up in Fort Wayne, Indiana, one of four daughters in a moderately wealthy family, none of whom ever married. After graduating from Johns Hopkins University Medical School, she came to Chicago to teach at the new Women's Medical School of Northwestern University. She moved into Hull-House and soon started a series of investigations of neighborhood medical conditions. She also developed a hopeless crush on Jane, who was nine years her senior.

"Miss Addams still rattles me, indeed more so all the time, and I am at my very worst with her," Alice wrote her cousin on October 13, 1897. "I really am quite school-girly in my relations with her . . . I know when she comes into the room. I have pangs of idiotic jealousy toward the residents whom she is intimate with. She is . . . well, she is quite perfect, and I don't in the least mind raving over her to you."

A sense of repressed sexuality shines from letters such as this one, and dozens were written to Jane. The fact that so many women were in thrall to her and responded to her so passionately suggests a sexual component on the part of her admirers that must have been sparked in part by a receptivity they sensed in her.

The relationship between Jane and Mary, however, was conducted with such scrupulous privacy that today it is almost impenetrable. Adding to the mystery, toward the end of her life, Jane destroyed most of Mary's letters to her. She never explained why. Perhaps she was trying to cover up the sexual nature of their love. On the other hand, she destroyed the letters at a time when a Freud-inspired awareness of homosexuality was spreading; it is possible that Jane didn't want anyone to misinterpret her friend's effusive Victorian expressions of affection.

Still, evidence of their deep bond shines through the bits of surviving correspondence and in the reminiscences of their friends. An 1895 poem that Jane wrote Mary, one of the few sentimental documents in her restrained papers, stands out as clear evidence that her feelings for her new friend were far more romantic than they ever were for Ellen:

One day I came into Hull-House,
(No spirit whispered who was there)
And in the kindergarten room
There sat upon a childish chair
A girl, both tall and fair to see,
(To look at her gives one a thrill)
But all I thought was, would she be
Best fitted to lead club or drill?
You see, I had forgotten Love,
And only thought of Hull-House then
That is the way with women folks
When they attempt the things of men;
They grow intense, and love the thing
Which they so tenderly do rear,
And think that nothing lies beyond
Which claims from them a smile or tear.
Like mothers, who work long and late
To rear their children fittingly,
Follow them only with their eyes,
And love them almost pityingly.

So I was blind and deaf those years
To all save one absorbing care,
And did not guess what now I know—
Delivering love was sitting there!

Jane's early letters to Mary are addressed to "My Dear Miss Smith" or "My Dear Friend" and often were signed by both Jane and Ellen. Most of these notes are acknowledgments of gifts and of Mary's volunteer activities at the settlement. In 1892, after Mary—suffering from a bout of asthma—was whisked away to a warm climate by her parents, Jane wrote her, "I am sure you know that we will miss you, not only for what you do, but for the interest and friendship which has come to mean a great deal to me."

But over time, the letters grew more intimate. "I miss you dreadfully and am yours "til death,'" Jane once wrote Mary. Another time, when she gave Mary a book, Jane asked her to accept it as a "token of my 'fondest love' and a feeble expression of my gratitude for our affection and friendship which has made life a very different thing for me during the last three years and has transformed the future." Eventually, she came to think of herself as married to Mary. "You must know dear, how I long for you all the time and especially during the last three weeks . . . there is reason in the habit of married folks keeping together," she wrote during one separation. And another time, "Maybe I am not homesick for you . . . [but] I almost cry for your ministrations at night when my conscience is bad and my spirits low."

Mary was perhaps more deeply attached to Jane. "You can never know what it is to me to have had you and to have you," she wrote Jane during Christmas, 1896, in one of her few letters Jane did not destroy. "I only hope I am thankful enough. I'm given to turning sentimental at this season, as you know, and I feel quite a rush of emotion when I think of you."

As passionate as these letters are, they offer no real clues to whether the relationship was sexual. The emotional bonds between women friends of this era often were as strong as, or stronger than, those between husband and wife. The thoroughly heterosexual novelist George Eliot, for example, referred to her closest woman friend as her "spouse." Scholars have long been familiar with the purple language Victorian women employed to describe their feelings for one another.

At the time, no one ever suspected that Jane and Mary were having sex, and it's impossible to know definitively. In a 1964 interview with Allen Davis, Alice Hamilton, then age ninety-four, denied that there had been any open lesbian activity among the Hull-House residents, though she acknowledged that the close relationships of the women involved an unconscious sexuality. For most women in Victorian romantic friendships, as Lillian Faderman noted in her history of lesbianism, *Surpassing the Love of Men*, genital sex remained the "great bugaboo," which they "preferred to ignore or deny." They either repressed their sexual urges or rationalized that what they were doing wasn't *really* sex, because a penis wasn't involved.

Jane's fierce determination to have a career perhaps grew from a deep-seated revulsion to heterosexual love—she knew she could never marry and wanted something more from life than being a spinster aunt. On the other hand, her strong ambitions might have short-circuited any erotic interest she had in men.

The books Jane read in childhood suggested that intense female love—even if it involved kissing, hugging, and sleeping in the same bed—was pure and noble, a chaste rehearsal for marriage. In Elizabeth Wetherell's popular 1852 girls' book, *The Wide, Wide World*, for example, two friends, anticipating spending the night together, "remained locked in each others arms." Louisa May Alcott, in *Work: A Story of Experience*, published in 1873, portrayed two young women casting amorous glances at each other, one wooing her friend "as gently as a lover might."

The Victorians had no trouble envisioning a romantic relationship without sex. Indeed, for women like Jane and Mary, the lack of sex in their lives was proof of their moral superiority to men. What's more, their sexual purity was linked to their moral purity, and it gave their reform activities the power of a religious calling.

One of Jane's contemporaries, Vida Scudder, a Wellesley professor, perhaps spoke for the majority of her generation of unmarried women when she wrote toward the end of her life that Freud had overemphasized "the sex instinct." From the perspective of a woman who'd been raised in the nineteenth century, she noted, "a life in which sex interests have never visited is a life neither dull nor empty nor devoid of romance."

A deep sisterly component underlay the love between Jane and Mary. Mary's family became a substitute family to Jane. She visited Mary's parents when Mary was out of town and traveled with her family. Though the two women slept in the same room and sometimes the same bed when they traveled (as they did with other friends, as well), in Chicago they were rarely alone. Mary never lived at Hull-House, and when she spent the night there, she often slept in a guest room; at Mary's home on Walton Place, a room opposite Mary's was kept available at all times for Jane.

THOUGH Mary teased about her "fortune," the fact that she was rich was important to Jane. At the time she met Mary, Jane had spent about $15,000 of her own money on Hull-House—a considerable sum for those days. (The money was probably drawn not only from rent from the Illinois farm she'd inherited from her father and interest on the $60,000 he'd left her, but also from her capital.) Some of the money was spent the first year to renovate and furnish the house; much of the rest went to cover the room and board of residents who were having financial difficulties. Florence Kelley, for example, didn't pay rent until nine months after she moved in. Jane had arranged a job for her and found donors—mostly rich members of the Chicago Woman's Club—to pay Florence's salary, but apparently Jane didn't have the heart to ask Florence to pay room and board. Florence needed every penny to support her children and pay the lawyers who were handling her divorce.

Hull-House was growing rapidly, and Jane's pocketbook could not keep up. During the settlement's first four years, the budget more than doubled, from $8,634 to $20,871. Jane's contribution steadily fell from 58 percent to 19 percent, but she was still paying almost $4,000 a year.

She was faced with the possibility of becoming absorbed by a larger, richer charitable institution or university and thus losing control of the settlement. This would be "an irreparable misfortune," she told William Rainey Harper, the president of the new University of Chicago, who had approached her about taking over Hull-House. The settlement's "individuality is the result of the work of a group of people, who had had all the perplexities and uncertainties of pioneers."

Hull-House was Jane's life, and she wasn't about to lose control of it. What she needed were donors who would give freely without putting restrictions on the money's use, donors who would let her exercise her vision.

Soon after she met Jane, Mary started contributing large sums of money to Hull-House, averaging about $4,000 a year, from 1891 to 1895, when she became a trustee of the settlement. She also persuaded her father to spend money on Hull-House, including financing construction in 1895 of the Children's Building, next to the Jane Club at Polk and Halsted Streets, which housed rooms for the kindergarten, nursery, and music school. Jane was somewhat self-conscious about her endless demands on Mary's resources. After Mary offered to pay the living expenses for a young resident, Jane wrote her in August 1895, "I went to bed quite determined not to do it, but after a three o'clock vigil found myself weakly accepting it." Mary eagerly fulfilled Jane's every request for money, from funding building projects to buying coal and food for destitute immigrants. She also paid many of Jane's personal expenses and lavished presents on her, occasionally buying her luxurious clothes. Jane had little vanity, but on a train trip to Niagara Falls in 1895, she wrote Mary of the pleasure she got in some recent gifts. "I have been homesick for you, and have meditated much on your unfailing goodness to me. I put on the blue dressing gown the other night in the cars thinking that I had accepted it too much as a matter of course and when I put on my black dress and fine new jacket in the morning both of which you had given me, I concluded that I had reached the limit of taking whatever you gave me without even so much as telling you how much I cared for them because they came from you."

Though Mary's contribution to Hull-House was large, she could not give enough to solve the settlement's financial problems. Fortunately, another woman came along who could. She was Louise de Koven Bowen, a fiercely energetic, strong-willed young wife and mother. Louise had been born in Chicago in 1861, when it was still a wilderness town where Indians lived in the woods and cattle roamed freely through the streets.

Louise's maternal grandfather, Edward Hadduck, had come from the East as a government agent in the early 1830s, arriving in Chicago in a covered wagon carrying his bride and $200,000 in gold—partial payment to the Indians for some of the five million acres they occupied in the area.

Chicago was growing rapidly, and within a few years, Louise's grandfather had become spectacularly rich through real estate investments. He built a massive brick mansion on the corner of Wabash and Monroe streets, where Louise's mother remained after her marriage to John de Koven, a banker, and the birth of Louise, their only child. One winter, as a little girl, she played with Tad Lincoln, the president's son, in the gardens stretching to sandy Lake Michigan. Tad's mother was living in a hotel, the Clifton House, a block away from the de Koven mansion. On mornings throughout her childhood, she rode her pony down to her father's bank on the corner of Clark and Washington streets. Trotting along the sidewalk, she would call her father's name, and he would open the window and tell her she was riding very well that day.

"Lulu," as Louise was called, had a sparkling intelligence and a strong sense of self that compensated for her plain appearance. Even as a child, she played the role of aristocrat. To keep up with her fashionable New York cousins, she convinced her father to buy a fancy carriage called a dogcart (it was the first one in Chicago), and with her allowance she bought a livery for the family footman. The neighbors were offended by this display of Eastern pretension, and sometimes they threw stones at the carriage as it rolled along. Once, the embarrassed footman abandoned the vehicle, but undaunted, Louise took the reins and drove on.

Paradoxically, the little girl's love of pomp was matched by a deep concern for the unfortunate. When she was eight, Louise raised $57 from her rich neighbors to pay the doctor bill for a poor child who'd been injured by a runaway horse. That early act of kindness was followed by many others.

In 1886 Louise married John T. Bowen, a businessman, and in 1891 they moved to a forty-room mansion on Astor Street and began having children—eventually three girls and one boy. Like many rich, idle young matrons of the era, she helped out from time to time for several charities. One day she visited a slum sweatshop, an experience that shocked her into devoting her life to public service. "I went into a kitchen where 20 women were sewing buttons on trousers, for a beggarly pittance," she later told a reporter. "The mother I had come to see took me into a bedroom. There, covered only with newspapers, lay a child so thin that it seemed as though her bones were sticking through her skin. On a chair beside her was a hunk of bread—her food for the day. The little girl, with dirty face and matted hair, held in her fingers a long spike which she was dressing in a soiled piece of tissue paper. This, she told me, was her doll."

Soon afterward, Louise went to Hull-House and offered to help Jane in any way she could. Jane asked her to lead the Woman's Club, a job she held for seventeen years. Every afternoon, Louise's carriage pulled up to Hull-House and she stepped to the pavement, an imperious-looking woman in expensive clothes with a long strand of pearls wound four times around her neck, the last loop hanging over her ample bosom. She also started giving large sums of money to the settlement, contributing an average of $15,000 a year. Eventually, Louise would become treasurer of Hull-House and would fund several large building projects. What's more, as a member of one of Chicago's oldest, richest families, her devotion to Hull-House helped the settlement maintain an aura of respectability and mitigated criticism that it was a haven for radicals.

• • •

WHILE Jane grew close to Florence Kelley, Julia Lathrop, Louise Bowen, and Mary Rozet Smith, her intimacy with Ellen Starr began to erode. Unlike Florence or Julia, Ellen didn't share Jane's worldly ambition. Unlike Louise, she wasn't rich and couldn't contribute financially to Hull-House; and unlike Mary, she couldn't be the serene companion that "the chief," as she called Jane, needed. Yet, if Ellen was jealous of these women, she suppressed the evidence of it. Indeed, she claimed to be glad that Jane had settled into a romantic friendship with Mary. After reviewing their correspondence at the end of her life, Ellen wrote Jane, "I can see by the way you overrate me in these letters that it was inevitable that I should disappoint you. I think I have always, at any rate for a great many years, been thankful that Mary came along to supply what you needed."

As Jane was moving farther away from religion, finding relief for her spiritual unease in ambitious involvement in the world, Ellen began and ended every day with meditation and prayers. She decorated her bedroom as a shrine, with a prie-dieu, crucifix, and candles. A Latin Breviary bound in red leather and tooled in gold sat on her night table.

Though the expressions of deep affection in their letters masks the cooled relationship, Jane and Ellen began spending a great deal of time apart. In the spring of 1892, Ellen sailed for Europe, first to visit Samuel Barnett and his wife, Henrietta, and then to travel to Italy. Jane was preparing to give two lectures at the School of Applied Ethics in Plymouth, Massachusetts, an earnest Victorian think tank run by the Society for Ethical Culture, the organization founded by Felix Adler in 1876 to foster ethics and morality. It would prove to be an important moment in Jane's life, one that would launch her as the head of a new movement for social justice.

II

Revolt of the Daughters

An unidentified resident greeting immigrants at Hull-House.
(Courtesy of University of Illinois at Chicago, the University Library, Jane Addams Memorial Collection)

Jane spent Sunday night, July 23, 1892, dictating the final drafts of her lectures to Edward Burchard, one of Hull-House's male residents, and the following morning boarded a train for Plymouth. She departed in the midst of a burning heat wave and typhoid epidemic, leaving behind Ellen Starr (who had returned recently from Europe) to cope with the crisis. "People are dying all the time," Ellen wrote Mary Blaisdell on July 26. "I went the day before yesterday to see a little girl who had been asking for me, but found her unconscious & she died in the night. I took her mother a white dress of [a Hull-House volunteer] to dress her in & some flowers & tried to have her buried today, but they wouldn't until tomorrow. They [the immigrants] are so obstinate."

The sordid reality of life in the tenements seemed far removed from the ethical culture school's high-minded gathering of professors, preachers, philosophers, and settlement workers. Subjects in the school's six-week summer session ranged from trade unions to Greek ethics, but a number of sessions were devoted to social justice and helping the poor. Among the participants were Bernard Bosanquet, an English advocate of "scientific charity," who had practiced his theories in the slums of East London; Father J. O. S. Huntington, an Anglican Christian Socialist; and Franklin Giddings, a sociologist and economist at Columbia University in New York. But thirty-two-year-old Jane Addams emerged as the leader of the group. Most of the conference's participants had kept up with the glowing articles about Hull-House in the journals devoted to charity and religion, and a few were plotting similar projects.

The settlement movement was about to take off. In 1892 there were only six settlements in the United States; within five years there would be seventy-four, and more than a hundred by 1910. The young, idealistic settlement workers were the most ardent advocates for the nation's exploited immigrants, and to many observers, they offered the best hope of mitigating the abuses of industrialism. At the time, no government programs—welfare, workers' compensation, or family aid—existed to help America's poor. Factories were unregulated, schools were overcrowded, the streets were filthy. The entire nation, as Jane later wrote, "seemed divided into two classes; those who held that 'business is business' and who were therefore annoyed at the very notion of social control, and the radicals, who claimed that nothing could be done to really moralize the industrial situation until society should be reorganized."

Jane was scheduled to speak twice. On the mornings of her talks, 150 people—double the number that attended the conference's other lectures—jammed an old school building in Plymouth's leafy town square. Several reporters in the crowd later wrote enthusiastic stories about Jane, "this daughter of the prairie [who] is one of those Americans like Dr. [Benjamin] Franklin, that make anything succeed which they undertake," as one put it.

In her first lecture, Jane described her motive—the "subjective necessity," as she called it—for founding Hull-House three years earlier. Primarily, she said, she wanted to provide meaningful work for herself and other idle young women. Quoting John Stuart Mill in *The Subjection of Women* (though without attribution), she said, "It is true there is nothing after disease, indigence and a sense of guilt so fatal to health and to life itself as the want of a proper outlet for active faculties."

She identified with the immigrants and felt a connection between her own powerlessness as a woman and theirs. College graduates like herself who had been "cultivated into oversensitive lives [and] shut off from the common labor by which most people lived," she explained, were, "to me, as pitiful as the other great mass of destitute lives," the urban poor. Settlements gave these "useless" women an opportunity to save themselves by getting back to the people.

Jane's second talk outlined what she called the "objective value" of settlements, to provide the poor with the same chance as the upper classes to develop their talents and pursue their dreams. Anticipating the civil rights movement seventy-five years into the future, Jane said, "The blessings which we associate with a life of refinement and cultivation can be made universal and must be made universal if they are to be permanent . . . the good we secure for ourselves is precarious and uncertain, is floating in mid-air, until it is secured for all of us and incorporated into our common life."

The talks were similar to ones Jane had been giving around Chicago since Hull-House opened, but in Plymouth she stated her views more forcefully than ever before. Storms of applause erupted each time she left the podium. With reporters and activists from around the country in attendance, the conference gave Jane her first opportunity to spread her ideas outside Chicago. The stirring reception she got sparked a bit of Midwest chauvinism from a reporter for the Springfield, Illinois, *Republican* who had come all the way to Plymouth: "Although nothing could be more modest than the way in which Miss Addams presented her enterprise to the attentions of her audience, it was good to see Chicago thus instructing the wise men and wise women of the East," he wrote. "New England has yet to recognize fully that the West, as we used to call that midland region, is in many things now at the front, and must be allowed to take the lead. Miss Addams, who for some reason or other puts one more d in her name . . . is an Illinois woman . . . with the quiet force of her sex, but also with that invincible energy for which Chicago is noted."

JANE arrived home in August to find Hull-House's residents plunged into a major investigation of the Halsted Street neighborhood. The project, led by Florence Kelley, was the first attempt in America to systematically study a slum, and three years later, in 1895, their findings were published as a book, *Hull-House Maps and Papers.* The work was modeled on Charles Booth's 1889 *Life & Labour of the People of London,* which developed the groundbreaking idea of the "poverty line"—the minimum income a family needed to live decently. Armed with census reports, the Hull-House residents conducted a house-to-house canvass of their neighborhood and charted income information on multicolored maps that also indicated the ethnic makeup of the area. The book received some respectful reviews, but it had none of the impact of *How the Other Half Lives,* Jacob Riis's anecdotal 1889 investigation of the dark lives of New York City's poor. Illustrated with dramatic photographs taken by the author, *How the Other Half Lives* was a blockbuster hit; *Hull-House Maps and Papers* barely sold a thousand copies. Still, it was a pioneering work, the first of many American urban surveys that later helped justify the nation's progressive social legislation.

In addition to the income information, the book contained a number of articles on specific subjects, including the Bohemians, the Italians, and the Russians. Ellen Starr had an essay on "Art and

Labour," Julia Lathrop wrote a piece on "Cook County Charities," and Jane contributed an article on "The Settlement as a Factor in the Labor Movement." Though she wrote about both men and women laborers, it was women workers who really sparked her imagination.

In the last twenty years of the nineteenth century, the number of women in the Chicago workforce had grown exponentially. A great prejudice against working mothers—which Jane shared with a majority of Americans—prevented all but the poorest married women from holding jobs, and most of the female wage earners in Chicago were young and single. They labored as domestics in private homes, in sweatshops, offices, and the new department stores. A great many of them worked in factories. Indeed, several industries—particularly dress manufacturing and bookbinding—built their labor force principally with women. In his 1900 novel, *Sister Carrie,* Theodore Dreiser evoked the dismal world of the Chicago factory, where the hours were long and the pay slight. It was, Dreiser wrote, "a place rather dingily lighted, the darkest portions having incandescent lights, filled in part with machines and part with work benches. At the latter labored quite a company of girls . . . drabby looking creatures stained in face with oil and dust, clad in shapeless cotton dresses and shod with more or less worn shoes. . . . They were a fair type of nearly the lowest order of shop girls—careless, rather slouchy, and more or less pale from confinement."

Jane first learned about the plight of working women from a tall, strapping redhead named Mary Kenney, who became at twenty-eight the first woman organizer of the American Federation of Labor. Mary Kenney moved to Chicago from Hannibal, Missouri, with her widowed mother, then fought for her rights in a series of exhausting factory jobs. She called the board of health to report unsanitary conditions. She demanded to be paid a just wage. She insisted she be addressed as Miss Kenney. Once, while working at a bookbindery, Mary was asked to take up an office job for an absent male employee. "I refused to do a man's job without a man's pay," she recalled in her memoirs.

Such experiences convinced Mary that the workers had to organize. She went from shop to shop, talking to women as they left their jobs, or sneaking into the factories at lunch breaks to invite the workers to union meetings. She took factory jobs for two weeks at a time so she could organize workers from the inside.

After hearing of Mary's work, Jane, who was eager to get to know her as "a genuine working person," invited Mary one evening to a concert at Hull-House. The young organizer distrusted rich do-gooders and was impatient with clubs that planned outings instead of working to improve conditions. But Jane quickly won her over by allowing Mary's bookbinders to meet at Hull-House and to use the settlement as a base for organizing other women's unions. In June 1892, Mary and Jane established a cooperative boardinghouse for working women in an apartment building on Ewing Street, near Hull-House. At the Jane Club, as the young women who lived there called it, rent was cheap, and an emergency fund supported members during payless periods when they were out of work or on strike. Like the settlement's residence quarters, the Jane Club created the atmosphere of a college dormitory, with communal dining facilities and a parlor, where the women could gather. The facility would grow over the years, eventually housing fifty women in a building adjacent to Hull-House.

In her memoirs, Mary Kenney recalled Jane's strong efforts on behalf of the workers. She "not only had the circulars distributed, but paid for them," Mary wrote. "She climbed stairs, high and narrow. Many of the entrances were in back alleys. There were signs to 'Keep Out.' She managed to see the workers at their noon hour, and invited them to classes and meetings at Hull-House."

Word that Hull-House championed women workers spread quickly through Chicago's factory district. When thirty-five young women walked off their jobs at the Star Knitting Works on Franklin Street in the spring of 1892, they went directly to the settlement. They were protesting the 35-cent fines levied against them whenever they were late. Taking up their cause, Jane "went over to see the firm, told them they had broken the law, arbitrated before [the judge] & had the girls all back in two days with the grievance removed & the world more the wiser & nobody the hungrier," Ellen later recalled. "That I call a pretty good job."

THE FEMALE factory workers were not unique in their efforts to take control of their lives. Throughout Chicago and across America, women were breaking out of the domestic sphere, becoming educated and holding down jobs. For the first time in history there were more than a handful of women business executives, lawyers, architects, painters, and scientists.

Many of their achievements were showcased at the 1893 World Columbian Exposition, held in Chicago to celebrate—one year late—the four hundredth anniversary of Columbus's discovery of the New World. Women from around the globe traveled to the city to visit the fair. Representatives from the General Federation of Women's Clubs, an organization with twenty thousand members, held a convention in Chicago in conjunction with the fair, and female celebrities from across the country flocked to the city. The notorious Victoria Woodhull, a spiritualist and free-love advocate, arrived with an entourage and declared her candidacy for president of the United States. The bespectacled, square-jawed Susan B. Anthony, president of the National American Woman Suffrage Association, also came to town, and drew large crowds to her speeches, which were widely covered by the press.

Almost on its own, Chicago had financed and built a 586-acre "White City" of huge alabaster pavilions filled with exhibits of American advances in science and technology. Frederick Law Olmsted, the eminent, white-bearded architect who'd designed New York's Central Park, had planned the exposition for Jackson Park, a swampy area eight miles south of the Loop. Following his design, an American Venice was constructed of interlinked canals, surrounding a reflecting basin decorated with symbolic fountains and statuary. The fair ran for six months, opening on May 2, 1893.

The morning of the opening, Jane and a group of Hull-House residents took a cable car to Jackson Park. A crowd of 200,000 had gathered in front of the massive white Administration Building, where President Grover Cleveland stood on the speaker stand with a gaggle of dignitaries, including the Spanish nobleman Duke Veragua, a descendant of Columbus. After a short address, the president pressed an electric button, setting in motion the machinery that powered the exposition. The flags of forty-seven nations unfurled, fountains shot water a hundred feet into the air, the drapery slipped from the huge statue of the Republic in the Great Basin, and guns boomed from warships in the harbor. Buffalo Bill Cody, in town for the summer with his Wild West Show, waved his huge white hat, and seventy-five Sioux Indians with black braids and war paint moved through the crowd as the band struck up "America the Beautiful."

For many women, the highlight of the exhibition was the Women's Building, a four-hundred-foot-long showcase of the talents of women designers, scientists, writers, artists, and architects. Women's domestic side was represented too, with the latest labor-saving devices, including the world's first gas oven.

The impresario of this exhibit was a remarkable woman who left a profound mark on Chicago and who would cross paths often with Jane in the years ahead. Bertha Honoré Palmer, president of the fair's board of lady managers, was born in Louisville in 1849, the eldest of three daughters of Henry Hamilton Honoré, a hardware merchant, and his cultivated wife, Eliza Carr. Attracted by stories of the fortunes being made in the West, Honoré moved his family to Chicago in 1855, when Bertha was six. One day, when the bright, dark-haired girl was thirteen, her father introduced her to a thirty-six-year-old tycoon named Potter Palmer, who'd made a fortune in real estate and a fashionable dry goods store, which he later sold to Marshall Field. Palmer, who'd never been married, immediately became smitten with the charming girl, and, as he later told his eldest son, decided to someday marry her.

Bertha grew up to be legendarily beautiful, brilliant, and ambitious. When she finally married Palmer in 1870, he was forty-four and she was twenty-one. Gossips sniped that the marriage was a business transaction, that Honoré, who was deeply in debt, had virtually "sold" Bertha to Palmer to ease the family's financial difficulties. But the union turned out to be solid and fulfilling for both partners. Bertha loved being rich and used her money not only to build a dazzling art collection but also to promote a series of progressive causes, from labor unions to women's suffrage.

With her buttery Southern voice, exotic, dark coloring, and fierce will, Bertha seemed more vivid than just about every woman around her, especially the mild wives of her husband's business associates. From her suite at the Palmer House Hotel on State Street, she supervised the governess in charge of her two sons, venturing out many times during the day to chat with the hotel's illustrious guests as they mingled in the lobby. In the evening, she presided over dinners and parties, dressed in velvet and satin, a diamond tiara nestled in her hair.

Bertha's romantic looks belied a cool, pragmatic nature. "I once heard her comment," a friend recalled, "upon the unforgivable folly of the marriage of a beautiful friend to a man without a fortune as if it belonged to the category of moral delinquency." Few men were as rich as her own husband. In 1882, Palmer built the largest house yet constructed in Chicago, a crenellated castle on Lake Shore Drive, featuring a cavernous foyer, a seventy-five-foot-long art gallery, and an immense bathtub in the shape of a swan.

Bertha reached her apotheosis in 1891 when the World's Fair officials named her head of the board of lady managers—a group of 115 women lawyers, artists, writers, community leaders, and wives of prominent men, who were charged with organizing the women's pavilion. Not everyone thought she deserved the job. In particular, professional suffragists scorned the flamboyant Bertha, who had little experience in public affairs. Isabella Beecher Hooker, the famous educator and Harriet Beecher Stowe's sister, and Elizabeth Cady Stanton, the seventy-six-year-old cofounder (with Susan B. Anthony) of the National Woman Suffrage Association, had opposed Bertha's appointment.

But Bertha proved to be an effective executive. She took the job seriously, seeing it as an opportunity to promote the advancement of her sex. From her office in the Rand-McNally building downtown, Bertha worked long hours, sending out letters from

New York to Siam, gathering information on the status of women throughout the world in industry, education, the arts, and business. She pressured the National Columbian Commission to include women on the committee that governed the exposition and lobbied legislators in Springfield into giving her an $80,000 appropriation. She went to Washington, where she had White House connections through her sister Ida, who was married to Ulysses S. Grant's son. She dazzled Senator J. W. Candler, chairman of the fair committee, and his fellow senators with her eloquence and charm. When questioned by Daniel Burnham, chief of construction for the fair, about her wish to have a woman architect design their section, "she whipped out a silver pencil and rapidly sketched the interior arrangement of [the proposed Women's] Building," noted her biographer. She added that her friend Mary Cassatt would happily contribute a mural.

In May 1891, Bertha traveled to Europe to win the support of foreign rulers and government officials. In London, she had tea with a daughter of Queen Victoria; in Paris she attended the opera with the president of France. She also visited artists' ateliers and began buying up Impressionist art. Many of her Degas, Monets, Renoirs, Pissarros, and Sisleys were displayed at the fair and now hang in the Art Institute of Chicago.

When Bertha returned from Europe, the secretary of the board of lady managers, Phoebe W. Couzins, a spinsterish St. Louis lawyer, complained to fair officials that Bertha had usurped too much power and was spending too much money. Bertha fired her. Couzins filed suit in Cook County Circuit Court, but lost her case. Again, many of the nation's leading suffragists came out against Bertha, and the breach brought headlines in the press. To placate the suffrage leaders, Bertha agreed to give them extra floor space in the Women's Building and to set aside a room where they could hold noonday meetings throughout the fair.

Jane stayed out of the conflict, maintaining good relationships with all the women involved. (Though they would later part company over Jane's defense of anarchists' rights to free speech, at this time Bertha was an ardent supporter of Hull-House and a great admirer of Jane's.) Jane took a backseat at the May Woman's Progress Congress, when women from around the world gathered in Chicago to discuss the progress and future of their sex, including the banning of "filth gathering" long skirts (which had already been outlawed in Hungary and Australia), property rights, divorce, salary rights, and, of course, the vote.

Jane had only a small role at the congress, reading a modest paper on "Domestic Service and the Family Claim" during one afternoon session. In her talk, Jane compared domestic and factory work, showing that "the latter possessed distinct advantages [for women] in point of hours, permanency of position, wages and the possibility of family and social life."

Overall, though the fair was supposed to celebrate world progress, little attention was given to social reform. There were only two small exhibits on model workers' housing and no exhibits on Hull-House. Discussion of social issues was confined to the series of international congresses held throughout the summer at the Memorial Art Palace (eventually renamed the Chicago Art Institute). Jane presided over seven sessions of the congress on social settlements during the week of July 17. Lectures were given on municipal corruption, tenement house reform, the relationship between settlements and charitable institutions, labor unions, and churches. But the talks were sparsely attended and virtually ignored by the press.

THE World Columbian Exposition was a dazzling spectacle in its day, and, indeed, it is still talked about as a shining example of American ingenuity and energy. It should have ended on a note of triumph. Instead, it closed with a shocking tragedy. On October 28, three days before the fair shut down, the city's charismatic mayor, Carter Henry Harrison, was shot to death in the hallway of his Ashland Boulevard mansion by a disgruntled office seeker. (The murderer, Patrick Eugene Prendergast, was a self-taught lawyer who was desperate to be the city's corporation counsel.) At sixty-eight, the Democrat Harrison had been mayor for nearly ten years (from 1879 to 1887, and after a hiatus of six years, reelected in 1893). Charming and youthful, he was known for riding around Chicago on a white mare, often at a full gallop. Harrison's extraordinary popularity cut across class, ethnic, and party lines. Working people liked him because he supported trades unions; the saloon-owning aldermen who controlled the city council liked him because he refused to enforce Illinois's Sunday closing laws for taverns. Yet, he was a millionaire who dined and played poker with the city's richest men.

Harrison died in the midst of a citywide crisis. The economic depression that had struck America by surprise on June 27, 1893, when the New York Stock Exchange crashed, was particularly acute in Chicago, where thousands of people who'd poured into the city to build the fair were left without work. Then, a smallpox epidemic raged through town. People ransacked garbage dumps for food; the newly appointed mayor, John Hopkins, allowed the homeless to sleep in City Hall and police stations.

At Hull-House, Jane faced daily hardship. "The suffering has been fearful and it is absolutely impossible to live in the midst of it and not do something about it," she wrote her friend Sarah Anderson. Since the founding of her settlement, Jane had struggled to avoid letting Hull-House become another charitable institution. But in the aftermath of the fair she found more and more of her time devoted to doling out relief—a situation that led to one of the most painful episodes of her career.

The City Bureau of Organized Charities opened a relief station at Hull-House, and it was constantly overrun with destitute people. One day, Jane refused relief to an out-of-work shipping clerk, urging him to take an available construction job. Jane thought he could handle it, even though the man insisted he could not endure outdoor work. As it turned out, after two days of digging a canal, the man contracted pneumonia and died. Jane never lost touch with the two small children he left behind. Still, as she wrote in her memoirs, she could never "see them without a bitter consciousness that it was at their expense I learned life cannot be administered by definite rules and regulations; that wisdom to deal with a man's difficulties comes only through some knowledge of his life and habits as a whole." The tragedy confirmed her belief in the damaging effects of traditional charity.

As SHE struggled with the increasing misery around Halsted Street, Jane had a new friend with whom to discuss her ideas. His name was William T. Stead, and he was the most famous journalist in Britain. The son of a Congregational minister, Stead looked as though he'd stepped from a Fra Angelico canvas—he was tall and muscular with a curly red beard and large, wide-set blue eyes. Fiercely evangelical, he'd recently published a sensational book about prostitution, *The Maiden Tribute in Babylon,* which prompted Parliament to raise the age of sexual consent for women. As editor of the news journal *The Review of Reviews,* he launched a series of moral crusades for his "senior partner in heaven," as he put it. He fought for the rights of widows, orphans, child laborers, and the unemployed; he railed against corrupt politicians and the wretched conditions in prisons and hospitals.

He had a talent for drawing attention to whatever he did. Nineteen years later his death would make front-page news around the globe—he would be among the passengers who went down with the White Star liner *Titanic.*

Stead had traveled to Chicago to cover the closing of the fair. But he was more interested in studying conditions in the city. He spent his nights touring the saloons and brothels of the Levee district, a shabby neighborhood of wooden cottages and low brick buildings just south of the Loop. Usually, he ended the evening by a visit to Hull-House, where he would arrive close to midnight "wet and hungry," as Jane recalled. Drinking endless cups of hot chocolate before a roaring fire in the settlement parlor, he would regale Jane and whoever else was up with monologues about his experiences "as an out-of-door laborer, standing in line without an overcoat for two hours in the sleet, that he might have a chance to sweep the streets; or his adventures with a crook, who mistook him for one of his own kind and offered him a place as an agent of a gambling house, which he promptly accepted," Jane wrote in her memoirs.

Stead was appalled at the lack of services for the poor, the corruption in city government, the indifference and ineffectiveness of civic leaders. He wrote a book, *If Christ Came to Chicago,* which came out the next year and was a best-seller. In it, Stead wrote that "the best hope" of the city "is the multiplications of Hull-Houses into all the slum districts." (He also suggested that Bertha Palmer be elected mayor.)

Before he sailed home, Stead organized two mass meetings at the Central Music Hall, and invited the representatives of business and labor, clergymen, society leaders, and a few prostitutes he'd befriended on his nightly forays into the Levee. Graham Taylor, the head of the Chicago Commons settlement, recalled that during the meetings, the floor and galleries of the Central Music Hall were "thronged by men and women of all grades, races, sects and conditions." Corporate kings sat next to labor leaders—one of them was Samuel Fielden, the recently pardoned Haymarket anarchist.

Standing at the podium, Stead announced that if he were a homeless wanderer, he would rather take his chances with the thieves and whores of the Levee "than with some persons in your churches and chapels." A hot-tempered socialist leader named Thomas J. Morgan shouted, "If you well-to-do people do not listen to the pleadings of editor Stead . . . may someone blow you out with dynamite." At that, wrote historian Donald Miller, "The audience rose as one, some persons cheering wildly, but most of the others hissing and shaking their fists at Morgan for daring to raise the specter of another Haymarket. It took all of Stead's persuasiveness to quiet the hall and secure the passage of a resolution designating a committee . . . to form a civic federation 'to drive Satan from Chicago,' as Stead put it."

Jane was one of the five people chosen at the meeting to form a group of one hundred civic leaders—the Civic Federation of Chicago. It had barely been organized when its members had to cope with a horrific labor strike.

Tensions that had been building among Chicago's unemployed

workers throughout the winter of 1894 exploded in June in the little neighborhood of Pullman, nine miles south of downtown Chicago, just within the recently expanded city limits. Pullman was a special place—a model town built in 1881 by railroad titan George Pullman for the workers of his Sleeping Car Factory. Acting on what seemed to the world at the time a progressive idea, Pullman had provided a church, a library, a school, stores, parks, and pretty brick town houses laid out along well-lit, leafy streets. But he ran the town as if he were a feudal lord. He required his workers to live there as a condition of employment. The rent was high, as were charges for gas and water. Pullman even tried to regulate the private behavior of his employees. He banned saloons from the town, and stories abounded about his monitoring church attendance and his bullying of employees to vote Republican.

During the winter following the closing of the fair, the depression set back the sleeping-car business. Pullman laid off scores of workers and slashed the wages of those remaining by 30 percent. But he refused to reduce rents, leaving many families destitute. A group of Pullman employees joined the new American Railroad Union, led by fiery, thirty-eight-year-old Eugene Victor Debs, and began to organize their colleagues. In May, Pullman announced another wage cut. The local union elected an employees' committee to discuss the situation with him, but Pullman refused to negotiate and fired the members of the committee. The next day, more than five thousand Pullman workers walked off their jobs.

Debs called for union members across the nation to detach Pullman cars from all trains, and quickly the strike escalated into a nationwide boycott. When the railroads fired employees who participated in the boycott, entire train crews quit, and eventually the national railroad system screeched to a halt, causing a disruption of the mails and food shortages throughout the country.

The Civic Federation appointed Jane to a six-member commission—also including several businessmen, a professor from the new sociology department at the University of Chicago, and Bertha Palmer—to explore the possibility of arbitration with both the workers and Pullman. Most likely Jane was chosen not only because of her status in Chicago as a moral leader, but because she knew Pullman. She had served on the board of the Chicago Visiting Nurses' Association with his daughter Florence, and during the previous year, Pullman had donated a small amount of money to Hull-House's relief fund, probably at Jane's request.

One evening after her appointment, Jane visited the Pullman workers' town, looked at a few houses, and ate dinner with some of the factory's female employees. She also investigated rents. "You can get two rooms [near Hull-House] for $6, while the cheapest two rooms I saw at Pullman were $7.50, and most of them $8.50. They were cleaner [in Pullman] because the surroundings were cleaner, but other facilities were no better," Jane later told a federal commission investigating the strike.

Another evening, Jane attended a railway union meeting in Pullman at which the workers voted to arbitrate with management. "I came back to the city, feeling that we had made a beginning toward conciliation," Jane told the commission, "and the other [male] members of the committee went to see Mr. Pullman."

He refused to arbitrate. Bertha Palmer, exasperated by his "pigheadedness," as she put it, moved to increase the pressure. She asked Ralph Easley, the Civic Federation secretary, to ask Marshall Field to reason with the sleeping-car king. But Pullman remained adamant.

After he directed his managers to bring in scabs, protecting them with Pinkerton guards, rioting broke out and mobs of young toughs attacked the train yards around Chicago, destroying hundreds of thousands of dollars of railroad property. In early July, several weeks after the strike started, President Cleveland sent federal troops to Chicago to get the trains running and the mail delivered. The troops set up white tents along the lakefront on the site of the World Columbian Exposition, which had been razed by the wrecking ball within days of the fair's conclusion. Meanwhile, George Pullman fled to his summer mansion on the New Jersey shore. Before he left, he installed guards around his Chicago château on Prairie Avenue and locked many of his valuables in his office safe downtown.

• • •

IN THE middle of the crisis, Jane's sister, Mary Linn, fell gravely ill with what turned out to be terminal cancer. Jane arranged for her to go to a hospital in Kenosha, Wisconsin, paid her bills, and visited her frequently. She had hoped Mary would recover, but in early July her condition deteriorated and doctors summoned the family to Mary's bedside. Jane found her way to Kenosha by a privately hired train car. But Mary's husband and four children, who were stuck in Chicago, could not reach her because of the blocked railways.

In anguish, Mary repeatedly asked Jane if her loved ones had arrived, and Jane had to tell her no. "I was filled with a profound apprehension lest her last hours should be touched with resentment towards those responsible for the delay, lest her unutterable longing should at the very end be tinged with bitterness," Jane later recalled. Finally, on July 5, after Mary's husband signed a document releasing the railroad from any responsibility for the family's safety, the Linns boarded a train for Kenosha. As a precaution against rocks thrown through the windows by rioters, the family sat on the floor the entire journey. But they arrived in Kenosha without incident. "It became known we were relatives of Jane Addams who was working for the strikers," recalled Esther Linn Hulbert, Jane's niece. By the time they arrived, however, Mary had slipped into a coma, and she died on July 6, Esther Linn noted, "without knowing any of us." The loss was devastating for Jane. Mary had been like a mother to her; they had loved each other deeply.

Two days after Mary's death, a riot broke out in Hammond, Indiana, an important railroad junction just south of Chicago. Ray Standard Baker, a reporter for the *Chicago Record,* arrived on the scene early in the morning as crowds choked the railroad yards. "The tracks from crossing to crossing were strewn with overturned freight cars, battered and burned coaches, twisted rails and broken switches," he reported.

> I heard hoarse voices shouting "Heave ho! Heave ho!" and saw that a crowd of men had thrown a hawser across the top of a Pullman car and were in the act of tipping it over to block a main railroad track. Hundreds of men were tugging at the rope. The heavy car would lift up on one side and then sag heavily back again. . . . Suddenly, I heard what seemed to me to be firecrackers exploding. A moment later a spectator, who was standing near me, slumped to the ground, and I saw blood spurt from his breast. Then another man fell. I looked up the track and saw a locomotive moving slowly down upon the mob. Blue-clad soldiers covered the fender, and the running boards, and the top of the cab. They had their rifles lifted and were firing directly at us. Instantly, there was panic, men running and women screaming.

When it was all over, one man had been killed and seven wounded.

Jane returned to Hull-House the next day to find "almost everyone on Halsted Street wearing a white ribbon, the emblem of the strikers' side," she recalled. Some of the Hull-House residents were closely involved in the conflict. Florence Kelley and Alzina P. Stevens had helped raise money for Debs's bail after he was arrested on a charge of conspiracy to obstruct the mails. Ellen Starr organized transportation out of town for other strike leaders. And Kelley, who had recently been appointed the state's chief factory inspector by Governor John Peter Altgeld, arranged work permits for the teenage children of the blacklisted workers, so they could be taken out of school to support their families.

One afternoon in the middle of the conflict, while Chicago's trolley operators were also on strike, Jane walked several miles from Hull-House to Lincoln Park, which runs along Lake Michigan. There, according to her memoirs, she sat alone in tranquility and contemplated Augustus Saint-Gaudens's statue of Abraham Lincoln. The statue stands at the southern entrance of the park in front of a large, curved stone bench by Stanford White, and it is reached by walking through a lovely garden. As Jane gazed at the statue, she drew strength from Lincoln's words, delivered at his second inaugural, which were carved on the sides of the bench: "Let us have faith that right makes might, and in that faith, let us to the end dare to do our duty as we understand it, with malice towards none, with charity for all, with firmness on the right as God gives us to see the right, let us strive on."

The Pullman strike had revealed a seething class bitterness that threatened many of the democratic principles Lincoln had come to stand for. Ironically, the martyred president's surviving child, Robert Todd Lincoln, was on Pullman's side. As a member of the board of directors of the Pullman Palace Car Company (and as Pullman's neighbor on Prairie Avenue), Robert Lincoln, a prominent lawyer who'd served as ambassador to Great Britain in the early 1890s, supported Pullman's decision not to arbitrate with the workers.

The battle in Hammond, Indiana, broke the strike, and by August the federal troops were gone. Despite the efforts of his brilliant young attorney (and Hull-House supporter) Clarence Darrow, Debs was locked away for six months in the county jail in Woodstock, Illinois, seventy miles northwest of the city.

On July 16, Lincoln and Pullman decided to reopen the sleeping-car factory and two days later they began hiring hundreds of new workers, all of whom signed a pledge never to join a union. Meanwhile, as the reporter Ray Standard Baker wrote, the strikers continued "more or less forgotten to starve in their model houses without any help from the man who said he loved his town like one of his own children."

Reflecting on the strike a few weeks later, Jane had the idea of comparing Pullman with one of Shakespeare's tragic heroes. In a speech she gave in October to the Chicago Woman's Club, Jane said Pullman, like King Lear, could not imagine that his child "should be moved by a principle obtained outside himself." Pullman could not fathom why the workers did not appreciate his generosity; why they wanted more independence, more freedom, more of a say in their own affairs. He was blind to his own selfishness,

Jane argued. For as the workers realized, the housing, parks, library, and other amenities of their neighborhood were really for Pullman, for the enhancement of his reputation and status, not for them.

Jane acknowledged that the labor movement had its faults, particularly in the violence that erupted during strikes, but nothing, she said, can "touch the fact that it started from an unselfish impulse"—the democratic ideal of letting men and women have a voice in their own affairs.

Though the speech was hardly inflammatory, Jane could not get it published until 1912, eighteen years after the strike. Editors of East Coast–based magazines like *The Atlantic Monthly,* one place where Jane had tried to place it, could not abide even her mild criticism of George Pullman, who was widely regarded outside Chicago, Bertha Palmer noted, as having saved America "from anarchy."

12

Battling the Ward Boss

The 19th Ward alderman, John Powers.
(Courtesy of University of Illinois at Chicago, the University Library, Lawrence J. Gutter Collection of Chicagoana)

No sooner had the Pullman strike ended than Jane was faced with caring for the children of her dead sister Mary, three of whom moved into Hull-House in September 1894. (The eldest, John, twenty-two, was attending an Episcopal Seminary in Chicago.) Mary's husband, John Linn Sr., was too distracted and ineffectual to cope with his brood, so it fell to Jane to make arrangements for the youngsters' education. She saw Esther, fourteen, off to school near Cedarville; settled James

Weber, eighteen, into quarters at the University of Chicago, and enrolled the youngest, Stanley, eleven, in a neighborhood school. Within weeks of his arrival, however, a typhoid epidemic hit Halsted Street, and Jane sent the frail child to boarding school in a peaceful, leafy suburb.

Later, as she walked through the tenements, Jane passed rickety doors to which pieces of white crepe had been pinned, signaling that a child had died inside. Jane was overcome with guilt, ashamed that she'd done nothing to save these children, who'd been torn from their families, not moved "into boarding school, but into eternity," as she put it in her autobiography. She vowed to attack Halsted Street's squalor.

Jane asked one of Hull-House's male residents to investigate the neighborhood's haphazard garbage collection system. He discovered that the ward's powerful alderman, Johnny Powers, had much to do with the horrific conditions. Powers had handed out the collection job as a political plum to a crony, who took the money but ignored the garbage.

The news was hardly surprising to Jane, and, indeed, it was just one instance of widespread corruption in the 19th Ward and throughout the city. From its earliest days, Chicago had been "this huge, incoherent city, always on the verge of lawlessness," as Jane once described it. A tradition of limited government had encouraged the city's rapid development, but also resulted in wretched municipal services—poorly paved streets, inefficient public transportation, unclean water. After Carter Harrison's murder, the city's historically weak mayor's office became even weaker. In five years, between 1893 and 1897, there were four mayors. Meanwhile, the city council, made up of sixty-eight aldermen from Chicago's thirty-four wards, ruled. The council was dominated by a ruthless Democratic machine, made up of a greedy mob of rough, uncouth "boodlers," who specialized in selling their votes to grant city franchises to companies that provided crucial services, from streetcars to electricity. The power of the corrupt aldermen relied on their ability to win votes from ordinary citizens, usually by doling out favors: they found jobs for the unemployed, bailed constituents out of jail, paid for lavish funerals, and distributed turkeys at Christmas.

In her first years on Halsted Street, Jane tried to avoid dealing with Johnny Powers, knowing him to be among the most ruthless and corrupt politicians in the city. Powers was short and stocky with heavy features and thick graying hair that he combed into a stiff pompadour. Even in grainy, century-old photographs, hardness and determination shine from his dark eyes. He was born in Kilkenny, Ireland, in 1851 and emigrated at nineteen to Chicago, where he got a job in a grocery store. Soon he was able to go into business for himself, buying two saloons. He was elected alderman in 1888, a year before Jane opened Hull-House. At the time, the city council was controlled by Alderman Billy Whalen. But Powers was ambitious and soon he had a chance to make his move. In 1890, Whalen collected a $30,000 kickback from the sale of a city franchise, but then died before divvying it up among his cronies on the council. Powers knew the money was in a safe in Whalen's saloon, so he bought out the saloon's furnishings. Instead of keeping the money for himself, however, he distributed it among Whalen's gang, thereby establishing himself as their new leader.

Powers quickly became chairman of the finance committee, the city council panel that handed out city contracts, and boss of the caucus that distributed the chairmanships of the other committees. He also was chairman of the Cook County Democratic committee. Though his salary as alderman amounted to $3 a week, Powers managed to buy a large house—the fruits of boodling. He collected $50,000 alone from Charles Yerkes, the crooked entrepreneur who built Chicago's elevated train system (and who was immortalized as Frank Cowperwood in Theodore Dreiser's novel *The Titan*).

The arrival in his ward of a mansion full of earnest, do-gooding women made Powers uneasy. At first he tried to befriend Jane in small ways. In December 1893, Powers visited Jane at Hull-House and offered her several thousand pounds of turkeys for her poor neighbors. When Jane mentioned the offer at the weekly residents' meeting, everyone agreed it should be turned down. Jane suggested an alternative—perhaps she could give Powers a list of needy families. In the end, though, the residents resolved, as Julia Lathrop said, that the settlement should "have nothing to do with Mr. Powers and his charities."

Indeed, when it came to serious reform of the neighborhood's worst conditions, Powers blocked Jane at every turn. The women of Hull-House wanted to replace a crowded, ramshackle school on Taylor Street, which served mostly the children of recent immigrants, who couldn't vote. Powers opposed and eventually crushed the effort, though he supported plans to build a parochial school that would serve the children of his supporters. But it was Powers's indifference to the filthy streets and to the ward's astonishingly high death rate that sparked Jane to fight him.

With the backing of two businessmen, she decided to try to win the garbage collection contract herself, and she put in a bid to the city council, estimating it would take sixteen collection teams to clean the ward thoroughly. Her bid was thrown out on a technicality, but the publicity she received in the newspapers led Mayor George Swift, a reform-minded Republican, to appoint her garbage inspector for the 19th Ward—the first woman to hold the $1,000-a-year job.

Every morning at six, Jane and her assistant, a young Hull-House resident named Amanda Johnson, started out on their rounds in a horse-driven buggy. Dressed "quietly and sensibly," according to one newspaper account, in shirtwaists with blue serge skirts that cleared the ground, they followed the collection teams on their rounds to make sure the work was done properly. Jane notified the contractor if any of the teams were not performing and, occasionally, she had to ask a judge to arbitrate disputes about the quality of the work.

Mayor Swift eventually gave her the use of eight emergency crews to haul away excess refuse. From one alley alone they took away fourteen truckloads. Jane kept meticulous records, drawing the collection wagons' routes in colored inks on maps so she could see at a glance which areas had been ignored. She also kept index cards on all the alleys in the ward—noting what improvements were needed, when a $5.50 new garbage box had been ordered, and whether or not it had been supplied and was in good repair. She pushed the city to have the alleys paved, and enlisted the three hundred children who belonged to Hull-House clubs to pick up tin cans and newspapers, organizing them into regiments with "official" badges and elected captains.

At the end of July, Amanda Johnson took over, and, refusing to break for vacation, "works on like a hero," Jane reported to Mary Smith. "The ward really is cleaner."

The neighborhood women were "much shocked by this abrupt departure into the ways of men," Jane recalled, but the press was charmed by the image of a courageous little woman battling the conniving politicians to protect the health of innocent people. "Miss Addams has achieved wonders in the ward," gushed one reporter.

Though Jane served in the post for only six weeks, her stint as garbage inspector brought her more attention than anything she'd done so far at Hull-House, and established her reputation as a determined reformer. Jane's extreme reserve and scholarly, philosophical bent made her slower to join the political fray than her more openly aggressive colleagues such as Florence Kelley. Indeed, she never felt totally comfortable with her ambition. The shadow of the Victorian angel hovered over her, even as she battled some of the city's roughest, most ruthless men. But the miserable conditions around Hull-House pushed her toward activism, and her confidence in her considerable powers to lead was growing daily.

IN THE summer of 1895 Jane served as a member of a commission investigating conditions in the Cook County poorhouse, which had been the subject of several sensational newspaper exposés, detailing the rancid food and cruel guards at the bleak institution. Every evening Jane returned home exhausted to find twenty or so people who had relatives in the poorhouse waiting to ask her if she had news of their loved ones. They were "all in such acute distress of mind that to see them was to look upon the victims of deliberate torture," Jane recalled.

At the same time she investigated the poorhouse, Jane insisted on overseeing every detail at Hull-House. Construction had recently begun on a four-story brick "Children's House," on the southwest corner of Polk and Halsted Streets. Financed by Charles Mather Smith, Mary Smith's father, and designed by Allen Pond, it housed a nursery, a kindergarten, club rooms, a kitchen, and a bathroom. Remodeling of the main house was also under way, with the construction of a new third story holding seven bedrooms and two bathrooms.

While she worried over floor plans and construction costs, Jane had to contend as well with a troublesome resident—a black doctor named Harriet Rice. Not much is known about Dr. Rice's background and personality. She arrived at the settlement in the early 1890s, and for a while roomed with Florence Kelley. Her job was to be on call for the women of the settlement and the Jane Club. Occasionally, however, Jane asked her to care for a sick neighbor, a task Dr. Rice invariably refused, probably because the immigrants, unused to seeing blacks in other than menial jobs, treated her like a servant. Jane was sympathetic to Dr. Rice's financial difficulties—"by the time she pays her room rent and her coal [she] probably does not eat enough," Jane told Mary Smith, who was partially subsidizing Dr. Rice. What's more, Jane sensed that as an educated black woman, Dr. Rice was isolated and lonely. She asked Julia Lathrop to talk to her about race, but Julia was too busy, and apparently never got around to it. Jane remained perplexed at Dr. Rice's inability to fit in, complaining to Mary Smith that Dr. Rice "has not the settlement spirit (if there is such a thing)."

Indeed, there was, and it was marked by obsessive cooperation and unfailing usefulness. "Duty above every other consideration in the world" was the motto the Hull-House women lived by. Devotion to the slum poor echoed the religious devotion most of them no longer practiced. But it also developed from their sense of being second-class citizens. Sacrifice became for them, as it did for George Eliot a generation earlier, a way "to locate women on a higher ground where men could not exert control," as Eliot's biographer Frederick Karl put it. At Hull-House, that meant staying extraordinarily busy. In a letter describing the "typical" Hull-House evening, Alice Hamilton captured something of the chronic bustle of settlement life:

> Here in the back parlour I am sitting at the table and opposite me is Miss Johnson, who is the street-cleaning commissioner. She is having a most killing time interviewing an old Irishman who wants a job from the city. . . . He says he never had any [naturalization papers]; his wife says they were lost in the snow out in Utah when Brigham Young was dedicating that temple. At the other end of the table sits Miss Brockway, the sweet little girl who is engaged to Miss Addams's nephew [John Linn]. In the front parlor are Mr. Deknatel and Mrs. Valerio . . . taking the names of the people who are registering for classes. Miss Addams is on the sofa with a very nice North End man. They are looking over plans for an addition to the coffee house. Miss Watson, Mr. Swope, Mr. Ball, Mr. Hooker, Miss Pitkin, Miss Gyles and all the others are managing classes and clubs in various rooms. In a few minutes a certain Dr. Blount is coming. [Dr. Blount] is a she-doctor and a socialist. I met her some time ago, and she it is whom Miss Addams destines to help me in some scheme for the amelioration of the condition of the Italian neighbors. Then at nine o'clock we are to have a residents' meeting to divide up the duty of tending the door and showing people over the house.

In addition to her unending role running Hull-House and working for reform, Jane responded to myriad daily crises, from caring for sick babies and alcoholic old men to breaking up domestic quarrels and giving eulogies at funerals. Indeed, though she had escaped the family claim, Jane had fallen into the clutches of the equally demanding claims of Hull-House and its neighborhood. Helen Gow, a visitor from an English settlement, thought the

Hull-House residents were extremely "weary-looking women," but that Jane was "tired beyond all the tired settlement workers I have seen." Once, she noted in her memoirs, Jane "came in looking scarcely alive. I have never seen one so death-like moving about."

Others, too, found Jane's whirlwind schedule alarming. After a visit to the settlement, the philosopher John Dewey wrote his wife, "I sh'd think the irritation of hearing the doorbell ring & never doing one thing without being interrupted to tend to half a dozen others would drive [the residents] crazy." After a late-summer 1895 visit to the settlement, Robert Woods, head of South End House in Boston, warned Jane that the residents' addiction to good works threatened their well-being. In a letter on September 4, 1895, two days before Jane's thirty-fifth birthday, Woods advised Jane to slow down: "It is my impression . . . that there is too much activity and not enough repose, and that you and all the other residents are spending creative vitality upon mechanical details to a rather large extent." The residents should stop thinking of themselves as "members of an emergency corps subject to call or bound to guard duty . . . There are times when the greater love must even leave the starving to starve."

The concern about Jane's condition was justified. A week after Woods's letter arrived, she collapsed with what Dr. Rice and another physician first diagnosed as typhoid fever, but which turned out to be appendicitis, the illness that had killed Jane's father fourteen years before. Shortly after noon on September 10, a doctor from a nearby hospital arrived at Hull-House with his surgical supplies (including a collapsible operating table), two attending physicians, and a nurse. After drawing the drapes in Jane's room against the hot afternoon sun, he gave her a mask of ether and removed her appendix, an extremely dangerous operation in 1895, and one that frequently resulted in death.

Jane weathered the operation well, though her recovery was slow. She canceled two speaking engagements in Denver and Kansas City and stayed in bed. Her spirits were lifted by visits from Weber and Alice. But it was three weeks before she was able to sit up in her William Morris chair, and she was still too weak on

October 12 to attend the wedding in the drawing room of the Hull-House nurse Annie Fryar to Dr. Edward Hutchinson.

Soon afterward, Mary Smith came to escort Jane by train to a friend's house on the North Shore, where Mary nursed her for a week before taking Jane back to Walton Street to recuperate further. As Jane lay in the big four-poster bed in the room opposite Mary's, she brooded about Johnny Powers. She'd been encouraged the year before when Frank Lawler, a member of the Hull-House Men's Club (a group of neighborhood men who got together once a week to hear lectures on a variety of topics), was elected alderman from the 19th Ward to serve beside Powers. But soon afterward rumors floated through the neighborhood that Lawler had joined Powers's machine. (Lawler died on January 17, 1896, with an estate of only $7,000—proof, his supporters insisted, that he had not boodled.) By then, Jane knew that the only way life would improve on Halsted Street was if she got rid of Powers.

At the time, Chicago was controlled by "some of the toughest, roughest politicians in the city's history. And there were no rules. The town was the widest open it had ever been," said historian Paul Green. But in the face of the disheartening corruption, a number of reform efforts began to heat up. The strongest operation was probably the Municipal Voters' League. This branch of the Civic Federation was dominated by Republicans and included some of Chicago's wealthiest businessmen. In 1896 it launched a vigorous campaign against boss rule, targeting fifty-eight of Chicago's sixty-eight aldermen as "unclean and unfit."

Interestingly, among Chicago's women reformers, there was little public agitation for the vote, an exasperating situation to Susan B. Anthony, who had attended a Civic Federation meeting the year before. Anthony wrote Jane on December 19, 1895, "Have those men had the thought enter their noodles yet that women could be of any help to them provided they had the ballot in their hands?"

Jane was a latecomer to organized suffrage, partly because she believed other issues—child labor, unions, sanitation, and factory regulation, to name a few—were more pressing. As Allen F. Davis notes, "She was the ultimate pragmatist who believed in solving the worst problems first." Unlike some suffrage leaders who supported votes for upper-class women only—in order to counteract the male immigrant vote—Jane supported votes for *all* women, including those from the lowest classes. Yet her public comments on suffrage were mild. In the few talks she gave on the subject before 1900, she emphasized that women were morally superior beings whose special intuitive powers should be channeled to solve the abuses of industrialization. She didn't even attend her first national suffrage convention until 1906.

Though Jane couldn't vote, she devoted her energies to working behind the scenes, and she became the guiding force behind the 19th Ward Improvement Club, which had been organized by community activists to lead the fight against Powers. The Improvement Club, which had offices in every precinct of the ward, was composed mostly of men and women affiliated with Hull-House programs. One of their chief activities was to find a candidate to run as an Independent against Powers.

Jane's first choice was George Cushing Sikes, a highly regarded writer for the *Chicago Record* whose wife had been a resident at Hull-House. When Sikes said he couldn't afford to leave his job, Jane secured a stipend for him from a wealthy friend. In the end, however, Sikes decided it was a conflict of interest for a newspaperman to run for political office, and he declined to join the race.

Afterward, the Improvement Club searched for a suitable candidate among the members of the Hull-House Men's Club, finally settling on William Gleeson, a forty-two-year-old Irish immigrant who was a former president of the Chicago Bricklayers' Union. Jane masterminded his campaign. She enlisted Henry Demarest Lloyd to help her persuade Hazen Pingree, the reform mayor of Detroit, and other speakers of "high moral tone" from society's "better element" to come to Chicago to speak on Gleeson's behalf. She also mobilized a group of professors to help the Hull-House residents hang campaign posters and distribute handbills. With the constant raging against "the Gang" in the newspapers and from the pulpits, Jane thought Gleeson had a good chance to win.

At one rally in the middle of the campaign, for example, a thousand people showed up on West Twelfth Street. The principal speaker was a popular circuit court judge, Murray F. Tuley, who once carried his invalid wife to a polling booth so she could vote for the trustee of Illinois State University, one of the few offices for which women had suffrage. Powers "never lost an opportunity to sell or give away the rights of the people," Tuley shouted to the crowd. Loud hissing from Powers's supporters split the air, only to be drowned out by wild applause from Gleeson's men.

Powers, meanwhile, was running scared. One newspaper said he spent $20,000 in the last two weeks of the campaign, bribing constituents and organizing gangs to corral the Italian vote, which was thought to be less firmly in Powers's camp. His bandwagon roamed the ward with Powers himself dressed in a black waistcoat, his chest straining against his diamond-studded shirtfront, standing in the center grinning and throwing nickels to the children. On the Saturday before the Tuesday election, his men distributed more than three hundred kegs of beer among the saloons around Hull-House. All weekend, drunken men wandered the streets, shouting and fighting. Through it all, Powers's heelers worked the crowds, making sure everyone knew who was supplying the drinks. At the same time, he bribed a member of the local temperance society to spread the rumor that if Gleeson was elected, the Hull-House candidate would shut down the saloons at ten o'clock every night. "I want to show the people of Chicago that the citizens of the nineteenth ward do not believe the stories that have been printed about me," Powers shouted to a large crowd gathered at a labor hall on the night before the election.

The polls opened at 6:00 A.M., April 7, 1896, a warm and sunny Tuesday. Ten policemen with billy clubs hanging from their belts stood guard at 189 Ewing Street, headquarters for the 19th Ward's 13th Precinct. At midmorning, Gleeson arrived in his carriage. A group of Italian men loitering on the sidewalk broke into cheers, hoisted Gleeson onto their shoulders, and carried him into the polling place. Seconds later, several of Powers's heelers rushed in and began flinging rocks at Gleeson's men, driving them out into the street. "Stand back, you dagos!" screamed a policeman, as he tried to subdue the Italians, according to one newspaper account.

Similar scenes played out throughout the 19th Ward and the entire city. In the first ward, the heart of Chicago's vice district, a man was shot and seriously wounded, but, amazingly, no one was killed.

Despite the violence, citizens turned out in large numbers at the polls, and all but five of the corrupt aldermen were defeated. Unfortunately, Powers was not among them, though his margin of victory had been reduced by nearly 60 percent. (He beat Gleeson by a vote of 4,064 to 2,703.) Powers seemed relieved and emboldened by his success. "My victory was a glorious one," he told a reporter. "Every man who voted for me did so because he knew and felt I was his tried and proven friend. The cry of boodle, boodle, cut very little figure. And say, I want to serve notice on the press of Chicago that from this time forth . . . that neither the press nor the pulpit will govern my actions. In return for the steadfastness of my friends I can only give my heartfelt thanks, and I will say that in the future, as in the past, I will look after their welfare as I have done heretofore."

As it turned out, Powers was as good to his enemies as to his friends. After the election, nearly every man who had been prominent in the campaign against him was bought off, receiving an office or a job. A printer who had played an important role in the reform campaign was appointed to a clerkship at city hall. A driver was given a new job and a large salary at the police barns. To repay the rumor-spreading temperance man (who also got a job at city hall), Powers donated $3,000 to buy uniforms and equipment for a boys' temperance brigade. Gleeson himself received a position in the city construction department.

Only then did Jane begin to understand Powers's hold on the average voter and realize the mistakes that she and the other reformers had made. "We doubtless depended too much upon the idealistic appeal for we did not yet comprehend the element of reality always brought into the political struggle in such a neighborhood where politics deal so directly with getting a job and earning a living," she later wrote.

BEFORE the election, Jane had accepted Mary Smith's offer to travel with her and her parents "on a nice little tour" of Europe, all expenses paid. As the day of departure approached, Mary's eagerness overflowed. "When I think of your going away with us I am quite overcome," she confessed to Jane. "It seems too good to be true, and I really can't take it in. I know you will be bored and homesick a lot of the time, but I believe you will get rested and that it will pay in the end. When I looked at you after the club today I wished you were going tomorrow."

The weeks before Jane set sail were frantically busy. In addition to organizing Hull-House to function without her, she spent time with her nephew Stanley, who was now living with her again and attending the Morgan Park School, a public elementary school in the neighborhood. She felt guilty leaving for four months. She took the little boy with her on a speaking tour at the end of March to Buffalo, Syracuse, and Philadelphia. Then she brought him to Cedarville to live with her brother Weber and his family.

Jane and the Smiths set sail from New York on April 29 and arrived in England ten days later. Immediately, Jane embarked on a whirlwind of speaking engagements (her fee was $25 plus expenses) and meetings with settlement workers, labor leaders, social activists, and writers, among whom her reputation was well known. She wrote to Ellen Starr on May 29 that "we buy a good deal of literature and 'cram up' before we meet the folks who have written the books." She was also feted at a round of lunches, lawn parties, and dinners, reporting that at one "I was the only 'lady' out of the eight who was not decollete."

In Oxford, she stayed with Sydney Ball, a friend of Arnold Toynbee's, and his wife. "It was in his rooms that Mr. Barnett read the first paper looking toward settlements," Jane wrote to the Hull-House resident Gertrude Barnum on May 22, 1896. She had lunch with Toynbee's widow and visited Toynbee Hall. She boasted to Gertrude that there were no "fresh air schemes as good and simple as ours," and, though she'd seen a lot of girls' clubs, "nothing approaching the Jane Club." In general, she found English settlements more patronizing than their American counterparts. The atmosphere at a settlement in Southwalk, she noted, was so cold "the poor might have been another name for microbes."

Through it all, she missed Hull-House. When she didn't get letters, she told Gertrude Barnum, she felt "fussy."

IN JULY, Jane and Mary traveled by train to Norway, and from there went to Russia, where they stopped at St. Petersburg and Moscow. Jane shopped for a fur for her sister Alice and observed the peasants. "It has been a very interesting trip opening up an entirely new people—the gentle and superstitious Slavs. It will give me quite a new insight into our neighbors when I get home," she wrote Alice. Aylmer Maude, Leo Tolstoy's translator, arranged for the women to visit the writer at his estate, Yasnaya Polyana, a popular stop at the time for European and American intellectuals, journalists, and reformers. Jane had read Tolstoy's philosophical writings between her two European trips and was greatly impressed by them.

By this time Tolstoy was a tormented, white-bearded egomaniac. He had disowned his masterpieces, *War and Peace* and *Anna Karenina,* and was in the grip of a Christian vision of an ideal world. Though Tolstoy remained at his ancestral home, he tried to live as much as he could like the peasants in the surrounding villages. He dressed like them, ate their simple food, and, while white-gloved servants roamed his mansion, he insisted on cleaning his own room and emptying his own chamber pot. He was also engaged in "a battle to the death," as he called it, with his long-suffering wife, partly over issues of inheritance regarding his literary and ancestral estates. Nevertheless, he had tremendous personal magnetism and always made time to talk to the many admirers who flocked to see him.

Yasnaya Polyana lies 120 miles south of Moscow. In the 1890s it included two thousand acres of farmland and forest, a two-story house, twenty outbuildings and a large stable, four ponds, and several villages containing 330 peasants. At the time of Jane's visit, Tsar Nicholas II was in power, and the Russian Revolution was twenty-one years away.

Jane, Mary, and Aylmer Maude arrived on a beautiful, sunny day and were ushered into a parlor where Tolstoy and his wife were waiting. As they sat on simple wood chairs under portraits of Tolstoy's ancestors, Maude explained to Tolstoy in Russian the purpose of Hull-House. Tolstoy listened gravely, his eyes fixed on the sleeves of Jane's traveling gown, "which unfortunately at that season were monstrous in size," she recalled.

Then the white-bearded sage "took hold of an edge and pulling out one sleeve to an interminable breadth, said quite simply that 'there was enough stuff on one arm to make a frock for a little girl' and asked me directly if I did not find such a dress a 'barrier to the people.'"

Jane explained that her sleeves were no bigger than "those of the working girls in Chicago and that nothing would more effectively separate me from 'the people' than a cotton blouse following the simple lines of the human form." Sensing Jane's embarrassment, Tolstoy's wife jumped in with a story about her own futile efforts to make clothes for poor girls from the superfluous train of *her* best gown.

Later, however, Madame Tolstoy was not around to rescue Jane when Tolstoy confronted her with a more personal question. Who supported her? he asked. When Jane told him she had an income from a farm she owned a hundred miles from Chicago, Tolstoy snapped, "So you are an absentee landlord? Do you think you will help the people more by adding yourself to the crowded city than you would by tilling your own soil?"

Jane's unease doubled when the guests sat down to dinner in the shaded garden. One of Tolstoy's daughters appeared, "coming straight from the harvest field where she had been working with a group of peasants since five o'clock in the morning," Jane recalled. "She was plainly much exhausted but neither expected nor received sympathy from the members of [her] family."

Two meals were served at the long, narrow dining table. The guests, including a group of Europeans, Countess Tolstoy, her children's governess, and her younger daughters, ate an elaborate upper-class meal. Tolstoy and the daughter who had worked all day in the fields ate porridge and black bread. The talk centered on the fate of a young Russian who had disguised himself as a country schoolmaster in order to obtain a copy of Tolstoy's *Life,* which the Russian authorities had banned. Later the young man had made a full confession to the police and was exiled to Siberia. Tolstoy raged about the injustice of punishing one of his readers, while he, the author of the forbidden book, remained free.

Jane thought Tolstoy was "more logical" than life warranted. Though his writings moved her deeply, she could not avoid feeling that he was something of a crank. In any case, Tolstoy's philosophy of nonresistance made no sense on Halsted Street, where the problems were overwhelming, and where Jane found herself drawn once again on her return into battle with Johnny Powers.

THE TROUBLE heated up in 1898 over Amanda Johnson, who had taken over from Jane the job of 19th Ward garbage inspector, and had dutifully carried out the work ever since. In January, Powers sent a letter to the Civil Service Commission demanding Johnson's removal, since the garbage-inspector post recently had been made a civil-service position. Powers charged that Amanda (who had taken the civil-service exam and passed at the top of the list) was using her position for improper "electioneering," that she had been making a house-to-house canvass of the neighborhood, advising people to vote against him in the upcoming April election. "Of course . . . the charges are false," Jane told a reporter. "It is a political move on the part of Mr. Powers, who never could stand the idea of having a woman hold a political job in what he is pleased to call his territory."

The Civil Service Commission found Amanda innocent of the electioneering charge. But soon after, ostensibly as a cost-cutting measure, the city council's finance committee, of which Powers was chairman, voted to fold the Bureau of Street and Alley Cleaning, which employed Amanda, into the larger Department of Streets. The shuffling put Amanda out of her job, while preserving the garbage-inspecting job of a Bohemian saloon keeper who was a friend of Powers's.

As the date of the April election approached, Jane once again mobilized forces to fight Powers, guiding the 19th Ward Improvement Club in its search for a candidate to run as an independent. The club finally settled on Simeon Armstrong, an Irish-Catholic former laborer and store clerk who'd struggled through night school to become a lawyer. Jane helped persuade the ward's Republican organization to endorse Armstrong so as not to divide the opposition vote. Then she imported a University of Chicago economics professor, William Hill, to make a study of the voters of the ward and to run Armstrong's campaign. She also organized her friends to go after the various ethnic voters. Signor Mastro-Valerio, the former editor of *L'Italia,* came in from Alabama, where he and his wife had started a farming commune, to campaign among the Italians. Mary Kenney, who was living in New York with her husband Jack O'Sullivan, a former seaman and labor organizer, moved into Hull-House for a few weeks to help win over the Irish-Catholics. Other residents worked until midnight every night addressing envelopes and stuffing them with Armstrong's campaign literature. Jane gave speeches and, on many days, "sallied forth" to raise money for Armstrong's campaign, shivering against the lake winds as she waited for streetcars, and returning late in the day, her skirts muddy and her handbag full of checks.

Jane recognized that Powers would be hard to unseat. In a speech to the Ethical Culture Society in January, which was later published in the prestigious *International Journal of Ethics,* she attacked Powers (without naming him) and astutely analyzed his hold over the 19th Ward. To the 19th Ward's poor, unsophisticated voters, Jane explained, Powers embodied the promise of the New World. He had arrived in America with nothing and within a few, short years had become rich and powerful. His constituents did not consider him corrupt. The Irish, in particular, she said, "through long custom at home, had come to look upon those who govern as rackrent landlords [those who demand the highest rents], and many had come to this country not only desiring to feed at the public crib but considering it perfectly legitimate to do so."

But the alderman's greatest power, she noted, was in being "a friendly neighbor"—in bailing constituents out of jail, providing jobs (at one time Powers boasted that he had 2,600 people in his ward on the public payroll, a third of all voters), paying for funerals, distributing turkeys at Christmas.

"Indeed, what headway can the notion of civic purity, of honesty of administration make against this big manifestation of human friendliness, this stalking survival of village kindness?" she asked. "The notions of the civic reformer are negative and impotent before it. They give themselves over largely to criticisms of the present state of affairs, to writing and talking of what the future may be, but their goodness is not dramatic, it is not even concrete and human."

As Allen F. Davis noted, the speech was one of the first attempts to explain the source of boss power, and it put Jane in the national spotlight. Jane repeated the speech several times in Chicago and once in Michigan, and it was widely excerpted in newspapers and magazines across the country.

Despite Jane's astute analysis of Powers's influence, Professor Hill's analysis gave Armstrong a good chance to win. Of the ward's approximately 10,000 voters, 2,500 were Irish, 1,000 were German, 3,000 were Jews, and 2,000 were Italians. Native Americans, Bohemians, and French made up the rest. Hill estimated that Armstrong would capture all 3,500 of the ward's Republican votes (divided among the various ethnic groups) and most of the Italian vote, and that he would split the 2,500 Irish votes that usually went to Powers. That combination alone would be enough to elect Armstrong, but Hill also counted on 1,000 additional votes from the Bohemians, the Jews, and the Germans.

But Powers, as Allen F. Davis noted, was not about to risk defeat, particularly since he was expecting a large payoff. The corrupt traction king, Charles Yerkes, was planning to ask the city council for an ordinance extending his street railway franchise for fifty years. Yerkes had offered Powers a substantial bribe to ensure that the council cooperated. But first Powers had to be reelected.

Powers realized he was in a ferocious battle, and he fought back. By now, he had long abandoned any notion of trying to win over the spirited do-gooders of Halsted Street, and he vowed to drive Jane Addams and Hull-House from the ward. "A year from now there will be no such institution!" he thundered at a reporter from the *Chicago Record,* adding that Jane was obviously jealous of his charities. He unsuccessfully tried to have the ward redistricted by cutting off the eastern, predominantly Italian end, where he faced his greatest opposition. Also, he gave his blessing to a ladies' auxiliary, which was instructed to publicly criticize the work of the Hull-House women. His heelers smashed the windows of shops displaying Armstrong's picture and broke up meetings in labor halls where political leaders stumped for Armstrong. He even bought up a batch of abandoned cottages and installed regiments of tramps to register to vote.

Jane paid a group of detectives to investigate the fraud, but "it is so hard to prove anything with everybody corrupt," she wrote Mary Smith, who was in Baltimore with her mother.

Jane was spending more money than she'd planned. Hull-House supporter Lydia Ward Coonley had given her $137, and she was trying hard not to use the $100 Mary had sent for some other expense, but she wasn't sure she could hold out. Jane was cheered when $1,000 came in from the editor of *The Railway Age,* a trade journal.

Meanwhile, Mary O'Sullivan was making headway with the Catholics. Four months pregnant and wearing an old dress of Mary Smith's, she spent long hours talking to the most powerful Jesuit priests in the ward. The priests for the most part supported Powers, and O'Sullivan discovered that their opposition to the Hull-House candidate sprung in part from jealousy of the success of Hull-House. They also had a sense of obligation to Powers, who routinely fed the churches' coffers. Still, the priests seemed to be responding to O'Sullivan's entreaties.

"For the first time I am beginning to have a little real hope," Jane wrote Mary on March 20. But she was exhausted. As today, paying to run a successful campaign could be hugely expensive and required constant hat-in-hand begging, which Jane found discomfiting. Her relentless schedule also included fund-raising for Hull-House, overseeing all the settlement's programs and building projects, plus speaking engagements. On top of that, she was wounded by the relentless criticism Armstrong and the reformers received throughout the campaign from *The Chicago Chronicle,* a newspaper with streetcar interests. The *Chronicle* knew how to play to the lingering prejudices against do-gooders, huffing that the reformers "profess to give psychological account of the people of the ward, as though they were . . . a species apart, to be looked upon with patronizing pity."

The morning mail also brought virulent attacks, most of them from men. One of the most obscene, signed "A Voter," arrived in the middle of January: "Did it ever occur to you while on a tour of inspection [of] such places where low depraved men with criminal records may be found . . . you might for a small sum induce one of such men to sell you his pecker and balls . . . You would then have the privilege of casting a vote. . . . Until you can do this you are a dead one."

BONE-TIRED and facing ugly personal attacks, Jane missed Mary terribly. "Dearest, I love you more than I ever did for in the midst of this horrible election and all the rest of it I find myself depending upon your moral fiber as never before," she wrote Mary in March. She'd commissioned an artist, Alice Kellog Tyler, to paint Mary's portrait, and one night at ten-thirty after collecting campaign funds all day, Jane slipped into the Hull-House art studio to gaze at the picture. Jane found Mary's youth and beauty to be in sharp contrast to the dirty business of campaign financing. "I almost sent back the money you looked so good & true," she told Mary.

On the Thursday before the Tuesday election, the entire settlement worked until midnight on campaign literature. Sitting at the dining room tables with the voter registration lists spread out before them, they addressed envelopes and folded flyers for twelve thousand households. The only break came when a few of the women escaped to see Frau Sorma portray Nora in Ibsen's new play, *A Doll's House,* at a theater downtown.

One evening a few nights later, Powers staged a parade in the neighborhood. It was the alderman's "last supreme effort," Alice Hamilton told her cousin, "and was very imposing indeed." As the parade marched down Polk Street and turned north onto Halsted, the women of Hull-House rushed outdoors to watch. The Jesuit Church's Boy's Temperance Band, resplendent in their new uniforms, paid for by Powers, led the way, followed by the Cook County Democrats dressed in cutaways and silk top hats and carrying canes. Then came a gaggle of carriages and a crowd on foot, some small boys among them shouting "Down with Hull-House" and others carrying banners reading "No Petticoat Government for Us!" A group of Hull-House men shielded Jane from the hecklers and blocked her view of a large placard depicting on one side Professor Hill dangling Simeon Armstrong from a string, and on the other, Jane tearing out Signor Mastro-Valerio's hair.

Election Day, Tuesday, April 5, was cold and sunny. Despite Mayor Swift's assurance that extra police would be on hand to enforce the peace, "everything is as bad as bad can be," Jane wrote Mary. "The saloons are all open." By midmorning a man had been arrested for drawing a gun at the polling place for the Hull-House neighborhood. Hill himself was struck in the face by a Powers supporter at another polling place. A policeman arrested the culprit, who managed to escape on the way to the Maxwell Street station house.

When it was all over, Powers had won easily, swelling his majority from the last election to nearly 80 percent of the vote. He lost only one of thirty-three precincts, the 17th, home of the largest number of Italians. No doubt, the vote was the result of substantial fraud, but Jane could not prove anything, despite her expensive detectives.

On the morning after the election, Jane called at 14 Walton Place, Mary's home. Mary was still in Baltimore, but Jane chatted with Mary's father about ward politics and Hull-House business. She felt so blue when she got back to Halsted Street that she slipped up to the art studio to retrieve Mary's portrait. She placed the unfinished picture over the mantel in her bedroom, where it would be the last thing she'd see in the evening and the first thing in the morning. It gave her, she reported to Mary, "a perplexing comfort."

PART III

Angel of the World

13

Spreading the Social Gospel

Jane, *second from right,* with unidentified friends in her apartment at Hull-House.
(Courtesy of University of Illinois at Chicago, the University Library, Jane Addams Memorial Collection)

After the 1898 election, Jane decided not to battle Powers again. Like many masterful people, she was uninterested in pursuits she couldn't control, and she knew that, as a woman without a vote, she could never hope to dominate ward politics. (Powers would remain in office for another twenty-four years, until his retirement in 1922.) What's more, Jane's five-year battle with the ward boss had convinced her that life on Halsted Street would never improve without larger, citywide and national reforms. She was developing a broad vision of the roots of poverty as sprouting from deep injustice at the core of American life, and she used her pen to push her ideas into the national spotlight.

As a new century dawned, she began producing a steady flow of magazine and journal articles on a wide array of subjects—children, unions, workers' rights, juvenile delinquency, political reform, education, militarism. Her literary ambitions had been sparked in part by the publication three years earlier, in 1895, of *Hull-House Maps and Papers.* But that had been a joint effort; now she was writing on her own. Jane's articles for *The Atlantic Monthly, Outlook, The American Journal of Sociology,* and other prestigious journals—at the time the only national media—turned her into a celebrity. She began traveling a great deal and spending less time at Hull-House. In many ways, the farther she got from Chicago, as historian Paul Green says, "the more successful she became." Hundreds of stories were written about her (Mary Smith paid for a clipping service to chart the publicity); parties and receptions were given in her honor whenever she traveled; she enjoyed easy access to important people. In July 1899, for example, she had no trouble getting an appointment with President William McKinley at the White House to see what he could do about finding a position for Florence Kelley, who lost her job as state factory inspector when Governor Altgeld left office. (Kelley took a job as the general secretary of the newly formed National Consumers League in New York.)

Jane's growing stature attracted visitors to Hull-House from around the world. The roster included John Burns, the British labor leader; Prince Petr Kropotkin, the Russian anarchist; Aylmer Maude, Tolstoy's translator; James Ramsay MacDonald, the first Labour prime minister of England; and the flamboyant Queen Marie of Rumania, who arrived one day wearing a floor-length fur and a rope of marble-sized pearls. Theodore Roosevelt, who was then as well known for his big-game hunting as for his political roles, came many times. During one visit, he was mobbed by a group of children who shouted, "Tell us what things you've killed!"

Jane began to receive extravagant adulation—flowery expressions of her virtue and spirit that echo, in their way, the lavish compliments of her Rockford classmates twenty years earlier. Her papers are filled with adoring letters, such as one written by Lillian Wald, head of New York's Henry Street Settlement, after a visit from Jane in 1898. "One small group has a deeper desire than ever to press its service into and for a fairer society for having touched you," Wald wrote. "Know that we want to be *good* and like children look up to you for guidance."

Sidney and Beatrice Webb, leaders of England's Fabian Socialist movement, stayed at Hull-House for a few days during their 1898 American tour. "Miss Jane Addams . . . is without doubt a remarkable woman, an interesting combination of the organizer, the enthusiast and the subtle observer of human characteristics," Webb wrote in her diary. "She has a charming personality, gentle and dignified, shrewdly observant: above all she excels in persistency of purpose and unflinching courage. She has made Hull-House; and it is she who has created whatever spirit of reform exists in Chicago." Halsted Street's unspeakable squalor, the choking summer heat, and the settlement's chaotic activity, lack of privacy, and unappetizing food (served "higgledepiggledy," the proper Englishwoman noted) made the Webbs' visit "seem like one long bad dream lightened now and again by Miss Addams' charming grey eyes and gentle voice and graphic power of expression."

These qualities made Jane a dazzling success as a speaker, and she spent a great deal of time crisscrossing the country on lecture trips. Louise Bowen often accompanied Jane to out-of-town lectures. In her memoirs, Bowen provides some of the few intimate glimpses of Jane apart from her public persona. The first time the two women shared a room, Mrs. Bowen recalled, Jane "went into the closet, which was unlighted, disrobed, went into the bathroom and took her bath, came out and got into bed. . . . In the morning Miss Addams got up first, shut herself in the unlighted closet and emerged fully dressed, with her hair neatly arranged, in spite of no light."

Another time, when Mrs. Bowen and Jane stood crammed against each other in a packed hotel lobby, the hooks of Jane's black dress got caught on the front of Mrs. Bowen's white dress, and, as Jane pulled away to enter the auditorium, she took the entire front panel of Mrs. Bowen's garment with her. As she stepped to the podium, Jane was unaware that a large piece of cloth was hanging on her back.

Her appearance rarely concerned her. As she approached her fortieth birthday, she'd begun to put on weight and wear wire-rimmed reading glasses. With her graying brown hair parted in the middle and pulled into a bun at the back of her head—the same hairstyle she'd had since college—her sensible shoes, and conservative, well-made dresses, she was the very picture of the Victorian spinster. Peering at her audience with those gentle gray eyes, Jane spoke in a low, strong voice with the clipped tones of an upper-class woman.

In March 1899, after an exhausting, two-week, seven-city lecture tour, Jane met Mary Smith and Eleanor Smith, the Hull-House music teacher, in Columbia, South Carolina, for a brief vacation. She read, slept, and relaxed in the sunshine on the patio of their rented house. She wrote Julia Lathrop that she was "not in the least tired . . . but in the best of spirits. The two good Smiths met me at the train, and we have been having a jolly visit ever since."

Mary felt extraordinarily protective of Eleanor Smith, chiefly, according to Mary's niece Ann Fischbeck, because Mary felt sorry for her. Eleanor Smith, Mrs. Fischbeck says, was "probably the ugliest woman I ever met. She had a full mustache and protruding teeth and a great deep voice. She had wire glasses, and wore her hair in a bun on top of her head." As a result, "Mary sort of adopted her," Mrs. Fischbeck says. She let Eleanor stay for long stretches at the Smiths' Walton Place house, where she had her own room, as Jane did. She took Eleanor on trips and gave her spending money. Mary's great passion "was the underdog," added Mrs. Fischbeck. "She liked to give herself to people who showed they were needy."

At thirty and eight years younger than Jane, Mary was still searching for a purpose in life, as Jane had been in her twenties. At one point, Mary considered adopting the baby daughter of an impoverished Hull-House neighbor (like many immigrants in the

Halsted Street area, the woman had named her child Jane); for a while, she thought about going to college. But Mary was hindered by family claims—her mother was a semi-invalid, who expected Mary to be her companion in Chicago and on long trips abroad. Her father, too, was unwell, as was an aunt who lived with the family. It fell to Mary to take care of them all. The effort, along with worry about her future, wore her out—a situation that was painfully similar to Jane's troubles when she lived with her stepmother in Baltimore. In a letter on July 22, 1897, during one of their many separations, Jane implored Mary to resist her family's demands, to stop drifting and take her advice:

> Darling,
> I suppose that one of the hardest things one has to learn in life is that one's experiences (even the bitterest ones) are of no use to anyone else. But I do find it hard that you insist upon repeating the self same mistakes I made over and over again until I caught a clue at H[ull]-H[ouse]. The medical college, the summer I did all the housework at Cedarville, my sheep farming, my studying languages and "art" in Europe, my drawing lessons in Baltimore to use my hands, would really seem less bitter to me to remember if I felt they had been of use to the person I love best. I really don't think you ought to put aside all my experience as of no avail . . . if you would just let me guide you and love you and cooperate with you I know I could be of use.

Soon after she wrote those words, Jane helped Mary secure a residency at Lillian Wald's Henry Street Settlement in New York. Mary's "physician thinks the change will do her good," as Florence Kelley noted. Mary left in September 1898. After a month in New York, she returned to Chicago briefly, and then spent the next seven months traveling with her mother. Jane would see little of her for more than a year.

Meanwhile, a new resident arrived who reminded Jane of some of the problems she'd had in her youth. Charlotte Perkins Stetson was a well-known writer on women's rights and a scandalous figure for having divorced her husband and given up her child. Charlotte had grown up in Connecticut and, on her father's side, was descended from a famous American dynasty, the Beechers. Her great-grandfather was the evangelist Lyman Beecher, and her aunts were Harriet Beecher Stowe, author of *Uncle Tom's Cabin,* Isabella Beecher Hooker, the prominent suffragist, and Catherine Beecher, an educator. At twenty-four, Charlotte had married a handsome artist, Walter Stetson. But after the birth of her daughter the following year, she had a breakdown. She was treated by Jane's former doctor, S. Weir Mitchell, but instead of returning to her family, as Mitchell had advised, she'd abandoned them. (Her daughter was raised by her husband's second wife.)

Charlotte (who would be known as Charlotte Gilman after her 1900 marriage to her cousin Houghton Gilman) spent three months at Hull-House in 1895, and, like virtually every other resident, became enthralled with Jane, whom she described as "one of the noblest, wisest, strongest, sweetest women in the world." Jane, however, did not entirely approve of Charlotte. As she told Mary Smith, she found the young divorcée "very interesting, but my opinion of her is as yet much mixed." (She didn't elaborate.) Still, Jane recommended Charlotte to be head of a new North Side settlement, Unity Settlement (later renamed the Eli Bates House). But Charlotte declined the offer, and spent the next couple of years traveling around the country, speaking and writing. She returned to Hull-House in 1898 having just published a groundbreaking book, *Women and Economics,* in which she called for an end to women's financial dependence on men and advocated cooperative housekeeping units that would allow women to pursue careers outside the home. Jane thought the book a "good piece of work" and lent one of Hull-House's two copies to Mary Smith.

THOUGH she had pushed Mary to go to New York, Jane was bereft without her. "You must never go off in this dutiful manner and desert Mr. Micawber again. Mr. Micawber does not stand it sufficiently well," Florence Kelley wrote Mary, likening Jane to the well-meaning but improvident comic character from Dickens's *David Copperfield.* Florence and others in Jane's intimate circle acknowledged that she and Mary were extremely close, but Jane was not eager to advertise it publicly.

For the first time, romantic friendship, which had provided an acceptable alternative to matrimony for several generations of women, was starting to become suspect. In the second half of the nineteenth century, several European sexologists identified a "third sex," which they said was characterized by a neurotic desire to reject society's accepted sexual roles and by an emotion which they called "inverted." In 1869 a German study claimed to find that "inversion" among men and women was a hereditary abnormality. Dr. Richard von Krafft-Ebing's 1892 *Psychopathia Sexualis,* a study of sexuality, pointed out that women who loved women were in fact homosexual, a "condition" that was due to "cerebral abnormalities," which were signs of "an inherited diseased condition of the central nervous system."

Though it wasn't until after World War I that the general public became aware of the sexologists' theories, it's likely that Jane, as a worldly ex–medical student, *was* aware of their writings. The knowledge may have led her to question her relationship with Mary and probably fed her doubts about her femininity. For years, Jane had been extremely uncomfortable about her interest in and talent for running things—the sorts of executive impulses that in the 1880s she could only conceive of as indicative of a masculine drive. The adulation showered on her by other women, though she was bolstered by it, also embarrassed her. Louise Bowen once saw her sitting on the windowsill at the foot of the main stairs of Hull-House, while a woman was leaning over her with both hands clasped around Jane's foot. "If you won't let me hold your hand, do let me hold your foot," the woman pleaded. Jane was appalled.

It's possible that Jane tried to distance herself from Mary because of her strong feelings for her; perhaps she worried that the relationship would be misconstrued; perhaps she felt guilty about the relationship and wanted to cover it up. Or perhaps she thought

Mary, who was sickly and self-denying, would be better off living a "normal life," married to a man. Jane once wrote of love leading to marriage as "the highest gift which life can offer to a woman." Toward the end of her own life, she explained why she and most of her friends had been denied this "gift": "For a considerable period after the door of opportunity began to be slowly opened to woman, she was practically faced with an alternative of marriage or a career," Jane wrote. "She could not have both apparently for two reasons. Men did not at first want to marry women of the new type, and women could not fulfill the two functions of profession and homemaking until modern invention had made a new type of housekeeping practicable, and perhaps one should add, until public opinion tolerated the double role."

There's no evidence, however, that Jane ever was romantically interested in a man. Reading through her letters, one gets the sense not that she sacrificed the "gift" of marriage for her work, but that her work saved her from becoming a bored spinster—a role that threatened to consume Mary Smith.

There's evidence, though sketchy, that Mary *had* considered marriage. One of her nieces says she inherited an engagement ring—gold, with a mid-sized diamond—that was given to Mary by a man she agreed to marry, but who was killed, perhaps fighting with the Illinois militia during the Spanish-American War. The man's identity is unknown, and Mary never mentioned him in her surviving correspondence.

Whatever Jane's motives, at about the same time Mary was moving to the Henry Street Settlement, Jane pushed her to become involved with Robert A. Woods, head of South End House, a Boston settlement. It's hard to understand why Jane thought Woods would be a good match for Mary. Though he had "the highest ideals and very clear, rational convictions," as Alice Hamilton noted, he was stern and austere and completely lacked the charm and playfulness that made Mary so attractive. "Mr. Woods . . . has no warmth, no human impulsiveness," Alice Hamilton complained.

But to Jane, who did not see men as romantic objects, Woods seemed like a good choice. Unlike her brother-in-law Harry, he didn't drink or chase women. Unlike her stepbrother George and her brother Weber, he wasn't mentally disturbed. Woods might have been stiff and dull, but at least he was reliable. What's more, he was prominent in the settlement movement. Though Mary would move to Boston if she married Woods, she would remain in the family of progressive reformers, and, presumably, she and Jane would have many opportunities to see each other.

Woods apparently became smitten with Mary when he first met her in Chicago several years before, and his interest in her was renewed when he saw her in Europe during the summer. Jane's surviving correspondence strongly hints that Woods confided to her his feelings for Mary and that he enlisted Jane's help in winning Mary's affection. "Bro[ther] Woods letters have been so ardent in regard to you," she told Mary, that she had "cherished a dream" that Mary would marry him. She urged Mary not to be "too frigid" to Woods. "Please don't be an iceberg nor a tombstone when the siege begins," she wrote.

It's especially puzzling that Jane would push Mary away at this time, when she was in need of warm friendship. Florence Kelley would soon leave Chicago to take up her duties at the National Consumers League in New York; Louise Bowen had a husband and children to look after; and Ellen Starr was becoming increasingly preoccupied with religion and a new passion—bookbinding.

In the spring of 1897, Ellen left Hull-House to move to London for fifteen months to study with the master craftsman T. J. Cobden-Sanderson at the prestigious Doves Press Bindery. When she returned to Chicago, she set up a bookbindery on the second floor of her duplex apartment at Hull-House, which was paid for by Mrs. Wilmarth, the widow of a man who had made a fortune in lighting fixtures and real estate.

The first floor had a living room, a bedroom, and a small kitchen. It was furnished with cast-off pieces from Mrs. Wilmarth's North Shore house and decorated with framed prints and William Morris wallpaper. A crucifix had pride of place on one wall of the living room, and a prie-dieu held candles, which Ellen lit every evening.

On the second floor was Ellen's bindery press and worktables piled high with imported European leathers. Few people in the neighborhood were interested in learning bookbinding, and after a while the classes Ellen had organized on her return from London stopped. From then on, she devoted herself to making books, working much of the day in her bindery. One of the first books she bound was a copy of Sappho's verses (popular among feminists at the time), a gift to her cousin Mary Allen. Though Ellen sold a few volumes, she couldn't make a living from her art, and Mrs. Wilmarth supported her with a monthly allowance.

Ellen's interest in bookbinding flowed from her devotion to the Arts and Crafts movement and the ideas of John Ruskin and William Morris. Yet other factors also might have been at work in her decision to distance herself from the daily routine at Hull-House. Ellen's passionate religious faith was out of step with the cool professionalism of the other residents. Alice Hamilton, for one, referred derisively to Ellen's "rosaries and prie-dieus." Jane herself occasionally expressed a mild prejudice toward Catholics—she thought they were superstitious and too devoted to hollow pageantry.

Even more disturbing to some of the Hull-House residents, however, was Ellen's volatile temperament. Alice Hamilton worried that Ellen would "act up" and embarrass her in front of visitors. Frederick Deknatel, a businessman who lived at Hull-House for a while after his wife died, "dreaded" Ellen's return from Europe in 1898. To avoid her at meals, he planned "to move down to our end of the table," Alice told her cousin. "I am so glad I am safely there already."

Ellen was aware that she could be difficult. Once, she confessed to a friend, she threw a temper tantrum that left her as yellow and acid as a lemon.

Throughout her life, Ellen insisted she wasn't jealous of Jane. But her letters hint that she resented being pushed aside at the settlement she helped found. Perhaps, as several historians have noted, she was drawn to labor protests because Jane remained ambivalent about them. Once, Ellen was arrested for disorderly conduct for picketing with striking waitresses at a Chicago restaurant. During the garment strike of 1910, she became directly involved, helping to raise money for the strikers and mobilize public support. After the strike was settled, a parade of garment workers marched up Halsted Street, passing Hull-House. "I was leaning out of my window all the time, recognizing my friends, waving to them, throwing kisses to the girls I know," Ellen told her father. "The men took off their hats to me & waved them, & cheered. It was great. I never had such an experience. They cheered the house three or four times, & Jane once, rather feebly. She said to me afterward, 'I am glad they cheered the house.' And I didn't say, 'I suppose you know why.'"

At the same time that Jane and Ellen were growing apart, Jane was becoming estranged from her family. Relations with her stepmother were particularly strained. Ann Addams blamed Jane for her son George's deteriorating mental health. Had Jane married George, Ann reasoned, she could have saved him from his crippling isolation. By the late 1890s, he'd given up all hope of a career and spent most of his time brooding in his bedroom at the Cedarville homestead, a tall, big-boned man who refused to bathe or cut his hair, which tumbled around his shoulders from a shiny bald pate. Sometimes, George wouldn't speak for days. On Christmas Eve, 1895, Ann reported to her son Harry that "George was down to dinner. He looked at all the gifts. But after dinner, he retired to bed. He does that almost every day. Some days he does not come down at all." A month later, she wrote, "Think George is feeling better but he says never a word." And in another letter, she noted, "George does not get strong. The least exertion and he gets so very tired." Occasionally, though, George would show flashes of enthusiasm for music and chess and, sometimes, a mordant wit. Once, staring at the homestead barn that had been built the year the alcoholic Harry had been born, George said, "Eighteen forty-eight—the birth of the stable and the unstable."

Worry over George was affecting Ann's health. She told Harry in 1899, "Sometimes I nearly go wild I can not eat or sleep. My power to resist depressing emotions is growing daily less. I have not one person who can give me any comfort or solace."

George did not blame Jane for his problems, and he "held frequent arguments on this point with his mother, who . . . nourished for years a strong bitterness," Marcet Haldeman recalled. "No doubt, as Aunt Jane's life broadened, an unadmitted jealousy mingled in my grandmother's attitude as she reflected on the great things her son, with his extraordinarily fine and scholarly mind, would have accomplished had it not been for this disaster."

George never criticized Jane, and, indeed, always was eager to hear news of her. When his mother spoke harshly of Jane, George would shake his head and say softly, "Now, now." Jane no longer corresponded with George, though she was saddened by his condition. She might have been willing to visit him, but that would have meant seeing Ann, whom she wanted to avoid.

On her frequent train trips to Cedarville to visit her brother Weber's family, Jane would often take the horse-drawn stage from the Red Oak station, passing the little cemetery where her parents and siblings were buried, and the house where she'd grown up. With Ann and George living there, she didn't set foot inside it for years. Whenever she was in town, she stayed with Weber.

The bitterness between Jane and Ann emanated from both women. Jane was angry that her stepmother refused to give money to Hull-House. She felt that had her father lived, he would have helped her. Ann sent Jane $10 to buy some silver spoons during Jane's first Christmas on Halsted Street, and she visited Hull-House once, in 1893, while she was in Chicago for the World Columbian Exposition. Soon after, however, they stopped speaking. Jane could not bring herself even to mention Ann's name, and referred to her sourly as "Harry's mother."

Alice and Harry Haldeman found themselves drawn into the conflict. Harry, who thought Jane's work sentimental and futile, sided with his mother. Alice, however, was loyal to Jane and in sympathy stopped speaking to Ann as well.

The older woman, meanwhile, seized on every bit of gossip to confirm the worst about her stepdaughters. "Laura and Esther [Linn, Mary Linn's daughter] were here for a short call today," Ann wrote Harry. "Laura said they had not heard a word from Jane or Alice since they left—tis a pity the lack of courtesy they exhibit and still [call themselves] refined. No matter—there is so marked a want of refinement in such treatment of others—that one has to credit it to lack of breeding."

The family relations grew more complicated still. Though united in their resentment toward their stepmother, Jane and Alice frequently bickered. After moving to Kansas in 1884, Alice, who had worked as her husband Harry's nurse and anesthesiologist, devoted herself to community service, and in 1895 she was elected president of the Girard board of education. Chiefly, Jane and Alice fought over questions about their sister Mary Linn's estate. Jane thought Alice should share more of the expenses and spend more time with Mary's children. Alice, who was envious of Jane's independence and fame, complained that Jane was neglecting her. Also, she seems to have been jealous of Jane's close relationships with the Hull-House women. "What is in your mind and why are your letters so reproachful?" Jane asked Alice at one point. "I cannot imagine why you would say 'that I fear the children and finances are cutting you off from your natural sister.' Why do you feel cut off? It seems to me that I deserve an explanation." And on another occasion, "I have many faults, but I am sure I am not snobbish and so it is always hard for me to comprehend why you imagine me sensitive about my relatives. I was really a little hurt by your first letter when you said you took pains *not* to say you were my sister."

Still, Jane remained devoted to Alice, shopping for her, buying her presents, trying to adjust her schedule so they could spend holidays together. When Alice discovered in 1898 that Harry was having an affair, Jane shared her outrage and invited Alice and Marcet, then eleven, to spend the summer with her at Hull-House, an offer Alice eagerly accepted.

Though Jane enjoyed their company, she was distracted by Hull-House affairs, and she didn't pay much attention to Marcet, who thought her aunt "hard and cruel." One of Mary Smith's nieces, Ann Fischbeck, also thought Jane cold. Mrs. Fischbeck says when she was a child, "Miss Addams was always [polite] to us," but she never showed much interest in Mrs. Fischbeck and her siblings.

Besides her sister Mary Linn's children, to whom she had always been close, Jane did not have emotional relationships with individual children. Her natural reserve and preoccupation with work led her to hold herself aloof from most of the children (also most of the adults) she met, even those who frequented Hull-House. At the same time, she remained passionately interested in *theories* about childhood and education.

"Child study" had become a fashionable pursuit for doctors, educators, psychologists, and settlement workers. Throughout most of history, children were thought to be miniature adults, who were born into the world with fixed natures. But the nineteenth-century writings of Friedrich Froebel (the German educator who sparked the kindergarten movement) and psychologist G. Stanley Hall suggested that childhood was a special time and that children's development depended as much on environmental influences as heredity. The idea that a child's personality, talents, intellect, and moral character could be developed through creative play, introduction to art and music, and a good education was new—and it appealed powerfully to Jane, who had vivid memories of her own precocious childhood.

She welcomed opportunities to observe children who could help clarify her ideas. Mrs. Fischbeck recalls once when Jane visited the Smith family's vacation home in Florida: "I remember seeing Miss Addams outside talking to some little colored children, the children of the man and woman who worked for us. She wanted to know what they thought, how they lived," Mrs. Fischbeck says.

Jane believed *all* children had the capacity for goodness, and that even the most unpromising, if nurtured properly, could grow up to be useful citizens. This romantic conviction led her into the most successful battle of her early career, one that had a profound effect on American justice.

• • •

SINCE THE opening of Hull-House, Jane and her friends had been greatly disturbed by the large numbers of young people in the neighborhood who were picked up by the police for trivial offenses—stealing vegetables, throwing snowballs, riding on train cars—and thrown into the Chicago City Prison with hardened criminals. For rural children, such mischievousness would have little consequence, but for children raised in poverty in the city, the minor offenses often led to a prison term, and the exposure to real criminals often pushed the children into lives of crime.

What was needed, the women believed, was to take the children out of the adult criminal system entirely, and handle their offenses through a special court. They wanted to see children who broke the law treated by the state in the same way wise and just parents dealt with their wayward offspring.

For years, judges, lawyers, and charity workers in Chicago also had complained about the city's harsh treatment of young offenders, and as far back as 1890, there had been talk about the need for a juvenile court. In the mid-1890s, public support for the plan was fueled by a series of newspaper exposés and investigations by the Chicago Woman's Club that turned up horror after horror: children as young as ten held in jail not because they were accused of a crime, but because they were homeless or abused; children witnessing executions; children being beaten by guards.

In 1898 the various groups calling for reform joined forces. That year, Jane served on a juvenile justice committee with members of the Chicago Bar Association. After researching the issue, the group drew up legislation to establish a juvenile court. The bill passed the Illinois state legislature in February 1899 and was signed into law by Governor John R. Tanner in July.

The law tried in any number of ways to eliminate the adult system when dealing with children. In bringing a child to justice, instead of a complaint or an indictment, a petition was filed. The child was not to be arrested, but rather brought in by a guardian. The law forbade keeping children in jails where adults were confined. In court, the state's case was handled by a probation officer instead of a prosecutor, and the child was not "convicted." Instead, he or she was found to be dependent, delinquent, or truant.

THE Cook County Juvenile Court, the first of its kind in the world, opened on July 1, 1899. The court was held in one of the downtown courthouse's regular courtrooms; the first juvenile judge was Richard S. Tuthill, an eminent Chicago jurist who had fought heroically for the Union during the Civil War. Louise Bowen recalled that "the courtroom was always crowded; the air was heavy; there was almost no ventilation. Women of many nationalities filled the place, accompanied by stolid looking husbands, and many times they held the women's babies in their arms."

The court proved to be an important model for the rest of the country. By 1920 all but three states had established special courts for young offenders. The idea soon spread to Europe, where juvenile courts had been set up in several countries by World War I.

Landmark though it was, the Illinois law was in many ways woefully inadequate. It made no provision for paying probation officers, for housing or educating the children awaiting hearings, or for arranging their transportation to and from court. Jane and the other Hull-House women stepped in to raise the money for these services.

They rented a house on Adams Street, which they set up as a detention home for all youthful offenders except those charged with murder (who remained until their trials in the city jail). The children were transferred to and from court hearings in a horse-drawn wagon, also paid for by the women. In her memoirs, Louise Bowen recalled the occasional comic moments during the court's earliest days: "We had only one horse, a little fellow, and it was too much of a job for him to draw that wagon, so we tried to get the county board to buy us another. The board refused. Finally, the firemen gave us an old lame firehorse and we harnessed the two together. Well, we started out with a wagonload of children and the firehorse apparently thought we were off to a fire. He began galloping and dragged the little horse off his feet, almost strangling him. We had to revive the little horse and then take the children to court by public transportation."

One Hull-House resident, Alzina P. Stevens, was named the juvenile court's first probation officer and another, Julia Lathrop, became the chairman of the first juvenile court committee, an advocacy group for juveniles. Eventually, the settlement, which by the turn of the century had branch offices for the city unemployment office and other welfare agencies, also housed a bureau of the Juvenile Protection Association, which fought to eliminate dance halls, poolrooms, bars, and other institutions that were thought to corrupt youth.

Jane followed the cases that went through the juvenile court and incorporated many of them into her 1909 book, *The Spirit of Youth & the City Streets,* her lyrical and sensitive exploration of adolescence. But she was not on good terms with Judge Tuthill. Nor did she get along with Florence S. Scully, a highly regarded teacher who gave lessons to the boys being held in the detention home. Though the details of their conflict are unknown, apparently Jane criticized Miss Scully's job performance, and Miss Scully complained to Judge Tuthill. "It may be the Juvenile Court School was outshining Hull-House, [but] no woman was more unkind to me than the Head Lady of Hull-House," Miss Scully later wrote. "I called upon the good Judge Tuthill, and when I repeated [Jane's] accusations he brot [*sic*] his fist down on his desk sufficient to break it so it seemed and exclaimed, 'The men have long known J.A. but it is taking the women a longer time to find her out!' "

Whatever it was that upset Judge Tuthill about Jane, it wasn't repeated with most other men. The near universal admiration for Jane's integrity and commitment to the unfortunate suggests that at least part of the judge's criticism stemmed from sexism—he was uncomfortable with powerful women like Jane.

THE JUVENILE court was Jane's last major Chicago battle, and it marked the end of the first part of her career. From this point forward, she became a national figure—pushed into the spotlight during the twentieth century by her best-selling books. The first, *Democracy & Social Ethics,* wasn't published until 1902, but much of the material in it was taken directly from a series of lectures Jane gave at the University of Chicago in the summer of 1899. At the heart of the lectures is Jane's unfailing faith in the common man—a faith that is, perhaps, her greatest legacy.

In the six lectures, Jane argued that the rapid changes overtaking America called for democracy to be interpreted in a new, broader way, one that would encompass a "social ethic." She was primarily concerned with the relationship of human beings to each other.

Generally, Jane's lectures each covered a separate "relationship category"—employer and employee, housewife and domestic servant, parent and adult child, charity agent and client, politician and voter. In each case Jane argued for more democratic relations between the parties.

For example, a new understanding of the causes of poverty required a new relationship between the charity agent and his client, she said. "Formerly, when it was believed that poverty was synonymous with vice and laziness, and that the prosperous man was the righteous man, charity was administered harshly with a good conscience; for the charitable agent really blamed the individual for his poverty, and the very fact of his own superior prosperity gave him a certain consciousness of moral superiority." Now, however, poverty was understood to flow from social causes, so "the relationship between those giving aid and those in need of help should be democratic," she said.

Jane's lectures were delivered to a group of college students during a period that has many social echoes of our own day. Though the middle and upper classes were comfortable (and the top tier was astoundingly rich), a growing underclass lived in degradation, cut off from even the basics of life—education, medical care, and safe housing.

Jane argued that everyone had a right to a decent standard of living and, at the same time, an obligation to contribute to the good of the whole. Education was key. In a separate lecture on the topic, Jane argued that "not only was it the right of every man to have his full powers 'freed' by education but also that society was the loser when *any* citizen was not educated so that the moral power . . . would be available," as scholar Anne Firor Scott wrote. "It was this moral power in all human beings which . . . she identified as the engine of social change."

Underlying Jane's lectures was her deep commitment to the basic equality of all Americans. At a time when multiculturalism was not an aspiration "but a widely regretted fact," as historian Alan Ryan has noted, she argued that the country would become stronger because of the diversity and talents of immigrants from many lands—a conviction that has been resoundingly affirmed throughout the twentieth century.

JANE struggled over the lectures, spending several hours a day at a walnut desk (which Alice had given her years before) in her Hull-House office. She had a habit of cutting up the pages, rearranging the paragraphs, and then piecing them back together again with straight pins. She was working on a typewriter for the first time, and the unfamiliar machine did not make the writing easier. "My first lecture . . . almost used me up and really didn't go very well," she reported to Mary, who had left the Henry Street Settlement in New York to travel in Europe for several months with her mother and Eleanor Smith. "The second one however went off with much more spirit and I am beginning to feel the swing. I am rewriting all of them practically and quite enjoying it."

While working on her lectures, Jane still had to cope with the whirlwind of Hull-House. Some days, she reported to Mary, were "very wild." One day there was a reception for the Woman's Club in the morning, a luncheon for a poet, and an outing for a group of boys to Buffalo Bill's Wild West Show. She did not let exhaustion and a bout of "lady trouble" on another day prevent her from giving a sermon at a Methodist church and entertaining a group of women from the Colored Women of the National Council, including Mrs. Booker T. Washington. Also, she was caring for her sixteen-year-old nephew, Stanley, who was out of school for the summer, and she was sitting for a new portrait by the artist Carl Lindon. She managed to find time, however, to bicycle along the lakefront with Helen Culver, now a spry sixty-nine. A group of Hull-House residents, led by Alice Hamilton, had taken up the sport and even bought bicycles. The hopelessly unathletic Jane, however, could manage only a tandem, and on one excursion relied on her partner, the twenty-something Gerard Swope, a resident who went on to become president of General Electric, to do most of the "spinning." Jane also made frequent trips to Winnetka, where the Smith family had a weekend home, to visit Mary's father, assuring him that it wasn't because she was trying to wrest more donations from him, but "because I much enjoy it."

Financially, and in every other way, Hull-House was thriving. Jane's building fund was up $6,515, and she was within $1,800 of raising the money she needed to complete a handsome wood-paneled coffee house with a theater above it. The Hull-House summer school in Rockford was full; a crowded schedule of adult and children's programs was in place in Chicago.

In the afternoons, children filled the settlement courtyard every day. "I went through the yard one day when it was full of Murphyes," Jane reported to Mary at the end of August. "In an attempt to avoid stepping upon Maud Cecelia and the hoop of Francis, I plunged into the hoop of Ruth. She looked up with a very large frown and said most ferociously, 'I wish that you would keep out of this yard.'" Jane was thrilled with the nearby playground, the first in Chicago, where "the willows wave in the breeze, likewise the clover, the children under gentle Mrs. Sly play in the sand, build block houses and the Mothers sit in the shelter and sew—quite like a storybook."

Other moments, however, were less than idyllic. On August 22, 1899, Jane wrote Mary that she was having "a devilish time over a strike connected with the new building. I have been trying to arbitrate between two sets of men who are dying to shoot each other and I am feeling very foolish and ineffective."

She was more effective with another troublesome man, a Western Electric worker who had impregnated a young girl from New Orleans. The girl had traveled to Chicago to find her lover and wandered into Hull-House one day. The settlement women contacted his employers and arranged for a wedding in the Hull-House parlor. It was not a happy event. As Jane reported to Mary, "The little bride sobbed throughout the ceremony in the most piteous way and would not look at the groom nor the white roses which he tried in vain to give her."

For a young mother at the end of the nineteenth century, a miserable marriage was better than no marriage at all. Indeed, it was difficult for *any* woman to live outside respectable convention. Perhaps that's why Jane urged Mary to consider marrying Robert Woods.

Yet, even as she was pushing Mary away, Jane yearned for her friend, whom she hadn't seen in three months, while Mary was traveling in Europe. Jane wrote Mary that when her train arrived in Chicago it would be "a little greedy" to go directly with her to her home in Winnetka, where her father was waiting, and that she would be "noble" and "wait for a later train."

Still, she was on the platform at the end of September, when Mary's train sputtered into the LaSalle Street station. The doors parted and people spilled from the cars. Jane saw Mary's hair—a flash of gold above the crowd—and then Mary's blurred form came into focus, tall and slender in a long, high-collared dress. A moment later they were standing side by side under the train shed's high dome. There was no more talk about Mary marrying Robert Woods or any other man.

Epilogue

Hull-House as it looked at the turn of the century.
(Courtesy University of Illinois at Chicago, the University Library, Jane Addams Memorial Collection)

With a flag-waving, foot-stomping crowd cheering her on, Jane Addams stood at the podium of the Chicago Coliseum on August 7, 1912, to second the nomination of Theodore Roosevelt for president on the Progressive party ticket. Roosevelt, who had already served two terms as a Republican president, from 1901 to 1909, was staging a comeback, running on a platform calling for the abolition of child labor, an eight-hour, six-day workweek for adults, housing reform, and the vote for women—"all the things I have been fighting for, for more than a decade," as Jane put it. It was the first time a woman had seconded a presidential nomination, and Roosevelt had chosen her for the job with good reason—Jane was probably the most revered woman in the world.

In the dozen or so years since the founding of the juvenile court, Jane spent a great deal of time away from Hull-House. Living primarily with Mary Smith in the Smiths' Walton Place house, Jane's focus had turned to national and even global issues. Her fame had spread mainly by the force of her pen—her best-selling books and dozens of magazine articles. To a modern ear, much of her writing seems anachronistic, partly because we take for granted the progressive causes, which were fresh and innovative in her time. However, two of her works, *Twenty Years at Hull-House,* her 1910 autobiography, and *The Spirit of Youth & the City Streets,* a discussion of the problems of inner-city youth published in 1909, speak very directly to readers today. *Twenty Years* derives a lasting power from the force of Jane's conviction that settlement work was the salvation for herself and the poor. *Spirit,* her favorite of her books, still resonates with Jane's lyrical meditation on being young.

Soon after the Progressive convention, Jane joined Roosevelt's campaign, sleeping on trains every night and delivering speeches all day as she crisscrossed the country. Wherever she went she was greeted by groups of female Roosevelt supporters who'd organized themselves into "Jane Addams choruses." Wearing red bandannas, the women sang at political rallies from *The Jane Addams Songbook,* which included such tunes as "Roosevelt Oh Roosevelt" and the hymn "Follow, Follow, We Will Follow Jesus."

Even after Roosevelt lost the election, Jane continued to travel the country, campaigning for women's suffrage. After the turn of the century, she had finally joined America's suffrage organization, and in 1911, she became vice president of the National American Woman Suffrage Association. She never wavered, however, from her conviction that women were profoundly different from men. Indeed, she based her support of votes for women on the grounds that women were morally superior beings, whose goodness had the power to change the world.

On April 1, 1911, Jane performed a monologue about suffrage on the stage of the Majestic, a vaudeville theater in New York. She also acted in a movie with Anna Howard Shaw, president of the National American Woman Suffrage Association. In the silent film, which was incorporated into a newsreel shown at theaters before the main feature, Jane and Anna Shaw played suffragettes who take an "anti" to the home of a widow and her two small children, who sew all night to supplement the widow's meager sweatshop wages. After observing the pitiful family, the "anti" is converted to the cause.

But Jane's enormous popularity was about to end. When war broke out in Europe in 1914, she opposed American involvement in the conflict and was elected chairman of the Women's Peace Party, an international group organized to wage a "women's war against war." While abroad in 1915 for a meeting of the organization, she toured battlefields and bombed-out villages along the front and interviewed soldiers and their families. In July, a few days after her ship docked in New York, she spoke to a large audience at Carnegie Hall. While describing her recent trip, she made an offhand remark that soldiers in every country she visited needed "stimulants," including liquor and "dope," before they could face combat.

The next day, newspapers across the country led with the story. TROOPS DRINK CRAZED, SAYS MISS ADDAMS, announced one headline. Without realizing it, she had attacked the sacred myth of the brave soldier, and the torrent of criticism heaped on her did not let up for a decade. She was vilified in the press, and ordinary citizens sent her angry letters. "My dear Miss Addams, believe me, you are an awful ass, truly awful," wrote one Chicago man. The most painful attacks, however, came from old friends. Even Teddy Roosevelt denounced her as "one of the shrieking sisterhood," "poor bleeding Jane," and "Bull Mouse."

The outrage reflected not only a national mood of superpatriotism but also America's deep ambivalence about the role she'd assumed. Many saw Jane as a foolish meddler in men's affairs. An English doctor who lectured on public health recalled, "In America in 1912 . . . it was unsafe to mention Jane Addams's name in a public speech unless you were prepared for an interruption, because the mere reference to her provoked a storm of applause. [But when I came back] after the war . . . , I realized with a shock how . . . her popularity had swiftly and completely vanished. The silence that greeted the name of Jane Addams! The few faithful who tried to applaud only made the silence more depressing."

She was deeply shaken by the hostility. It revived her girlhood depression, and she responded as she had as a young woman, by getting sick. Poor health plagued her for the rest of her life. Still, she never abandoned her pacifist position, and she continued to work for peace. In April 1919, she was elected president of the Women's International League for Peace at a meeting in Zurich, Switzerland. The league embodied Jane's continuing belief that women were the world's nurturers, that their gentleness and cooperation could be channeled to civilize aggressive men. The group passed a resolution condemning the harsh nature of President Wilson's treaty ending World War I, which called for the disarmament of only one side and enforced economic penalties on the Central Powers. Jane went to Paris to give Wilson the league's resolutions, but couldn't get an audience with the president and had to leave them with one of his advisors.

A few years later, when the Red Scare gripped the country, Jane again was cast in a malevolent light. She'd never wavered in her support of labor unions and the right of free speech for anarchists, and now she found herself denounced as a communist, "the Reddest of the Red," and "the most dangerous woman in America." She led the list of subversives on War Department spiderweb charts, which, with tangled lines resembling spiderwebs, attempted to show a giant conspiracy of pacifist, progressive, and women's organizations.

She was out of step with the mood of the country in other ways as well. Personal freedom, not moral duty, represented the new code; the flapper, not the Angel in the House, was the new feminine ideal. Jane seemed hopelessly old-fashioned, an overweight, frumpy spinster who stood on podiums talking about social justice and was appalled by the Freudian era's "astounding emphasis upon sex," as she put it.

Like many intellectuals of the day, she spent much of the 1920s abroad. In 1922 she went around the world with Mary Smith, and she traveled to Japan and the Philippines, where her popularity had never dimmed. When she was in Chicago, Jane dropped in at Hull-House, but she lived mostly on Walton Place with Mary, sleeping in the bedroom that had been kept reserved for her since the 1890s. Both women suffered serious health problems. Mary had a double mastectomy after the war; Jane had a breast removed in 1923, though her tumor turned out to be benign. Asthma continued to torment Mary; Jane suffered a tubercular kidney, and after a heart attack in 1926, she had chronic angina and bronchitis.

Every summer the friends left the city behind for a charming clapboard house in Bar Harbor, Maine. Mary owned the house, but Jane considered it *their* home, writing once to her friend, "'Our House'—it quite gives me a thrill to write the words, it was our house wasn't it in a really truly ownership." It was the first time they'd lived alone together, and the experience deepened their relationship. "Dearest," Jane wrote Mary in 1904, "you have been so heavenly good to me all these weeks. I feel as if we had come into a healing domesticity which we have never had before and, as if it were the best . . . affection had offered us."

Jane was able to relax at Bar Harbor as she couldn't anywhere else. She read, wrote letters, enjoyed the beautiful garden, and even dabbled a bit in the occult—at the time séances and Ouija boards were fashionable among feminists, who believed women had special intuitive powers. Sometimes Jane and a group of friends tried to get in touch with "spirits." They'd sit in the dark with their hands spread in front of them on a tabletop and wait for the rappings—a signal that a spirit was trying to make contact. "Oh, it's my stepmother, of course, it always is," Jane remarked wryly during one session. "Now she will be reproaching me again for not having married George."

By then, Ann, George, and nearly everyone else in the Addams-Haldeman clan were dead. Harry Haldeman had died in 1905 at fifty-seven of acute alcoholism, and George passed away at forty-eight four years later. After her husband's death, Alice Haldeman took over as president of the Girard National Bank in Kansas, a position she held until her own death from cancer in 1915. Weber, the last of Jane's siblings, died in 1918, and Ann Haldeman Addams the following year, at ninety-two.

Jane had reconciled with her stepmother long before. Over the years, Jane's feelings for Ann had softened, and she began seeing her regularly and even bringing friends to Cedarville for visits. Yet, despite the rapprochement, Jane did not mention Ann in her autobiography, published a year after George's death. Her niece Marcet was disturbed by the omission and asked Jane if it were not true "that grandmother had been a constructive force in her life—in some ways, even more than had [John Addams]." Jane answered "Yes," but added, Marcet recalled, "that it was 'all too complicated.' We two were sitting at the moment on the porch of the homestead at Cedarville and I remember yet the little breeze of emotional coolness that blew between us."

Despite chronic ill health, Jane outlived nearly all her friends. Both Florence Kelley and Julia Lathrop died in 1932. Of the early Hull-House group, Ellen Starr was one of the few who survived Jane. Ellen remained at Hull-House until 1920, when she underwent a spinal operation that left her paralyzed from the waist down. She retired to the Convent of the Holy Child in Suffern, New York, becoming a Benedictine oblate, passing her days writing long letters to friends and painting still lifes of flowers.

DURING the Great Depression, Jane's commitment to the unfortunate made her once again an admired figure, and in the last years of her life she was showered with honors and treated like a saint. But Hull-House was not the same. Many donors who were upset by Jane's pacifism and eager to support patriotic causes like the Red Cross stopped giving money to the settlement. What's more, settlement work was no longer fashionable and daring. The brilliant, ambitious young women who were the backbone of America's late-nineteenth-century settlement movement were more likely after the war to move to Paris or Greenwich Village than the inner city.

Indeed, settlements across the country were closing. But Jane had a genius for fund-raising, and with the loyal support of such wealthy friends as Louise Bowen and Mary Rozet Smith, she kept Hull-House going. Though the settlement complex of thirteen buildings is gone, Charles Hull's original mansion still stands, and is now a museum. Jane's spirit survives through the Jane Addams Hull-House Association, which, operating out of offices in downtown Chicago, serves as a refuge for battered women, destitute children, prostitutes, drug addicts, and recent immigrants.

After World War I, Hull-House was no longer the force for activism it had once been. The residents were more likely to be professional social workers than idealistic reformers. And there was a feeling of hopelessness, not hope, around Halsted Street, where the poverty and degradation had only deepened. It stood, as Edmund Wilson wrote after a visit in 1932, "with proud irrelevance . . . only a few blocks from a corner made famous by a succession of gangster murders."

In May 1931 Jane was awarded the Nobel Peace Prize, an award that seemed to her friends a long-overdue vindication of her pacifism. That month, however, she was operated on for ovarian cancer, and she was too sick to travel to Oslo to collect the prize. Her health continued to deteriorate. Severe bronchitis and angina kept her bedridden in her room at Mary Smith's house for four months in 1933. Mary, too, was suffering from bronchitis, and in February she suddenly became gravely ill with pneumonia. One afternoon, in the room across the hall from Jane's, Mary died. At that moment, Jane told her nephew, "I suppose I could have willed my heart to stop beating, and I longed to relax into doing that, but the thought of what she had been to me for so long kept me from being cowardly."

Jane lived for another year, rallying long enough to complete her last book, *My Friend, Julia Lathrop,* a memoir of the devoted

Hull-House resident. She died on May 21, 1935, following an operation for a recurrence of cancer. Hundreds of mourners filed past Jane's coffin as it lay on a bed of tulips in a Hull-House auditorium. After a funeral service in the settlement courtyard, it was taken to Cedarville to the little cemetery on the hill near her childhood home. At the gravesite, a group of village children stood in the brilliant sunshine singing "America the Beautiful." As Jane was lowered into the ground next to her parents and eight siblings, their soft, thin voices filled the air with the anthem's last refrain: "And crown thy good with brotherhood, from sea to shining sea." Few Americans have embodied that spirit more fully than Jane Addams.

Abbreviations of Frequently Cited Sources

Archival Collections

CHS	Chicago Historical Society
JAMC	Jane Addams Memorial Collection Special Collections, the University Library University of Illinois at Chicago
SCPC	Jane Addams Collection Swarthmore College Peace Collection Swarthmore, Pa.
JAPM	Jane Addams Papers Microfilm Edition University of Illinois at Chicago
HJ Papers	Haldeman-Julius Family Papers Special Collections, the University Library University of Illinois at Chicago

AH Papers	Alice Hamilton Papers Hamilton Family Papers The Arthur and Elizabeth Schlesinger Library on the History of Women in America Radcliffe College Cambridge, Ma.
FK Papers	Florence Kelley Papers Rare Book and Manuscript Library Columbia University, New York
EGS Papers	Ellen Gates Starr Papers Sophia Smith Collection Smith College, Northampton, Ma.

People

AHA	Anna Haldeman Addams
JA	Jane Addams
JHA	John Huy Addams
JWA	John Weber Addams
LB	Louise de Koven Bowen
AAH	Alice Addams Haldeman
GH	George Haldeman
HH	Harry Haldeman
AH	Alice Hamilton
FK	Florence Kelley
JL	Julia Lathrop
MAL	Mary Addams Linn
MRS	Mary Rozet Smith
EGS	Ellen Gates Starr

Books

TYAHH	*Twenty Years at Hull-House*

Note on Sources

Jane Addams's correspondence, and the correspondence of many of her associates, is extremely difficult to read; in fact, some of the sentences are virtually indecipherable. In preparing the manuscript for publication, Maree de Angury of the Jane Addams Papers Project checked my transcripts against those completed by her office. Like many people of the nineteenth century, Jane and her friends were creative spellers. In many cases, I have cleaned up the punctuation and spelling for the sake of clarity.

Endnotes

Prologue

"a failure in every sense": JA diaries, JAPM
"the problem that has no name": Friedan, *The Feminine Mystique,* p. 15
"stunting or evasion . . .": *Ibid.,* p. 76
"the subjective necessity and the objective value": Addams, *Philanthropy and Social Progress,* pp. 1–56

chapter 1 – Sarah

"Let her in . . . invented it": Linn, *Jane Addams,* p. 22
"Integrity above all else . . . the above": John Addams diaries, SCPC
"spent the afternoon . . .": *Ibid.*
"in fulfillment of their destiny . . .": *The Present Advantages and Future Prospects of the City of Freeport, Illinois,* 1857, p. 15, CHS
"You would wonder where . . .": C. Kibblehouse to "Dear Sir," Apr. 26, 1856, SCPC

"Picked potatoes . . . for a town": John Addams diaries, 1844, SCPC

"You would no doubt laugh . . .": Sarah Addams to Enos and Elizabeth Reiff, Jan. 12, 1845, Sarah Alice Haldeman Collection, The Lilly Library, Indiana University

"We moved to Cedarville . . .": *History of Stephenson County, 1970*, p. 27, CHS

"The gentle wife who decks . . .": Patmore, *The Angel in the House,* George Bell and Son, London, 1896 edition, p. 135.

"No, I won't . . .": Linn, *Jane Addams,* p. 17

"so far forgetting . . .": *Ibid.,* p. 25

"I could not endure . . .": MAL to AAH, Aug. 21, 1871, HJ Papers

"They were all . . .": Marcet Haldeman, "The Two Mothers of Jane Addams," p. 10, HJ Papers

"a very pretty cloak . . .": TYAHH, p. 13

"abominable ugly . . . egotistical": JHA to Sarah Addams, Feb. 20, 1869, SCPC

"the king gentleman of the district": Linn, *Jane Addams,* p. 21

"kiss the children . . . your time": JHA to Sarah Addams, Jan. 7, 1857, private collection

"There was a great crowd . . .": JHA to Sarah Addams, Jan. 6, 1857, private collection

"Mr. Lincoln's letters . . . pointing": TYAHH, p. 31

"They left on the ten . . .": *Freeport Bulletin,* Apr. 22, 1861

"in the harvest field . . .": Linn, *Jane Addams,* p. 18

"engraved roster of names . . .": TYAHH, pp. 23–24

"the horses going very fast . . .": MAL to AAH, Nov. 19, 1869, HJ Papers

"It was perfectly safe . . .": MAL to AAH, Oct. 15, 1868, HJ Papers

"a sudden and gory death": TYAHH, p. 9

"She walked across the yard . . .": Haldeman, "The Two Mothers of Jane Addams," pp. 6–7, HJ Papers

"Oh it was very hard . . .": George Weber to brother and sister, Jan. 17, 1863, SCPC

"chastisement . . . plain": *Ibid.*

"that mysterious injustice . . . universality": TYAHH, pp. 26–27

"Mrs. Addams was a woman . . . mourning friends": *The Freeport Journal,* Jan. 21, 1863

"the shadow of her wings": A generation later, many women still struggled with the code of Victorian womanhood. In a speech to professional women in 1931, Virginia Woolf spoke of "the Angel in the House" looking over her shoulder as she tried to write: "the shadow of her wings fell upon the page; I heard the rustling of her skirts in the room . . . I turned upon that Angel and caught her by the throat. I did my best to kill her . . . If I had not killed her, she would have killed me—as a writer."

CHAPTER 2 – ANN

"mother would have liked it": MAL to AAH, Apr. 27, 1867, HJ Papers

"Take good care . . .": MAL to AAH, Feb. 4, 1869, HJ Papers

"If you bathe . . .": *Ibid.*

"all that careful imitation . . . marks": TYAHH, p. 11–12

"horrid . . . him": TYAHH, p. 2

"he was very glad": *Ibid.,* p. 3

"filled with admiration . . . little girl": *Ibid.,* pp. 6–8

"the greatest man in the world . . .": *Ibid.,* p. 23

"out of all the men in the world . . .": *Ibid.,* p. 26

"no one to love me": JA to AAH, Aug. 20, 1890, JAPM

"Though [Martha] . . . is happy": MAL to AAH, Apr. 17, 1867, HJ Papers

"Just one month . . .": MAL to AAH, Apr. 24, 1867, HJ Papers

"one of the most common": Hedrick, *Harriet Beecher Stowe,* p. 191

"She had everything she wanted . . . petted": Minutes, Sept. 6, 1935, Women's International League for Peace and Freedom Papers, U.S. Section, SCPC

"I never saw her . . .": Haldeman, "The Two Mothers of Jane Addams," p. 13, HJ Papers

"Barbara was put on the bed . . . same day": AHA to HH, n.d., 1884, HJ Papers

"Whatever is beautiful . . .": Haldeman, "The Two Mothers of Jane Addams," p. 13, HJ Papers

"in getting up imaginary . . .": William Haldeman to AHA, Aug. 30, 1861, HJ Papers

"Aunt Ann has been talking so ugly to Mother . . .": Journal of Anna Martha Bowman, Mar. 5, 1862, HJ Papers

"Music and drawing . . .": AHA to GH, Dec. 30, 1884, HJ Papers

"What a wonderful wife . . .": Haldeman, "The Two Mothers of Jane Addams," p. 12, HJ Papers

"Dear Madam . . .": JHA to AHA, Sept. 9, 1868, SCPC

"all the tastes and manners": Lasch, *The New Radicalism in America,* p. 6

"the precious freight . . .": AHA to JHA, Feb. 27, 1869, HJ Papers

"I am very much obliged to you . . .": JWA to AHA, Feb. 21, 1869, HJ Papers

"Down on the lakefront . . .": Henry Sill poem, Paul Fry, *Generous Spirit: The Life of Mary Fry,* p. 34, Mary Fry Collection, University of Illinois at Chicago

"but downstairs to try . . .": AHA to JHA, Feb. 18, 1869, HJ Papers

"To be termed 'Mother' . . . about me": AHA to JHA, Jan. 2, 1869, HJ Papers

"it never seems . . .": JA to Vallie Beck, Mar. 16, 1876, JAPM

"as I am a little inclined . . .": *Ibid.,* Mar. 30 and Apr. 2, 1876, JAPM

"Jennie and Georgie . . .": MAL to AAH, Aug. 21, 1871, HJ Papers

"scarcely wait . . .": MAL to AAH, Apr. 9, 1867, HJ Papers

"Long before we had begun . . . powers": TYAHH, p. 18

"for any intimation . . . happened": *Ibid.,* pp. 14–15

"the great change came . . . that": TYAHH, pp. 19–20

"magic protection from . . . election": *The Long Road of Woman's Memory,* p. 152

"poverty which implies squalor . . . these": TYAHH, pp. 3–5

"She is brave . . . keep it": MAL to AAH, May 29, 1872, HJ Papers

"which is simply a piece . . .": JA to Vallie Beck, Mar. 21, 1877, JAPM

"I would store my mind . . . Sure!": TYAHH, p. 6

"the gravest and most somber . . .": AHA to JHA, Feb. 18, 1869, HJ Papers

"I do hate the nigger . . .": HH to AHA, Nov. 8, 1868, HJ Papers

"I don't feel a bit more sorry . . .": Fry, *Generous Spirit,* p. 38, Mary Fry Collection, University of Illinois at Chicago

"We have tried about everything . . .": JA to Vallie Beck, Mar. 16, 1876, JAPM

"It was his great delight": John Linn to JA, Aug. 26, 1881, JAPM

"conscientiousness . . . at last": Phrenological Reading, Jul. 28, 1876, JAPM

CHAPTER 3 – ROCKFORD FEMALE SEMINARY

"At no time of life . . .": Mitchell, *Wear and Tear or Hints for the Overworked,* p. 40

"elevate and purify . . .": Miss Sill, *Memorials of Anna Peck Sill: First Principles of Rockford Seminary, 1849–1889,* Rockford, Ill.

"She does everything . . .": JA Notebooks, JAPM

"They all looked . . .": Lucy Townsend, "Anna Peck Sill and the Rise of Women's Collegiate Curriculum," Ph.D. thesis, p. 120.

"was considered . . .": GH to AHA, Mar. 12, 1882, HJ Papers

"Must I then exercise": Poem from JA Notebooks, quoted in Lucy Townsend, "The Education of Jane Addams: Myth and Reality," *Vita Scholastica: The Bulletin of Educational Biography, Vol. 5,* 1986, pp. 225–46

"Where Is My Place? . . . Sphere": *Rockford Seminary Magazine,* 1, Jan. 1873, pp. 11–14

"Why should not a woman . . .": *Rockford Seminary Magazine,* 8, May 1880

"I think it is just wicked . . .": Ralph Emerson to his wife, Feb. 2, 1876, quoted in *A Power Not of the Present,* edited by Elizabeth M. Asprooth, p. 19

"this passive resistance of mine . . .": TYAHH, p. 56

"consistently . . . opposed to privilege": Biographical information on Ellen Gates Starr, n.d., Ellen Gates Starr Collection, University of Illinois at Chicago

"Give the ballot to women . . . creatures": Biography of Caleb Starr by EGS, EGS Papers, Sophia Smith Collection

"as if I had participated . . .": EGS to JA, Mar. 6, 1881, JAPM

"certain characters . . .": EGS to JA, Jul. 27, 1879, JAPM

"You long for a beautiful faith . . .": JA to EGS, Jan. 29, 1880, JAPM

"God is more a reality . . .": EGS to JA, Jul. 27, 1879, JAPM

"I can work myself into . . .": JA to EGS, Aug. 11, 1879, JAPM

"I have been trying an awful experiment . . .": JA to EGS, Jan. 29, 1880, JAPM

"I was somewhat shocked . . .": JA to EGS, Nov. 22, 1879, JAPM

"he said it . . .": JA to EGS, Nov. 22, 1879, JAPM

"remark that it . . .": EGS to JA, Aug. 20, 1879, JAPM

"After I had besought you . . .": EGS to JA, Jul. 27, 1879, JAPM

"as I do on the Sun . . .": Sarah Anderson to JA, Apr. 11, 1882, JAPM

"However mopey . . .": Linn, *Jane Addams,* p. 47

"I am disappointed . . .": JA to EGS, Aug. 11, 1879, JAPM

"[This] will be a week . . .": JA to AHA, Jan. 14, 1880, JAPM

"I have learned . . .": JA to AAH, Jan. 23, 1880, JAPM

"There is some thing in Carlyle . . .": JA to EGS, Aug. 11, 1879, JAPM

"butchery . . . them": "The Present Policy of Congress," Dec. 5, 1877, JAPM

"The country is flooded with tramps . . .": "Tramps," Apr. 10, 1878, JAPM

"that at least . . . Jane Addams": Quoted in Linn, *Jane Addams,* p. 60

"We backed her up . . .": Linn, *Jane Addams,* p. 48

"Life's a burden . . .": *Ibid.*

"Solitude is essential . . .": JA Notebooks, JAPM

"with a stern command . . .": TYAHH, p. 46

"state of ecstatic . . . service": *Ibid.,* p. 50

"an impediment . . .": Quoted in Townsend, "Anna Peck Sill and the Rise of Women's Collegiate Curriculum," Ph.D. thesis, Mar. 1985, p. 88

"then I was excited . . .": JA to Eva Campbell Goodrich, Jul. 25, 1879, JAPM "is the primitive meaning . . .": JA to AAH, Jan. 23, 1880, JAPM

"passed from accomplishments . . .": "Breadgivers," Apr. 20, 1880, JAPM

"Gentlemen, I graded . . .": In Lucy Knight, "Voices and Silences: Jane Addams and William Jennings Bryan as College Orators," Aug. 1996, p. 27

Over the years there has been much confusion about whether Jane Addams debated William Jennings Bryan—some of it sparked by Jane's own muddled memories. In TYAHH she writes that she faced Bryan in an intercollegiate oratorical contest in Jacksonville, Illinois, in which she came in "fifth," and Bryan took a "prior place." After the contest, she noted, she visited institutions for the blind and the deaf and dumb. But the original contest was in October in 1880 in Galesburg, Illinois, not Jacksonville. She didn't visit the institutions in Jacksonville until the following spring, after both she and Bryan had been eliminated from the competition. I am indebted to Lucy Knight for this information.

"scared . . . for fear . . .": Henry W. Read to JA, Apr. 9, 1917, JAPM

"the progress of Woman's Cause . . . middle": TYAHH, p. 55

"My highest aspirations . . .": Mary Downs to JA, Nov. 14, 1880, JAPM

"Have you heard . . .": EGS to JA, Jul. 20, 1880, JAPM

"serious not to say priggish": TYAHH, p. 49

"I am a great admirer . . .": JA to Vallie Beck, May 3, 1877, JAPM

"lacked carnal motivation . . . 'glory'": Nancy F. Cott, "Passionlessness," p. 227

"was anxious for a career . . . life": Quoted in Farrell, *Beloved Lady,* pp. 35–36

"strong barrier . . .": Quoted in Ann Douglas Wood, "The Fashionable Diseases," p. 48

"symbol . . .": "The College Woman and the Family Claim," pp. 3–7

"As there are such . . .": JA to JHA, Mar. 20, 1881, JAPM

"Do not think . . .": JA to JHA, May 8, 1881, JAPM

"The brave warriors . . . mad": "Cassandra," *Rockford Seminary, Thirtieth Commencement, Essays of Graduating Class,* Wed., Jun. 22, 1881, pp. 36–39

CHAPTER 4 – THE REST CURE

"I remember how . . .": L. D. Cummings to JA, Aug. 20, 1881, JAPM

"The poignancy of your grief . . .": John Linn to JA, Aug. 26, 1881, JAPM

"By a word you spoke . . .": Caroline A. Potter to JA, Aug. 20, 1881, JAPM

"absolutely at sea . . .": TYAHH, p. 64

"Your first letter reached me . . .": JA to EGS, Sept. 3, 1881, JAPM

"is a trifle esoteric . . .": JA to GH, Dec. 19, 1884, JAPM
"utter failure . . .": JA Notebooks, JAPM
"approbation . . .": John Linn to JA, Aug. 26, 1881, JAPM
"powers of darkness . . .": "The College Story," an address to the graduating class, Women's Medical College of Pennsylvania, Mar. 17, 1881
"very severely . . .": Sarah Blaisdell to JA, Dec. 24, 1881, JAPM
"traces of it . . .": TYAHH, p. 66
"the aberration . . .": Dr. William A. Hammond, *Spinal Irritation*
"slight, pale lad . . .": Burr, *Weir Mitchell,* p. 37
"obstinately clung . . . New Woman": *Ibid.,* pp. 373–74
"nervous, exhausted . . . hopeless and helpless": Mitchell, *Lectures on Diseases of the Nervous System (Especially in Women),* 17, pp. 265–83: "The Treatment of Obstinate Cases of Nervous Exhaustion and Hysteria by Seclusion, Rest, Massage, Electricity and Full Feeding"
"the shawl and the sofa": Mitchell, *Wear and Tear or Hints for the Overworked,* p. 29
"self-conceit . . . blood": Quoted in Ann J. Lane, *To Herland and Beyond: The Life and Work of Charlotte Perkins Gilman,* p. 113
"Wise women . . . questions": Mitchell, *Doctor and Patient,* p. 48
"destroy the soil . . . flourish": Mitchell, *Lectures on Diseases of the Nervous System (Especially in Women),* 17, pp. 265–83
"an effort to lift the health . . .": *Ibid.*
"means with me . . . a time": *Ibid.*
"to lie abed . . . mandate": Mitchell, *Fat and Blood,* pp. 40–41
"If the patient . . . relief . . .": Mitchell, *Lectures,* 17
"with bolted doors . . .": Quoted in Ann Douglas Wood, "The Fashionable Diseases," pp. 25–52
"to absolutely perfect use . . .": Mitchell, *Lectures,* 14, p. 227
"I will be dreadfully . . .": JA to EGS, Mar. 19, 1882, JAPM
"Live as domestic a life . . .": Gilman, *Autobiography,* p. 96
"I am a failure . . .": JA Notebooks, 1883, JAPM
"You will grow . . . shell": AHA to GH, Jan. 15, 1884, HJ Papers
"We can set a watch . . .": JA Notebooks, JAPM
"[Harry] has thought of that back . . .": AAH to JA, Sept. 10, 1882, JAPM
"ashamed to show . . .": JA to EGS, Jan. 7, 1883, JAPM
"grew so interested . . .": *Ibid.*
"I have had the kindest care . . .": *Ibid.*
"becoming quite absorbed . . . air": JA to EGS, Apr. 24, 1883, JAPM
"feeling splendidly . . .": JA to AAH, May 1, 1883, JAPM
"She afterwards apologized . . .": JA to AAH, May 29, 1883, JAPM
"My experiences of late . . .": JA to EGS, Jul. 11, 1883, JAPM
"It seems quite . . .": *Ibid.*

"large enough . . .": JA to AAH, Jul. 11, 1883, JAPM
"I am more convinced every day . . .": JA to EGS, Nov. 3, 1883, JAPM
"Ma and I . . .": JA to AAH, Jun. 5, 1883, JAPM
"They will keep . . . dogs": JA to AAH, Jul. 18, 1883, JAPM
"pounded and rubbed . . .": JA to AAH, Aug. 8, 1883, JAPM
"I quite feel as if . . .": JA to EGS, Aug. 12, 1883, JAPM
"the big, beautiful . . .": JA to AAH, Aug. 22, 1883, JAPM

CHAPTER 5 – GRAND TOUR I

"We have a great big room . . .": JA to AAH, Sept. 10, 1883, JAPM
"blood thirsty little . . . swelling": JA to AAH, Jul. 12, 1884, JAPM
"How I have wished . . .": AHA to HH, n.d., 1884, HJ Papers
"Jane is growing . . .": AHA to HH, Jan. 27, 1884, HJ Papers
"Jane . . . makes every effort . . .": AHA to HH, Feb. 7, 1884, HJ Papers
"I feel convinced . . .": JA to GH, Oct. 8, 1883, JAPM
"from the kitchen . . .": JA to John Weber, Oct. 14, 1883, JAPM
"smothered and sickened . . . morning": TYAHH, p. 73
"contains more privileges . . .": JA to EGS, Nov. 3, 1883, JAPM
"Monster City . . . people": JA to Weber Addams, Oct. 14, 1883, JAPM
"hideous human need . . .": TYAHH, p. 68
"At the very moment . . .": *Ibid.*, pp. 70–71
"The white porcelain stoves . . .": JA to MAL, Jan. 13, 1884, JAPM
"We are all . . .": JA to MAL, Dec. 6, 1883, JAPM
"Jane looks . . .": AHA to HH, Dec. 24, 1884, HJ Papers
"faces and hands . . . speak": TYAHH, p. 74
"I would invariably . . .": *Ibid.*, p. 75
"They are perfectly . . .": JA to AAH, Dec. 14, 1883, JAPM
"opera glass . . .": JA to AAH, Dec. 26, 1883, JAPM
"Some days . . .": JA to AAH, Jan. 8, 1884, JAPM
"spring burst . . . July": JA to MAL, Feb. 27, 1884, JAPM
"the use and good . . .": JA to GH, Mar. 8, 1884, JAPM
"It may be partly owing . . .": JA to EGS, Mar. 9, 1884, JAPM
"never fail . . . goodness": *Ibid.*
"May be it is . . .": JA to Sarah F. Blaisdell, Apr. 26, 1884, JAPM
"It smokes . . .": JA to AAH, May 7, 1884, JAPM
"My teeth have . . .": JA to EGS, Jun. 10, 1884, JAPM
"is fascinating . . .": JA to AAH, Jun. 22, 1884, JAPM
"nerve force . . . himself": AHA to GH, Jan. 7, 1884, HJ Papers
"T'will be so pleasant . . .": AHA to HH, n.d., 1884, HJ Papers
"the role of male in charge": GH to AHA, Apr. 13, 1884, HJ Papers

"As last year . . . in it": JA to AAH, Nov. 16, 1884, JAPM
"as modern and busy as Chicago itself": JA to AAH, Oct. 1, 1884, JAPM
"two English . . . time": JA to MAL, Oct. 10, 1884, JAPM
"almost a boarding school . . .": JA to GH, Oct. 17, 1884, JAPM
"I seem to be about as busy . . .": JA to AAH, Nov. 16, 1884, JAPM
"Your kind and regular . . .": JA to GH, Nov. 15, 1884, JAPM
"I have been idle . . .": JA to EGS, Jun. 8, 1884, JAPM
"no more heats . . .": JA to EGS, Feb. 21, 1885, JAPM
"is just now . . .": *Ibid.*
"dress and jewelry of . . .": JA to JWA, Apr. 19, 1885, JAPM
"the little round table . . . water": JA to AAH, May 1, 1885, JAPM
"All the delicacies . . .": JA to AAH, May 19, 1885, JAPM

CHAPTER 6 – BALTIMORE

"I am afraid . . .": JA to AHA, Oct. 16, 1885, JAPM
"What reading I do . . .": JA to AAH, Oct. 23, 1885, JAPM
"The first real experience . . .": EGS to JA, Oct. 23, 1885, JAPM
"positively forlorn . . . work together": EGS to JA, Nov. 28, 29, 1885, JAPM
"I had almost forgotten us": EGS to JA, Dec. 3, 1885, JAPM
"For many years . . .": JA to EGS, Dec. 6, 1885, JAPM
"immediately . . . degree": EGS to JA, Dec. 3, 1885, JAPM
"[Eliot's] books give me . . .": JA to AAH, Oct. 23, 1885, JAPM
"[You are] so much above me . . .": EGS to JA, Dec. 3, 1885, JAPM
"a merry old fashioned . . .": JA to AAH, Dec. 26, 1885, JAPM
"I had seemed to have reached the nadir . . .": TYAHH, p. 77
"There is a sentiment here . . .": JA to AAH, Feb. 17, 1885, JAPM
"superior . . . Virginia": JA to AAH, Feb. 10, 1886, JAPM
"The pleasant ladies . . .": JA to AAH, Feb. 17, 1886, JAPM
"I have had the strangest . . .": JA to EGS, Feb. 7, 1886, JAPM
"did all the housework . . .": JA to MRS, Jul. 22, 1897, JAPM
"who is under . . . long": "The College Woman and the Family Claim," pp. 3–7
"all sorts of plans . . .": JA to AAH, Jan. 1887, JAPM
"I had such a pleasant . . .": JA to AAH, Nov. 24, 1886, JAPM
"I heartily approve . . .": JA to AAH, Dec. 28, 1886, JAPM
"after a lecture . . .": EGS to Mary Blaisdell, Feb. 23, 1889, EGS Papers
"about twilight . . . chest-nutting": JA to AHA, Oct. 24, 1886, JAPM
"If you don't . . .": JA to EGS, Apr. 3, 1887, JAPM
"I don't often remember . . .": Josephine Starr Notes, EGS Papers
"How dear . . . happy": JA to AAH, Dec. 13, 1887, JAPM

CHAPTER 7 – GRAND TOUR II

"I went to this hotel . . .": JA to AAH, Jun. 6, 1888, JAPM
"a cathedral . . . solidarity": Linn, *Jane Addams,* pp. 85–86
"I have seldom . . .": JA to AAH, Jan. 6, 1888, JAPM
"vulgar nude women": AHA to HH, Feb. 7, 1884, HJ Papers
"We have simply . . .": JA to AAH, Jan. 6, 1888, JAPM
"to an absurd . . . her": EGS to AHA, Jan. 30, 1888, EGS Papers
"Ellen always overestimates . . .": JA to AAH, Mar. 22, 1888, JAPM
"stopped crying . . .": *Ibid.*
"what God wanted . . .": MAL to JA, Feb. 23, 1888, JAPM
"I'm beginning to think . . .": JA to AAH, Feb. 27, 1888, JAPM
"the satisfaction . . .": JA to JWA, Mar. 1, 1888, JAPM
"the impropriety of . . .": JA to AAH, Feb. 27, 1888, JAPM
"She is neither . . .": JA to AAH, Apr. 6, 1888, JAPM
"the great event . . .": JA to Laura Addams, Apr. 25, 1888, JAPM
"a beautiful creature . . .": *Ibid.*
"the bull was so . . . in it": *Ibid.*
"stern and pale . . . self seeking": TYAHH, p. 86
"where many primitive . . .": TYAHH, p. 85
"spiritual crisis . . .": Deborah Epstein Nord, *The Apprenticeship of Beatrice Webb,* p. 21.
"Nothing among . . .": TYAHH, p. 69
"seemed destined . . .": Himmelfarb, *Poverty and Compassion,* p. 237
"ranting preacher . . .": Quoted in J. A. R. Pimlott, *Toynbee Hall,* p. 8
"the religion of humanity" and ff: This paragraph relies on two works by Himmelfarb: *Poverty and Compassion* and *The Demoralization of Society.*
"implied no denial . . .": Himmelfarb, *Poverty and Compassion,* p. 243
"It is true of people . . .": "Outgrowths of Toynbee Hall," Dec. 3, 1891, JAPM
"the solace of daily activity": TYAHH, p. 88

CHAPTER 8 – CHICAGO

"At this moment . . .": TYAHH, pp. 78–79
"But do you believe . . .": Marcet Haldeman, *Jane Addams As I Knew Her,* p. 29, HJ Papers
"It seems to me . . .": JA to AAH, Feb. 19, 1889, JAPM

"ragged and dirty . . .": Newspaper clipping, HH Scrapbooks, JAPM
"I am dreadfully disappointed . . . salvation": JA to EGS, Jan. 24, 1889, JAPM
"I must stop . . .": JA to EGS, Jun. 7, 1889, JAPM
"I don't know . . .": EGS to Mary Allen, Sept. 15, 1889, EGS Papers
"attacks of obstinacy . . .": *Ibid.*
"I remember . . .": EGS to JA, Apr. 12, 1935, JAPM
"ordinary . . . together": EGS to Mary Allen, Sept. 15, 1889, EGS Papers
"the term 'Boston marriage' . . . singlehood": Ware, *Partner and I,* pp. 57–58
"The ideal old maid . . .": J. H. Kellog, *The Ladies Guide in Health and Diseases,* p. 317
"some of the conditions . . .": Kaplan, *Lincoln Steffens: A Biography,* p. 51
"demonstrably male . . .": Wills, *The New York Review of Books,* Oct. 21, 1993, p. 20
"thirteen blessed babies . . .": *Chicago Tribune,* HH Scrapbooks, JAPM
"the mother . . .": Julian Ralph, quoted in Donald Miller, *City of the Century,* p. 416
"Our manner of getting . . .": Louise Bowen Scrapbooks, CHS
"I was hurrying . . .": Anne Forsyth, "What Jane Addams Has Done for Chicago: A Fight for the Betterment of a Great City," *Delineator,* 65, Oct. 1907
"I took him this morning . . .": JA to MAL, Apr. 1, 1889, JAPM
"They saw the living conditions . . .": Hofstadter, *Social Darwinism in American Thought,* p. 106
"all sorts of . . .": JA to MAL, Feb. 26, 1889, JAPM
"saintly drivellers . . .": EGS to Mary Blaisdell, Feb. 23, 1889, EGS Papers
"The scheme is progressing . . .": JA to AAH, Feb. 19, 1889, JAPM
"rational moral being[s] . . .": Himmelfarb, *The Demoralization of Society,* p. 158
"The reporter came twice . . .": JA to MAL, Mar. 13, 1889, JAPM
"A Project to Bring . . .": *Chicago Tribune,* Mar. 8, 1889
"long after Hull-House . . .": TYAHH, p. 66
"the supposed treachery . . .": Nancy F. Cott, *The Roots of Bitterness,* p. 7
"Miss Addams's rarest . . .": Lelia G. Bedell, "A Chicago Toynbee Hall," *The Woman's Journal, 20,* May 25, 1889
"I positively feel . . .": JA to EGS, May 3, 1889, JAPM
"the conception . . .": Davis, *American Heroine,* p. 61
"Everybody who comes . . .": EGS to Mary Allen, Sept. 15, 1889, EGS Papers
"the neurotic turmoil . . .": Woolf, *Sowing: An Autobiography of the Years 1880–1904,* p. 48
"spiritual . . .": Davis, *American Heroine,* p. 61

"After we have been there . . .": EGS to Mary Blaisdell, Feb. 23, 1889, EGS Papers

"He said he had a perfect horror . . .": JA to MAL, Feb. 26, 1889, JAPM

"that he could . . .": JA to MAL, Feb. 12, 1889, JAPM

"English speaking persons . . .": *Chicago Tribune,* Oct. 26, 1889

" 'Americans' never came . . . innocent": JA to MAL, Mar. 13, 1889, JAPM

"It was exactly . . .": *Ibid.*

"about ten thousand . . .": TYAHH, p. 98

"The Mayor and the Alderman . . .": Hilda Polacheck, *I Came a Stranger,* p. 30

"'Tis the struggle . . .": AHA to HH, Jan., n.d., 1884, HJ Papers

"I stood about . . .": EGS to Mary Allen, Sept. 15, 1889, EGS Papers

"by *far* the prettiest . . .": JA to AAH, Sept. 13, 1889, JAPM

CHAPTER 9 – HULL-HOUSE OPENS

"in a most formal manner . . .": EGS to her parents, Nov. 3, 1889, EGS Papers

"miniature Italians . . .": Addams, "Hull-House Chicago: An Effort Toward Social Democracy," *Forum, 14,* Oct. 1892, p. 235

"Friday afternoon . . . them of": JA to AAH, Nov. 23, 1889, JAPM

"The little Italians . . .": EGS to Mary Blaisdell, Jan. 2, 1895, EGS Papers

"with the rich . . .": EGS to Mary Blaisdell, Jan. 1, 1895, EGS Papers

"the rollicking crew . . .": HH Scrapbooks, JAPM

"Bisno has renewed . . .": EGS to Mary Blaisdell, Jul. 26, 1892, EGS Papers

"Let us not acknowledge . . .": *Unity, 42,* Dec. 22, 1898

"seemed to incline . . .": EGS to Mary Blaisdell, Dec. 19, 21, 1890, EGS Papers

"It ended . . . in . . . our . . .": *Ibid.*

"The truth of the . . .": *Ibid.*

"a German parent . . .": *Ibid.*

"none of the honest . . .": TYAHH, p. 110

"The appeal of the bloodshed . . .": Leibowitz, *Fabricating Lives,* p. 137

"something impersonal . . .": Caroline F. Urie to EGS, May 25, 1935, EGS Papers

"an almost indescribable personal magnetism": HH Scrapbooks, JAPM

"She is the greatest . . .": Madeline Wallin Sikes to George Sikes, Oct. 27, 1896, CHS

"Miss Addams . . .": Bowen, *Open Windows,* pp. 219–20

"Thank you very much, sir . . .": Josephine Starr, *Biographical Notes,* EGS Papers
"My dear, you . . .": *Ibid.*
"She believed . . .": Davis, *American Heroine,* p. 352
"they are all . . .": EGS to her parents, Nov. 3, 1889, EGS Papers
"I love Francesco . . . children": EGS to Mary Allen, Dec. 7, 1890, EGS Papers
"One is so overpowered . . .": JA to GH, Nov. 24, 1889, JAPM
"wouldn't do at all . . .": EGS to Mary Allen, Dec. 7, 1890, EGS Papers
"she highly . . . overpopulation": EGS to Mary Allen, Dec. 7, 1890, EGS Papers
"hobnobs delightfully . . . time being": *Ibid.*
"self-subordinating . . .": Quoted in Bryan and Davis, *One Hundred Years at Hull-House,* p. 61
"Curious visitors . . . yet": Linn, *Jane Addams,* pp. 118–19
"just naturally . . .": AH to Agnes Hamilton, Mar. 30, 1898, AH Papers
"a great prejudice . . .": *Ibid.*
"a great mingling of economy . . .": Helen Culver to Nelly (last name unknown), Jan. 19, 1891, JAMC
"the moral effect . . .": JA to AAH, Jan. 22, 1890, JAPM
"Miss Addams was really . . .": Bowen, *Open Windows,* p. 252
"While the strain and perplexity . . .": Addams, *Democracy and Social Ethics,* p. 12
"at the great wells . . .": *Ibid.,* p.11

CHAPTER 10 – WOMEN WITHOUT MEN

"was a dreadful . . .": Kelley, *The Autobiography of Florence Kelley,* p. 78
"She has to pay . . .": EGS to Mary Blaisdell, Jul. 26, 1892, EGS Papers
"bigness, manliness . . .": AH to Agnes Hamilton, Mar. 30, 1898, AH Papers
"I wonder . . .": EGS to Mary Blaisdell, Jul. 26, 1892, EGS Papers
"From the age of eighteen months . . .": Kelley, *The Autobiography of Florence Kelley,* p. 80
"stench that shouts to heaven . . .": Newspaper clipping, HH Scrapbooks, JAPM
"do not seem . . .": John Dewey to his wife, Oct. 19, 1894, Dewey Family Letters, Center for Dewey Studies, Southern Illinois University
"sit around . . . part of the work": AH to Agnes Hamilton, Jun. 13, 1897, AH Papers
"a revolt of [America's] daughters . . .": J. Ramsey MacDonald, "American Social Settlements," *Commons, 2,* Feb. 1898, pp. 4–6

"false social . . .": JA to MRS, n.d., 1891, JAPM

"Of course, you would *rather* starve": Addams, *My Friend, Julia Lathrop,* p. 51

"She was not playing at life . . .": Davis, *American Heroine,* p. 77

"in making life . . .": Linn, *Jane Addams,* p. 149

"Why didn't you wait . . .": Bowen, *Open Windows,* p. 227

"This is a very fine plan . . .": MRS to JA, n.m., n.d., 1896, JAPM

"never did anything . . .": Monroe, *A Poet's Life,* p. 193

"Miss Addams still rattles me . . .": AH to Agnes Hamilton, Oct. 13, 1897, AH Papers

"One day I came . . .": Poem, n.d., JAPM

"I am sure you know . . .": JA to MRS, May 26, 1902, JAPM

"token of . . . low": JA to MRS, May 26, 1902, JAPM

"You can never know . . .": MRS to JA, Dec., n.d., 1896, JAPM

"great bugaboo . . .": Faderman, *Surpassing the Love of Men,* p. 252

"remained locked . . .": Wetherell quoted in Faderman, *Surpassing the Love of Men,* p. 173

"as gently as . . .": Alcott quoted in Faderman, p. 173

"the sex instinct . . . romance": Scudder quoted in Faderman, p. 251

"an irreparable . . . pioneers": JA to William Rainey Harper, Dec. 19, 1895, JAPM

"I went to bed quite . . .": JA to MRS, Aug. 15, 1895, JAPM

"I have been homesick . . .": JA to MRS, Feb. 21, 1895, JAPM

"I went into a kitchen . . .": Bowen, Louise Bowen Scrapbooks, CHS

"I can see by the way . . .": EGS to JA, Apr. 12, 1935, JAPM

CHAPTER II – Revolt of the Daughters

"People are dying . . .": EGS to Mary Blaisdell, Jul. 26, 1892, EGS Papers

"seemed divided into . . .": TYAHH, pp. 183–84

"this daughter of the prairie . . .": *Boston Transcript,* Jul. 30, 1892, HH Scrapbooks, JAPM

"It is true there is nothing . . .": "The Subjective Necessity for Social Settlements" and "The Objective Value of a Social Settlement," *Philanthropy and Social Progress,* pp. 1–56

"Although nothing could . . .": *Republican,* Jul. 30, 1892, HH Scrapbooks, JAPM

"a place rather dingily . . .": *Sister Carrie,* Penguin Classics edition, 1986, p. 25

"I refused to do . . .": *Mary Kenney,* O'Sullivan autobiography, Schlesinger Library, Cambridge, Ma., p. 32

"not only had the circulars . . .": *Ibid.,* p. 55
"went over to see . . .": EGS to Mary Blaisdell, Jul. 26, 1892, EGS Papers
"I once heard her comment . . .": Mrs. Reginald de Koven, *A Musician and His Wife,* p. 101
"she whipped out . . .": Ishbel Ross, *Silhouette in Diamonds,* p. 72
"the latter possessed . . .": *The World's Congress of Representative Women,* Vol. 2, edited by May Wright Sewall, pp. 626–31
"The suffering . . .": JA to Sarah Anderson, Jun. 23, 1894, JAPM
"see them without . . .": TYAHH, p. 162
"wet and hungry . . . accepted": *Ibid.,* p. 160
"thronged . . .": Graham Taylor, *Pioneering on Social Frontiers,* pp. 28–33
"than with some persons . . .": *Chicago Record,* quoted in Miller, *City of the Century,* p. 536
"If you well-to-do . . .": *Ibid.*
"The audience rose as one . . .": *Ibid.*
"You can get two rooms . . .": *United States Strike Commission Report on the Chicago Strike,* June–July 1894, Washington, D.C., Government Printing Office, 1895
"I came back to the city . . .": *Ibid.*
"I was filled with a profound . . .": TYAHH, pp. 216–17
"It became known . . . any of us": Esther Linn Hulbert, *The Autobiography of an Unknown,* n.d., p. 11, SCPC
"The tracks from crossing . . .": Baker, *American Chronicle,* pp. 39–40
"almost everyone on Halsted Street . . .": TYAHH, p. 217
"more or less forgotten . . .": Baker, *American Chronicle,* p. 41
"should be moved . . .": "A Modern Lear," pp. 131–37
"touch . . .": *Ibid.*

CHAPTER 12 – BATTLING THE WARD BOSS

"into boarding school . . .": TYAHH, p. 284
"this huge, incoherent city . . .": Addams, *The Excellent Becomes the Permanent,* p. 75
"have nothing to do with Mr. Powers . . .": Minutes of Residents' Meeting, Sept. 1893, JAMC
"works on like a hero . . .": JA to MRS, Aug. 8, 1895, JAPM
"much shocked by . . .": TYAHH, p. 287
"Miss Addams has achieved . . .": HH Scrapbooks, JAPM
"all in such . . .": TYAHH, p. 166

"by the time . . .": JA to MRS, Feb. 3, 1895, JAPM
"has not the settlement spirit": *Ibid.*
"to locate women . . .": Karl, *George Eliot,* p. xiv
"Here in the back parlour . . .": AH to Agnes Hamilton, Oct. 13, 1897, AH Papers
"weary-looking . . .": Helen J. Gow diaries, Apr. 11, 17, 1897, Duke University, Durham, N.C.
"I sh'd think . . .": John Dewey to his wife, Oct. 7, 1894, John Dewey Letters, Dewey Family Letters, Center for Dewey Studies, Southern Illinois University, Carbondale, Ill.
"It is my impression . . .": Robert Woods to JA, Sept. 4, 1895, JAPM
"some of the toughest . . .": Interview with author, Summer 1998
"Have those men . . .": Susan B. Anthony to JA, Dec. 19, 1895, CHS
"She was the ultimate . . .": Interview with author, Summer 1998
"never lost . . .": *Chicago Tribune,* Apr. 4, 1896
"I want to show . . .": *Chicago Times Herald,* Apr. 6, 1896
"Stand back . . .": *Chicago Daily News,* Apr. 7, 1896
"My victory . . .": *Chicago Tribune,* Apr. 7, 1896
"We doubtless . . .": TYAHH, p. 316
"on a nice little tour": MRS to JA, Feb., n.d., 1896, JAPM
"When I think of . . .": MRS to JA, Mar., n.d., 1896, JAPM
"We buy a good . . .": JA to EGS, May 29, 1896, JAPM
"I was the only 'lady' . . .": JA to MRS, Jun. 27, 1896, JAPM
"It was in his rooms . . .": JA to Gertrude Barnum, May 22, 1896, JAPM
"fresh air schemes . . .": *Ibid.*
"the poor might . . .": JA to MRS, Jun. 22, 1896, JAPM
"It has been . . .": JA to AAH, Jul., n.d., 1896, JAPM
"which unfortunately . . . 'family'": TYAHH, pp. 267–80
"Of course . . .": *Chicago Daily News,* Jan. 14, 1898
"through long custom . . .": "Ethical Survivals of Municipal Corruption," pp. 273–91; "Why the Ward Boss Rules," pp. 879–82
"a friendly neighbor . . .": *Ibid.*
"A year from now . . .": Quoted in Scott, "Saint Jane and the Ward Boss," *American Heritage,* Dec. 1960, p. 96
"it is so hard . . .": JA to MRS, Apr. 3, 1898, JAPM
"For the first time . . .": JA to MRS, Mar. 20, 1898, JAPM
"profess to give . . .": *Chicago Chronicle,* Mar. 13, 1898
"Did it ever occur . . .": A voter to JA, Jan. 17, 1898, JAPM
"Dearest, I love you . . .": JA to MRS, Mar., n.d., 1898, JAPM
"I almost sent . . .": JA to MRS, Apr. 11, 1898, JAPM

"last supreme effort": AH to Agnes Hamilton, Apr. 3, 1898, AH Papers
"Down With Hull-House": *Ibid.*
"everything is as bad . . .": JA to MRS, Apr. 3, 1898, JAPM

CHAPTER 13 – Spreading the Social Gospel

"the more successful . . .": Interview with author, Summer 1998
"One small group . . .": Lillian Wald to JA, Nov. 15, 1898, Lillian D. Wald Papers, the New York Public Library
"Miss Jane Addams . . .": Webb quote in Bryan and Davis, eds., *One Hundred Years at Hull-House,* p. 61
"went into the closet . . .": Bowen, *Open Windows,* pp. 206–7
"not in the least . . .": JA to Julia Lathrop, Mar. 6, 1899, JAPM
"probably the ugliest . . ." and ff: Interview with author
"Darling . . .": JA to MRS, Jul. 22, 1897, JAPM
"physician thinks the change . . .": FK to Caroline B. Kelley, Sept. 28, 1898, FK Papers
"one of the noblest . . .": Charlotte Perkins Gilman to C. Houghton Gilman, Jul. 27, 1897, quoted in Hill, p. 275
"very interesting . . .": JA to MRS, Aug. 8, 1895, JAPM
"You must never . . .": FK to MRS, Aug. 28, 1899, FK Papers
"cerebral abnormalities . . .": Quoted in Faderman, *Surpassing the Love of Men,* p. 241
"If you won't . . .": Bowen, *Open Windows,* p. 227
"the highest gift . . .": JA, quoted in Ann Firor Scott's introduction to *Democracy and Social Ethics,* Harvard Library, 1964, p. xxxi
"For a considerable period . . .": *The Second Twenty Years at Hull-House,* p. 196
"the highest ideals . . .": AH to Agnes Hamilton, Jun. 18, 1899, AH Papers
"Bro[ther] Woods letters . . . frigid": JA to MRS, Aug. 24, 1899, JAPM
"Please don't be an iceberg . . .": JA to MRS, Jul. 28, 1899, JAPM
"act up . . . already": AH to Agnes Hamilton, Nov. 26, 1898, AH Papers
"I was leaning . . .": EGS to Caleb Starr, Dec. 9, 1910, EGS Papers
"George was down . . .": AHA to HH, Dec. 24, 1895, HJ Papers
"Think George . . .": AHA to HH, Feb. 7, 1898, HJ Papers
"George does not . . .": AHA to HH, Oct. 28, 1899, HJ Papers
"1848 . . .": Fry, *Generous Spirit,* p. 37, Mary Fry Collection, University of Illinois at Chicago
"Sometimes I nearly . . .": AHA to HH, Oct. 28, 1899, HJ Papers

"held frequent arguments . . .": Haldeman, *Jane Addams As I Knew Her,* p. 5, HJ Papers
"Laura and Esther . . .": AHA to HH, n.d., HJ Papers
"What is in your . . .": JA to AAH, Feb. 16, 17, 1896, JAPM
"I have many faults . . .": JA to AAH, Sept. 23, 1900, JAPM
"Miss Addams was . . .": Interview with author
"I remember seeing . . .": Interview with author
"the courtroom was always . . .": Bowen in *Child, the Clinic & the Court,* pp. 305–6
"We had only one horse . . .": Louise de Koven Bowen Scrapbooks, CHS
"It may be . . .": Florence S. Scully, handwritten note at the bottom of letter from Richard S. Tuthill, to "whom it may concern," Jul. 19, 1912, small manuscripts, JAMC
"Formerly, when it . . .": *Charities, 8,* May 24, 1902, pp. 517–20
"not only . . .": Ann Firor Scott, introduction to *Democracy and Social Ethics,* p. iv
"but a widely regretted fact": Alan Ryan, *John Dewey and the High Tide of American Liberalism,* p. 24
"My first lecture . . .": JA to MRS, Jul. 28, 1899, JAPM
"because I much . . .": JA to MRS, Aug. 8, 1899, JAPM
"I went through the yard . . . storybook": JA to MRS, Jul. 31, 1899, JAPM
"a devilish time . . .": JA to MRS, Aug. 22, 1899, JAPM
"The little bride . . .": JA to MRS, Aug. 14, 1899, JAPM
"a little greedy . . . train": JA to MRS, Sept. 26, 1899, JAPM

Epilogue

"all the things . . .": Quoted in "Jane Addams Tells Why," *New York Post,* Aug. 8, 1912
"Troops Drink Crazed . . .": *The New York Times,* Jul. 13, 1915
"My dear Miss Addams . . .": John Henry Hopkins to JA, Jun. 11, 1917, JAPM
"one of the shrieking . . .": Quoted in Davis, *American Heroine,* p. 223
"In America in 1912 . . .": *Ibid.,* p. 269
"the Reddest of the Red": *Congressional Record,* 69th Congress, first session, 1926, 12946–47
"the most dangerous woman in America": Quoted in Davis, *American Heroine,* p. 251
"'Our house' . . .": JA to MRS, Aug. 14 [1904], JAPM
"Dearest . . . affection had offered us": JA to MRS, n.d., 1904, JAPM

"Oh, it's my stepmother . . .": Linn, *Jane Addams,* p. 33
"that grandmother . . .": Haldeman, *Jane Addams As I Knew Her,* pp. 10–11, HJ Papers
"with proud irrelevance": Edmund Wilson, "Hull-House in 1932," *The New Republic,* Jan. 18, 1932, p. 262
"I suppose I could have . . .": Linn, *Jane Addams,* pp. 407–8

Select Bibliography

Works by Jane Addams

Democracy & Social Ethics. New York: Macmillan, 1902.
Excellent Becomes the Permanent. New York: Macmillan, 1932.
Ed. by Jane Addams and Florence Kelley. *Hull-House Maps and Papers.* New York: Thomas Y. Crowell & Co., 1895.
Jane Addams: A Centennial Reader. New York: Macmillan, 1960.
The Long Road of Woman's Memory. New York: Macmillan, 1916.
My Friend, Julia Lathrop. New York: Macmillan, 1935.
A New Conscience & an Ancient Evil. New York: Macmillan, 1912.
Newer Ideals of Peace. New York: Macmillan, 1907.
Peace & Bread in Time of War. New York: Macmillan, 1922.
Philanthropy & Social Progress. New York: Thomas Y. Crowell & Co., 1893.
The Second Twenty Years at Hull-House. New York: Macmillan, 1930.
Social Thought of Jane Addams. Indianapolis: Bobbs-Merrill Co., 1965.
The Spirit of Youth & the City Streets. New York: Macmillan, 1910.
Twenty Years at Hull-House. New York: Macmillan, 1910.

Books

Abbott, Edith. *Historical Aspects of the Immigration Problem.* New York: Arno Press, 1969.

Addams, Jane, et al. *Child, the Clinic & the Court.* New York: New Republic Inc., 1927.

Asprooth, Elizabeth M., ed. *A Power Not of the Present.* Rockford: Rockford College Press, 1973.

Baker, Ray Standard. *The American Chronicle: The Autobiography of Ray Standard Baker.* New York: Charles Scribner's Sons, 1945.

Barnett, Henrietta. *Canon Barnett: His Life, His Work and His Friends.* Boston: Houghton Mifflin, 1919.

Beam, Ronald H. *Cedarville's Jane Addams . . . Her Early Influences.* Freeport: Wagner Printing Co., 1966.

Bisno, Abraham. *Union Pioneer.* Madison: University of Wisconsin Press, 1967.

Blanc, Marie Therese de Solms. *The Condition of Women in the United States: A Traveler's Notes, 1895.* Reprinted, New York: Arno Press, 1972

Bowen, Louise. *Growing Up with a City.* New York: Macmillan, 1926.

———. *Open Windows: Stories of People and Places.* Chicago: Ralph Fletcher Seymour, 1936.

Boyer, Paul, and Janet Wilson James. *Notable American Women 1607–1950.* Cambridge: Harvard University Press, 1971.

Breuer, Josef, and Sigmund Freud. *Studies in Hysteria.* London: Penguin Freud Library, 1974.

Briggs, Asa, and Anne Macartney. *Toynbee Hall, the First One Hundred Years.* London: Routledge & Kegan Paul, 1984.

Bryan, Mary Lynn McCree, ed. *The Jane Addams Papers: A Comprehensive Guide.* Indianapolis: Indiana University Press, 1996.

Bryan, Mary Lynn McCree, and Allen F. Davis, eds. *One Hundred Years at Hull-House.* Bloomington: Indiana University Press, 1969.

Burr, Ana Robeson. *Weir Mitchell: His Life and Letters.* New York: Duffield & Co., 1929.

Bym, Nina. *Women's Fiction: A Guide to Novels By and About Women in America (1820–1870).* Ithaca: Cornell University Press, 1978.

Carson, Mina. *Settlement Folk: Social Thought and the American Settlement Movement.* Chicago: University of Chicago Press, 1990.

Cott, Nancy F. *The Roots of Bitterness: Documents of the Social History of American Women.* New York: Dutton, 1972.

Cott, Nancy F., and Elizabeth H. Pleck, eds. *A Heritage of Her Own: Toward a New Social History of American Women.* New York: Simon & Schuster, 1979.

Crocker, Ruth Hutchinson. *Social Work and Social Order: The Settlement Movement in Two Industrial Cities.* Urbana: University of Illinois Press, 1992.

Davis, Allen F. *American Heroine: The Life and Legend of Jane Addams.* New York: Oxford University Press, 1973.

———. *Spearheads for Reform: The Social Settlements and the Progressive Movement 1890–1914.* New York: Oxford University Press, 1967.

Dedmon, Emmett. *Fabulous Chicago.* New York: Random House, 1953.

De Koven, Mrs. Reginald. *A Musician and His Wife,* New York: Harper & Bros., 1926.

D'Emilio, John, and Estelle B. Friedman. *Intimate Matters: A History of Sexuality in America.* New York: Harper & Row, 1988.

DeMuth, James. *Small Town Chicago.* Port Washington, N.Y.: Kennikat Press, 1979.

Dreiser, Theodore. *Sister Carrie.* New York: Doubleday, 1900.

Earnest, Ernest. *S. Weir Mitchell, Novelist and Physician.* Philadelphia: University of Pennsylvania Press, 1950.

Faderman, Lillian. *Odd Girls and Twilight Lovers: A History of Lesbian Life in Twentieth Century America.* New York: Columbia University Press, 1991.

———. *Surpassing the Love of Men: Romantic Friendship and Love Between Women From the Renaissance to the Present.* New York: Morrow, 1981.

Farrell, James C. *Beloved Lady: A History of Jane Addams's Ideas on Reform and Peace.* Baltimore: Johns Hopkins Press, 1967.

Flexner, Eleanor. *Century of Struggle: The Woman's Rights Movement in the U.S.* Cambridge: Belknap Press, 1959.

Friedan, Betty. *The Feminine Mystique.* New York: Dell Paperback, 1984.

Gilman, Charlotte Perkins. *The Living of Charlotte Perkins Gilman: An Autobiography.* New York: Arno Press, 1972.

Ginger, Ray. *Altgeld's America: The Lincoln Ideal Versus Changing Realities.* New York: Funk and Wagnalls Co., 1958.

Green, Carol Hurd, and Barbara Sicherman, eds. *Notable American Women, the Modern Period: A Biographical Dictionary.* Cambridge: Harvard University Press, 1980.

Green, Paul M., and Melvin G. Holli. *The Mayors: The Chicago Political Tradition.* Carbondale: Southern Illinois University Press, 1987.

Haller, John S. and Robin. *The Physician and Sexuality in Victorian America.* Urbana: University of Illinois Press, 1974.

Hamilton, Alice. *Exploring the Dangerous Trades: The Autobiography of Alice Hamilton, M.D.* New York: Little, Brown & Co., 1943.

Hammond, William, Dr. *Spinal Irritation.* Detroit: George S. Davis, 1891.

Hedrick, Joan D. *Harriet Beecher Stowe.* New York: Oxford University Press, 1994.

Hill, Mary Armfield. *Charlotte Perkins Gilman: The Making of a Radical Feminist, 1860–1896.* Philadelphia: Temple University Press, 1985.

Himmelfarb, Gertrude. *The Demoralization of Society: From Victorian Virtues to Modern Values.* New York: Knopf, 1994.

———. *The Idea of Poverty: England in the Early Industrial Age.* New York: Knopf, 1984.

———. *Poverty and Compassion: The Moral Imagination of the Victorians.* New York: Knopf, 1991.

History of Stephenson County. Published by the County of Stephenson, 1972.

Hofstadter, Richard. *Social Darwinism in American Thought.* Boston: Beacon Press, 1955.

Horowitz, Helen. *Alma Mater: Design and Experience in the Women's Colleges From Their Nineteenth Century Beginnings.* New York: Knopf, 1894.

———. *Culture and the City: Cultural Philanthropy in Chicago From the 1880s to 1917.* Chicago: University of Chicago Press, 1976.

———. *The Power and Passion of M. Carey Thomas.* New York: Knopf, 1994.

Howe, Irving. *World of Our Fathers.* New York: Harcourt Brace Jovanovich, 1976.

Johnson, Mary Ann, ed. *The Many Faces of Hull-House: The Photographs of Wallace Kirkland.* Urbana: University of Illinois Press, 1989.

Kaplan, Justin. *Lincoln Steffens: A Biography.* New York: Simon & Schuster, 1974.

Karl, Frederick. *George Eliot, Voice of a Century.* New York: W. W. Norton, 1995.

Kelley, Florence. *The Autobiography of Florence Kelley.* Reprint. Chicago: Charles H. Kerr Publishing Co., 1986.

Kellog, J. H. *The Ladies Guide in Health and Diseases.* New York: Modern Medicine Publishing Co., 1895.

Lane, Ann J. *To Herland and Beyond: The Life and Work of Charlotte Perkins Gilman.* New York: Pantheon Books, 1990.

Lasch, Christopher. *The New Radicalism in America 1880–1963.* New York: Knopf, 1965.

———, ed. *The Social Thought of Jane Addams.* New York: Bobbs Merrill Co., 1965.

Leibowitz, Herb. *Fabricating Lives: Explorations in American Autobiography.* New York: Knopf, 1989.

Levine, Daniel. *Jane Addams and the Liberal Tradition.* Madison: University of Wisconsin Press, 1971.

Linn, James Weber. *Jane Addams.* New York: D. Appleton Century, 1935.

Lowe, David. *Lost Chicago.* Boston: Houghton Mifflin, 1975.

McCarthy, Kathleen D. *Lady Bountiful Revisited: Women, Philanthropy and Power.* New Brunswick: Rutgers University Press, 1990.

Miller, Donald L. *City of the Century: The Epic of Chicago and the Making of America.* New York: Simon & Schuster, 1996.

Mitchell, Silas Weir. *Doctor and Patient.* Philadelphia: J. B. Lippincott & Co., 1886.

———. *Fat and Blood: An Essay on the Treatment of Certain Forms of Neurasthenia and Hysteria.* Philadelphia: J. B. Lippincott & Co., 1877.

———. *Lectures on Diseases of the Nervous System (Especially in Women).* Philadelphia: Lea Brothers & Co., 1885.

———. *Wear and Tear or Hints for the Overworked.* Philadelphia: J. B. Lippincott & Co., 1871.

Monroe, Harriet. *A Poet's Life: Seventy Years in a Changing World.* New York: Macmillan, 1938.

Muncy, Robyn. *Creating a Female Dominion in American Reform 1890–1935.* New York: Oxford University Press, 1991.

Nasaw, David., ed. *The Course of U.S. History.* Chicago: Dorsey Press, 1987.

Nevins, Allan. *The Emergence of Modern America, 1865–1878.* New York: Macmillan, 1927.

Nord, Deborah Epstein. *The Apprenticeship of Beatrice Webb.* Amherst: University of Massachusetts Press, 1985.

Patmore, Coventry. *The Angel in the House.* London: George Bell and Son, 1896.

Pimlott, J. A. R. *Toynbee Hall, Fifty Years of Social Progress, 1884–1934.* London: J. M. Dent & Sons, Ltd., 1935.

Polacheck, Hilda Satt. *I Came a Stranger.* Urbana: University of Illinois Press, 1991.

Riis, Jacob. *How the Other Half Lives: Studies Among the Tenements of New York.* New York: Charles Scribner's Sons, 1890.

Ross, Ishbel. *Silhouette in Diamonds.* New York: Harper Bros., 1960.

Ryan, Alan. *John Dewey and the High Tide of American Liberalism.* New York: W. W. Norton, 1995.

Salvatore, Nick. *Eugene Debs: Citizen and Socialist.* Urbana: University of Illinois Press, 1982.Schlesinger, Arthur. *The Rise of the City, 1878–1898.* New York: Macmillan, 1933.

Schlesinger, Arthur. *The Rise of the City, 1878–1898.* New York: Macmillan, 1933.

Scudder, Vida. *On Journey.* New York: E. P. Dutton & Co., 1937.

Sewall, May Wright. *The World's Congress of Representative Women.* Chicago: Rand McNally & Co., 1894.

Sklar, Kathryn Kish. *Florence Kelley and the Nation's Work.* New Haven: Yale University Press, 1995.

Smith-Rosenberg, Carroll. *Disorderly Conduct: Visions of Gender in Victorian America.* New York: Oxford University Press, 1986.

Taylor, Graham. *Pioneering on Social Frontiers.* Chicago: University of Chicago Press, 1930.

Townsend, Lucy. *The Best Helpers of One Another: Anna Peck Sill and the Struggle for Women's Education.* Chicago: Educational Studies Press, 1988.

Ware, Susan. *Partner and I: Molly Dewson, Feminism and New Deal Politics,* New Haven: Yale University Press, 1987.

Wend, Lloyd, and Herman Kogan. *Lords of the Levee: The Story of Bathhouse John and Hinky Dink.* Bloomington: Indiana University Press, 1943.

Woods, Robert. *The City Wilderness.* New York: Arno Press, 1898.

Woolf, Leonard. *Sowing: An Autobiography of the Years 1880–1904.* London: Hogarth Press, 1960.

Ziff, Larzer. *The American 1890s: A Life and Time of a Lost Generation.* New York: Viking, 1968, 1979.

Articles, Dissertations, Unpublished Material by Jane Addams

"The Chicago Settlements and Social Unrest." *Charities and the Commons, 20* (May 2, 1908): pp. 155–66.

"The College Woman and the Family Claim," *Commons, 3* (Sept. 1898).

"Ethical Survivals of Municipal Corruption." *International Journal of Ethics, 8* (Apr. 1898).

"A Function of the Social Settlement." *Annals, 13* (May 1889).

"Hull-House, Chicago: An Effort Toward Social Democracy." *Forum, 14* (Oct. 1892).

"A Modern Lear," *Survey, 29* (Nov. 2, 1912).

"A New Impulse to An Old Gospel," *Forum, 14* (Nov. 1892).

"One Menace to the Century's Progress." *Unity,* 47 (Apr. 4, 1901).

"Outgrowths of Toynbee Hall." Speech delivered before the Chicago Woman's Club on Dec. 3, 1891. JAPM.
"The Subtle Problems of Charity," *Atlantic Monthly, 83* (Feb. 1899).
Testimony of Jane Addams [on the Pullman Strike], in United States Strike Commission, *Report on the Chicago Strike of June–July 1894*, by the United States Strike Commission (1895).
"Trades Unions and Public Duty." *American Journal of Sociology, 4* (Jan. 1899)
"Why the Ward Boss Rules." *Outlook, 58* (Apr. 2, 1898).
"With the Masses." *Chicago Advance, 25* (Feb. 18, 1892).
"Woman's Work for Chicago." *Municipal Affairs, 2* (Sept. 1898).

Works by Others

Baker, Ray Standard. "Hull-House and the Ward Boss." *Outlook,* 58 (Mar. 28, 1898).
Cook, Blanche Wiesen. "Women Alone Stir My Imagination: Lesbianism and the Cultural Tradition." *Signs* (Summer 1979): pp. 719–20.
Cott, Nancy F. "Passionlessness." *Signs, 4* (Winter 1978).
Davis, Allen F. "Jane Addams v. The Ward Boss." *Journal of the Illinois State Historical Society,* 53 (Autumn 1960).
Fry, Paul. *Generous Spirit: The Life of Mary Fry.* Mary Fry Collection, University of Illinois at Chicago.
Knight, Lucy. "Voices and Silences: Jane Addams and William Jennings Bryan as College Orators." (Aug. 1996, publication forthcoming).
Martin, Franklin H., M.D. "Hystero-Neurasthenia or Nervous Exhaustion of Women, Treated by the S. Weir Mitchell Method." *Journal of the American Medical Association, 8, no. 14* (Apr. 2, 1887).
Nelli, Humbert S. "John Powers and the Italians: Politics in a Chicago Ward, 1896–1921." *Journal of American History, 57* (June 1970): pp. 67–84.
Roberts, Sidney I. "The Municipal Voters' League and Chicago's Boodlers." *Journal of the Illinois State Historical Society, 53* (Summer 1960).
Rosenberg, Charles E. "The Place of George M. Beard in 19th Century Psychiatry," *Bulletin of the History of Medicine* (1962): p. 36.
Scott, Anne Firor. "Saint Jane and the Ward Boss." *American Heritage, 12* (Dec. 1960).
Sicherman, Barbara. "Career Patterns of the Progressive Generation of Women." Paper delivered to the Women's History Institute, Princeton University (Jul. 23, 1980).

———. "The Uses of a Diagnosis: Doctors, Patients and Neurasthenia." *Journal of the History of Medicine and Allied Science, 32, no. 2* (Jan. 1977).

———. "Women's Contribution to Social Reform." Paper delivered to the Cambridge Forum (Oct. 14, 1981).

Sklar, Kathryn Kish. "Hull-House in the 1890s: A Community of Women Reformers." *Signs, 10* (1985).

Smith-Rosenberg, Carroll. "The Female World of Love and Ritual: Relationships Between Women in Nineteenth Century America." *Signs, 1* (Autumn 1975).

———. "The Hysterical Woman." *Social Research, 39* (1972).

Townsend, Lucy. "Anna Peck Sill and the Rise of Women's Collegiate Curriculum." Ph.D. thesis, Loyola University (Mar. 1985).

Welter, Barbara. "The Cult of True Womanhood 1820–1860," *American Quarterly, 18, no. 2* (Summer 1966).

Wood, Ann Douglas. "The Fashionable Diseases: Women's Complaints and Their Treatment in Nineteenth Century America." *Journal of Interdisciplinary History 4, no. 1* (1973): pp. 25–52.

Acknowledgments

Many people contributed to this book. First of all, I would like to thank Mary Lynn McCree Bryan, editor of the Jane Addams Papers Project, who has spent more than two decades gathering and organizing Jane Addams material. Her work has been invaluable to everyone working on Jane Addams and Hull-House. Mary Lynn also spent many hours discussing the material with me, directing me to sources, reading the manuscript, and correcting errors. Her assistant, Maree de Angury, checked my transcripts of Jane Addams's letters and helped with the endnotes.

Allen F. Davis, author of the last biography of Jane Addams, *American Heroine: The Life and Legend of Jane Addams,* published in 1973, responded to my many requests for information, read the manuscript, and corrected mistakes. Paul Green also read *A Useful Woman,* and talked to me about nineteenth century Chicago politics. Mary Rozet Smith's nieces, Jan Ann Detmer, Ann Fischbeck, and Sally Wood, cheerfully answered my questions, shared some family correspondence, and provided a living link to the young Jane Addams.

The real heroes of biography are librarians, and many aided my project by tracking down obscure sources, checking facts, and pointing out material I had overlooked. At the University of Illinois at Chicago, where the bulk of Jane Addams's papers are housed, I am indebted to Mary Ann Bamberger, curator of special collections, and her staff, especially, Pat

Bakunas, Zita Stukas, and Alan Kovac. I'd also like to thank librarians at the Swarthmore College Peace Collection, the Lilly Library at Indiana University, the Sophia Smith Collection at Smith College, the Arthur and Elizabeth Schlesinger Library on the History of Women in America at Radcliffe College, the Chicago Historical Society, and Rockford College.

Once again, my agent, Rhoda Weyr, has seen me through a long and difficult project, and, as always, she's provided unfailingly astute advice. My dear friend Dinitia Smith patiently endured long monologues about Jane Addams and never let me lose faith that I'd complete the book. Dinitia's husband, the historian and writer David Nasaw, first suggested I write about Jane Addams's early life, and also corrected many errors in the final manuscript.

Everyone at Scribner has been a delight. I am grateful especially to Lisa Drew for her wisdom and care in shepherding the book through publication, and for coming up with the perfect title.

My husband, Richard Babcock, was there at every stage of the project—he discussed the material with me, read all drafts, and sent me back to the computer to rewrite, and rewrite again. His love and guidance enabled me to realize my vision of the book. Indeed, without him, it wouldn't have been possible.

Index

Note: Page references to photographs are in *italics*.
See also the photographic insert.